KU-255-059

German Unification

German Unification

The Destruction of an Economy

Edited by
Hanna Behrend

Pluto **Press**
LONDON • EAST HAVEN, CT

First published 1995 by Pluto Press
345 Archway Road, London N6 5AA, UK
and 140 Commerce Street,
East Haven, CT 06512, USA

Copyright © Hanna Behrend 1995

The right of the individual contributors to be identified as the
authors of this work has been asserted by them in accordance
with the Copyright, Designs and Patents Act 1988

British Library Cataloguing in Publication Data
A catalogue record for this book is available from the British Library

ISBN 0 7453 1004 4 hardback

Library of Congress Cataloging in Publication Data
Applied for.

Designed and produced for Pluto Press by
Chase Production Services, Chipping Norton
Typeset from author's disk by
Stanford DTP Services, Milton Keynes
Printed in the EC by T J Press, Padstow, England

Contents

Abbreviations   vi

Notes on Contributors   viii

Foreword   x

1   Inglorious German Unification   1
  Hanna Behrend

2   East German Political Parties and Movements Before
  and After the Fall of the GDR   35
  Manfred Behrend

3   An Unparalleled Destruction and Squandering of
  Economic Assets   80
  Harry Nick

4   Changing the East German Countryside   119
  Christel Panzig

5   Rolling Back the Gender Status of East German Women   139
  Anneliese Braun, Gerda Jasper and Ursula Schröter

6   The End of a European Tradition in Scholarship
  and Culture?   167
  Horst van der Meer

7   Right-wing Extremism in East Germany Before and
  After the '*Anschluß*' to the Federal Republic   199
  Manfred Behrend

Index   223

Abbreviations

ARD	Association of German Broadcasting Companies
BDI	Federal Association of Industry
BFD	Alliance of Free Democrats – the Liberals
CDU	Christian Democratic Union
CSU	Christian Social Union
DA	Democratic Awakening *or* German Alternative
DBD	Democratic Farmers' Party
DFD	Democratic Women's Federation
DGB	German Trade Union Council
DJ	Democracy Now
DNP	German National Party
DSU	German Social Union
DVU	German People's Union
EALG	Law on Compensation and Conciliation
EKO	Iron Foundry Works East at Eisenhüttenstadt (GDR)
FAP	Freedom-loving German Workers' Party
FDGB	Free German Trade Union Council (GDR)
FDJ	Free German Youth
FDP	Free Democratic Party
FMJ	Support Scheme Central German Youth
FTA	Science and Technology Park at Berlin-Adlershof
GdNF	Community of Adherents of the New Front
GDR	German Democratic Republic
IAB	Institute for Job Market and Vocational Research
IFM	Initiative for Peace and Human Rights
ILO	International Labour Organisation
IM	unofficial informant (of the *Stasi*)
ISDA	Institute for the Analysis of Social Data
KPD	Communist Party of Germany
KPF	Communist Platform of the PDS
LAG	Law on the Structural Adjustment of Agriculture in the German Democratic Republic to the Social and Economic Market Economy

LDPD	Liberal Democratic Party of Germany
LPG	agricultural cooperative (GDR)
MBO	management buy-out
MND	Central German National Democrats
NABU	Society for the Protection of Nature
NDPD	National Democratic Party of Germany (GDR)
NF	Nationalist Front *or* New Forum
NPD	National Democratic Party of Germany (FRG)
NSDAP	National Socialist German Workers' Party
NSDAP-AO	NSDAP Organisation for Expansion Abroad
ORB	East German radio and TV channel
PDS	Party of Democratic Socialism
RAF	Red Army Fraction
REP	Republican Party
SED	Socialist Unity Party of Germany
SPD	Social Democratic Party of Germany
SRP	Socialist Reich Party
Stasi	Ministry of State Security (GDR)
UFV	Independent Women's Association
VdgB	Farmers' Mutual Aid Association
VEG	State farm (GDR)
VL	United Left
ZAST	Central Reception Point of Asylum Applicants
ZIE	Central Institute for Electron Physics

Notes on Contributors

Hanna Behrend, historian and literary scholar, spent a decade in Britain as a refugee from nazi oppression, taught English literature and women's studies at Humboldt University in Berlin and was a founding member of the East German Independent Women's Association (UFV) in 1989. She has published on German history, English language textbooks and English literature. Since the *Wende* she has published and lectured on East German women and on German politics in Germany and abroad and has chaired a research project on race, class and gender.

Manfred Behrend, historian and political scientist, has worked in radio and in publishing. In 1962, he joined the Institute for Contemporary History, which later merged with the Institute for International Politics and Economics, researching West German conservative and right-wing parties. After the Institute closed in 1990, he published and has lectured widely on neofascism and right-wing extremism in East and West Germany.

Anneliese Braun was Professor of Economics and researcher at the GDR Academy of Sciences in national economy and the economy of labour, particularly relating to the employment of women. She had to take early retirement when her institute was closed and has since co-founded a team, attached to the Unemployed Association, committed to investigating and publicising the situation of redundant women. She publishes and lectures on various aspects of this subject and on the nature of employment in present-day society.

Gerda Jasper, a trained accountant for agrarian enterprises, taught economics while undertaking extra-mural studies in economics. She then became a post-graduate student in Moscow. After her doctorate she took on a researcher's post at the Academy for Social Sciences (dissolved in 1990) investigating the economics of labour, and comparative studies in free market and planned economies. Since 1990 she has undertaken studies in feminist theory and on the situation of women in gainful employment. At present she is employed under a job-creation scheme.

Harry Nick, retired Professor of Political Economy at the Academy for Social Sciences, has published on economic and social problems arising from scientific and technical development. Since 1991 he has been on the board of a scholarly association dealing with economics and democracy. His special subject, on which he publishes and lectures, is investigation into the causes of the economic failure of the GDR.

Christel Panzig, a historian and sociologist, worked on the agrarian and social history of East Germany, focusing on women, and was on the staff of the Academy of Agrarian Sciences until that institution was closed. She was appointed chairperson of a research team financed by the Council of Science of the Federal Republic of Germany on a project dealing with the effects of the transformation of the rural areas of the ex-GDR, especially on the gainful employment of women and their everyday lives. She also runs a research project for Potsdam University on historical and socio-anthropological investigations into rural areas in East Germany.

Ursula Schröter studied mathematics and worked in a national enterprise in Thuringia in this field. She moved to Berlin to work on a doctorate on statistics and the methodology of sociology. When the Academy for Social Sciences was dissolved, she co-founded the Institute for the Analysis of Social Data (ISDA) and committed herself to feminist politics. She is in the process of investigating whether East German women are the losers of German unification and to what extent they may have gained. She has subsisted, since the *Wende*, on a job under the job-creation scheme, on unemployment benefit, and on temporary employment. She has been unemployed since October 1994.

Horst van der Meer, who was born in the (West German) Rhineland, studied economics in East Germany. His first doctorate was on the International Federation of Christian Trade Unions under the influence of the German Christian trade unions, and his second doctorate was on monopoly capitalist enterprises in the Federal Republic of Germany. He worked as a researcher at the now defunct Institute for International Politics and Economics in Berlin. Since his early retirement, he has been involved in aid to Third World countries, and reports on these countries and on German politics for various publications.

Foreword

There are scores of books by British, US and (West) German authors on recent European and German history that cover German unification; some even specialise in the events leading to and arising from that unification. So far as I am aware, all these works approach the subject from the outside; necessarily so in the case of British or US authors. The (West) German authors' discourses, even if they sympathise with the left, are, at best, struggling to be fair. Outsiders too, they are exposed to the full weight of the official legend proliferated by all the German media with the exception of the handful of East German periodicals which have survived the backlash following unification.

This legend – of 16 million East Germans, oppressed for 40 years, unanimously desirous of merging with the Federal Republic, liberated by selfless West Germany, their decrepit economy reconstructed at huge cost to the ordinary West German brothers and sisters – has displaced what really happened. The West German media have succeeded in erasing from (particularly West German) public consciousness the fact that many hundreds of thousands of GDR citizens took to the streets chanting 'We are the people and we are staying'. The East Germans rid themselves of the gerontocratic regime and set about democratising public affairs.

The halcyon days were brief; the attempt to reform the GDR and to create a truly alternative German state was doomed. The delicate plant of true self-determination which had emerged was quickly torn out by its roots, for a few months later 40 per cent of the East Germans voted for Herr Kohl's party, persuaded by West German promises that German unity would given them Deutschmark-prosperity. Many of those who voted for the quick merger were out for a new start, eager for conditions as different from the repressiveness the GDR stood for as could be possible. They wanted no democratic socialist reforms or experiments; capitalism to them meant good wages, full shops, free travel and more lifestyle options.

West German big business took over. Under *Treuhand*[1] management, geared to the interests of the dominant faction of West German capital, East Germany's productive potential was considered an actual or potential competitor and, therefore, deliberately destroyed or, at best, segmented into minor units dependent on the West German monopolies and, anyway, in West German hands. Cooperative agriculture was also largely destroyed or discriminated against and the return of former landlords was made legally possible.

The West German Constitution, its legislation, its inferior social system, its bureaucracy and its monetary system, were imposed on the East Germans. The impending economic crisis in West Germany was delayed for almost two years by the simple expedient of taking over from one day to the next the entire GDR retail trade, lock, stock and barrel, and dumping surplus commodities on the East Germans eager to test the West.

The dominant factions of German industry are no longer interested in investing capital in German production except in the sector of high-tech commodities. In this field, West German industry is by no means competitive and has failed, in a number of export deals, to get contracts while French or US firms had their tenders accepted.

German capitalism can make more money by importing and selling cheap industrial commodities from the Third World and ex-Second World countries (19 Russian workers' earnings equal one average West German wage packet; an East German worker earns an average of 60 per cent of the West German wage) than by adapting East German enterprises to West German market conditions.

By creating a huge labour reserve in the East, not only was the establishment able to keep East German wages down in defiance of election promises, but also employers' federations thereby blackmailed the German trade unions into agreeing to undermine what working-class rights had been won in the past 40 years both in the West and in the East. Mass unemployment with impecunious local and regional governments in its wake increases the national debt, a safe source of profit to banking and investors.

This policy, however, has obvious shortcomings. It destroys the home markets and undermines civil consensus. From this short-term and therefore short-sighted point of view, the capitalist restructuring of East Germany by steamrolling the country and turning it into a colonised backyard makes sense. From the more political, longer-term vision of a Greater German economic supremacy and global political influence this unification policy, however, is counterproductive.

The irrationality of the dominant faction of German capitalism in destroying capital assets and industrial research capacity on so huge a scale – some of which they already find themselves obliged to reconstruct – is due to the desire to take revenge for having been deprived of those means of production for more than a generation. They want to discipline those who had dared to defy them by building up a noncapitalist industry and agriculture from the debris left after the Second World War and training a generation of first-rate industrial researchers they never tired of braindraining away. They intend to make sure that the attempt to build up an alternative system is never repeated. This motive has influenced them more than their long-term politico-economic sense. In their very own interest, they would have been well advised not to ride roughshod over the GDR economy, which, through in need of rehabilitation, constituted an unexpected windfall not to be despised if one was set on dominating, if not globally, then, at least, the European economy.

These motives and the subsequent policy pursued coincided with the pressure a number of hitherto profitable sectors of industry found themselves under world-wide, e.g. the steel, car, aircraft and airline industries, coal and potash mining. Without doubt while both the rational and the irrational facets described are specific features of German capitalism, they are options arising from the contradictions international capital has for some time been confronted with.

Until about 1992 the people of East Germany were stunned by the rapid and total changes which had overcome them. Since then, a growing number have woken from their stupor and have begun to evaluate these changes in the light of gains and losses. Though they are aware of their losses in social security and in solidarity they also realise that the old system had come to a dead end. The majority of East Germans, irrespective of whether they are in gainful employment or unemployed, old age pensioners, disabled, men or women, young or elderly, consider themselves second-class citizens in Greater Germany. The political stage in Germany is shifting. Though on the surface, the results of the 1994 general elections point towards continuity rather than change, stale political structures are being eroded by new political organisations, new coalition models have emerged, a new defiance on the part of an unexpectedly large number of people against intervention by those in authority can be observed; changes which are more evident in the East than in the West.

The contributors to this book are five women and three men. Their biographies bear the stamp of GDR socialisation. Economists, historians, a mathematician, an agricultural expert and a literary scholar, all of working-class or lower middle-class background, they taught at universities or at other institutions of higher education and research, or worked in industrial or agricultural research. Notwithstanding their personal records of integrity, or their individual involvement in reform, they all lost their jobs in 1990. They are, at present, either unemployed or in badly paid temporary part-time work under some job-creation scheme; three were coerced into early retirement, or became victims of the pension cuts suffered by those close to the state.

They have two basic motives in writing this book and presenting the case of the East Germans: the first is to speak on behalf of those whose voices have been muted in their own country and are hardly ever heard abroad.

The second motive arises from their awareness that what has happened to the East Germans is by no means unique. Similar and even more heart-rending processes of appropriation and social backlash are taking place in many parts of the world. West German capitalist-style unification reveals, in a national context, all the features and trends of the contemporary global contradictions which the capitalist system is, as present, confronted with. In displaying the way in which German unification took place, we do not, as some critics might think, bewail the passing away of hierarchical, patriarchally constructed state socialism, which deserved its downfall. The short-lived democratic GDR which succeeded the Honecker state, however, did show, if inadequately, the potential of popular power under conditions of self-determination.

We were all involved in this brief episode of popular democracy in the GDR from October 1989 to March 1990 and witnessed West German capitalism and its political spokesmen taking advantage of the political and economic inexperience of the GDR reformers and of the people's rightful wrath against those who had failed them in 40 years of state socialism which merged with their ignorance of capitalism. We belong to those in the GDR who foresaw more or less clearly that German capitalism would ruthlessly annihilate every democratic feature which had snowballed into existence after the disposal of the gerontocrats. We watched apprehensively the undermining and eventual disappearance of those features of the GDR social, educational, health, cultural and even legal system which would have been well worth preserving.

We share, therefore, the unique historical experience of having been exposed, in half a decade, to far more radical and irreversible changes of situation, values, prospects and viewpoints than most people in the Western industrial countries experience in their entire lifetimes. Our report on what has happened in Germany should be listened to.

Hanna Behrend
Berlin, February 1995

Note

1. *Treuhand* was the holding company in charge of reprivatising the entire nationalised property in the GDR. See Chapter 1, pp. 9–15.

1 Inglorious German Unification

Hanna Behrend

The End of the Second World War

The implosion of the socialist experiment in East Germany and Eastern Europe set the European and German stage anew. Although state socialism had provided stable employment for everybody, and built up a more (GDR, Czechoslovakia, Hungary) or less (USSR, Poland, Romania, Bulgaria, Albania) efficient welfare state with free and equal education, health and social services, it had alienated itself progressively from the people. East Germans, Czechs, Hungarians, Poles, Bulgarians, Albanians and the nations comprising the Soviet Union, including the dominant Russians themselves, had come to hate the fossilised geriatrics who ruled them on behalf of a rapacious nomenklatura motivated only by their desire to retain power. The subjects of this political class, even if never personally affected by discrimination or other repressive measures, resented the ever-widening gap between the official picture of their alleged liberty, equal opportunities and increasing prosperity, of their country's just and democratic constitution, and the truth as they experienced it. This truth consisted in the arbitrary power of the rulers, who could waive the considerable formal individual rights and collective privileges of co-determination in public and management decisions, and the lack of effective constitutional safeguards for the individual citizen's rights; the censorship imposed on the media and the prevention of any public criticism which arose from the pathological fear of those in authority of conspiratory associations jeopardising their power.

The complete disintegration of civil consensus was also brought about by the manner in which those in authority coped with the policy of economic sanctions the West imposed on the COMECON countries including the GDR. To circumvent the ban much hard currency was needed. No means was too dishonest or fatal in its effects on the non-capitalist character of the country for the rulers to stoop to it. They promoted the disintegration of the country's currency system and the corruption of the people by officially admitting the Deutschmark as means of payment. They sold dissident prisoners to the West for hard cash. These and similar practices also undermined the system in the GDR. The erosion not only affected the mass of the people and the handful of civil rights activists under the roof of the churches, or within the ranks of the leading Socialist Unity Party of Germany (SED), or working autonomously, it also undermined the political and repressive apparatuses of the GDR.

By the end of the summer of 1989 the opening of the Hungarian/Austrian border turned the steady trickle of GDR citizens voting against the system by leaving the country into a flood involving tens of thousands. Young men and women with their children crossed the dismantled 'Iron Curtain' firmly convinced they would find a new Jerusalem on West Germany's rich and hospitable lands. Were not their West German relatives the living evidence of the West German utopia? There you earned good Deutschmarks which allowed you to buy 'real' cars (instead for waiting for years on end for your turn to get one of the processed cardboard Trabants), and to spend your holidays in exotic places (instead of being reduced to the COMECON countries). Last but not least, the migrants would gain access to the free and enjoyable community of consumers. For them there would be no more pre-Christmas queues for oranges and bananas, no more need to bribe the plumber for a supply of bathroom tiles. Instead, there would be the lifestyle which, watching Western television for years, they had enviously assumed existed but could not experience.

Of course, the majority of the population stayed put for all kinds of reasons. Of these a small but growing and increasingly articulate minority took to the streets defiantly intoning 'We are the people and we are staying!'. They rallied by the hundred thousand, conquering the streets from the early October days of 1989, when the authorities still tried to disperse them by the usual brutal police methods, to about mid-December, when, as we shall see, the demos began to change in character. These activists of the so-called 'velvet revolution' contributed decisively to the implosion of the GDR state socialist system by forcing those in power to first get rid of the most compromised figureheads and then to tear down the wall they had erected 27 years before to protect the system which, even then, failed to win the support of the majority of its citizens.

The *Wende*[1] of 1989

As so often in history, power lay on the streets for anyone to pick up. The left-wing faction of the 'velvet revolutionaries' were united only in wishing to reform the GDR and turn it into a truly alternative society to the other German state. Discredited in the eyes of the general public, even the reform-oriented members of the former ruling party were by that stage certainly no rallying point for a viable reformers' party. The newly established political organisations arising from former dissident and civil rights groups had no concepts that went beyond the negation of the past, and the speedily Westernised former satellite parties and the newly formed SPD quickly became the mouthpieces in the East of their West German big brothers.

By early December, the mood of the 'Monday demos', which had become a standing ritual, changed radically. From 'We are the people', the chant changed to 'We are one people'. At the same time, an invasion of West German advisers, representatives of big business, real estate agents, racketeers of all description, top-echelon politicians of the established parties, right down to neonazis, flooded the country. While the business people paved the way for the general appropriation of GDR property which took place later, Messrs Kohl, Brandt and company canvassed for East German support for speedy unification which alone was to guarantee that the former East would become a 'thriving land'. They warned the people not to believe those who would encourage them to vote for 'yet another socialist experiment'.

Thus prepared, over 40 per cent of the GDR electorate voted for the East German CDU, i.e. for speedy unification in March 1990 and, thereby, unwittingly, for their own expropriation. The coalition of Christian Democrats, Free Democrats and Social Democrats (CDU-FDP-SPD) quickly degenerated into dogsbodies assiduously taking orders from their West German headquarters, whipping momentous decisions like the monetary union or the Unification Treaty through parliament at a pace which gave the deputies no time to even read the documents properly, never mind debate their possible effects.

German unification was internationally accepted, not only by the Gorbachev government, preceded by the meek capitulation by Premier Modrow and the Provisional GDR Government. Returning from the USSR in January 1990 he proclaimed, under Soviet pressure, his new policy of Germany as united fatherland. The death-knell to any other, more gradual form of fusion of the two German states in dignity and equality was also sounded by the agreement of Federal Germany's Western allies, albeit a reluctant agreement on the part of France and Britain.

The precipitate speed with which West Germany was rushing the weaker East German state into unification is generally explained not only by the 'insistence of the people' but also by the need to take advantage of the favourable international political constellation. Whether this was really uppermost in the minds of those in power or not, the really pressing problem was that Germany had been sliding into a recession, and Herr Kohl's government was at an extremely low ebb in popularity. Cashing in on the GDR 'velvet revolution' and acting as midwife to German unification after nearly half a century of segregation would have boosted governments far nearer their end. So unification would, it was hoped, also stop or at least postpone the impending economic crisis.

It did, indeed, delay the West German recession by about two years. This delay, however, was achieved by speedily taking over, with the help of gullible or corrupt managers, GDR retail trade and exporting the West German surplus commodities to that new market until it was sated. Subsequently, policies which had the effect of de-industrialising the East also kept such competitive potential as it had at bay. In the meantime, both West and East were overtaken by the recession from which the whole industrialised world was suffering.

The New 'Greater Germany'

After the incorporation of the GDR, not only had the map of Europe changed, more importantly, Germany pursued, less reticently than before, a major power policy in Europe and in the world with potentially worrying implications. Almost simultaneously with the '*Anschluß*', united Germany helped, some feel, to escalate the conflicts in former Yugoslavia by insisting that Slovenia's and Croatia's independence be acknowledged. Germany took the opportunity of the war in Somalia to send its army 'out of area', thus exercising its new international status. The pre-unification formula of 'never shall another war be unleashed from German soil', so glibly uttered only half a decade before by German statesmen, had disappeared from their vocabulary. Instead, both the Coalition Government and the established opposition parties, the SPD and Alliance 90/the Greens, approved of the *Bundeswehr* taking part in military actions 'designed to bring about peace'. Thus, even the established opposition parties were no longer strictly against the transformation of the *Bundeswehr* from a purely domestic defence service to an international commando troop entitled to its share of international police actions. More recently, the German parliament also relaxed armament exporting conditions to 25 OECD countries for German arms manufacturers.[2]

That Germany had a fair chance of eventually achieving its wish to be accorded a seat on the Security Council showed how much the balance of power had changed.

No doubt the international role the Federal Republic will eventually play will depend on many imponderables relating to its future relationship to the US, to Eastern Europe, within the EC, etc. However, the character of unification as an '*Anschluß*', i.e. an act of incorporating an economically weaker state with little reference to the interests of the people concerned and in no way as a merger towards which both parties contribute as equal partners, throws light on its prospective motives. They are geared to power politics and market strategies in the interests of West German big business.

Already, land is being bought up in pre-1945 German territories in Poland and the Czech Republic by German resettlers. Neonazi organisations have opened branches, too, producing some of their propaganda material there to save costs.

For decades, there have been warnings from the Club of Rome and others of the scale of problems for the world that a continued and unrestricted policy of industrial expansion could lead to. United Germany's promotion of global ecological policies, like those of its competitors, has consisted, by and large, of verbal professions while it continues to export its poisonous waste to poor countries (some of which have lately taken to returning these consignments).

Conservative and neoliberal economic representatives, already in the early 1980s or before, were calling for a reduction of the rights of trade unions to conclude binding wage agreement with employers' federations for entire industries, there was a cry for cheap government, i.e. for whittling down the social side of the budget, and a privatisation drive covering more and more public services.

Neoliberalism and Germany's '*Anschluß*' Policy

By 1992 the optimistic forecasts of an East German economic miracle which would prove the truth of the Chancellor's promises, justify the high hopes of his East German voters in 1990 and stun the rest of the world had subsided.

To succeed in the global competition, German capitalists were stepping up post-fordist production strategies.[3] Joining the neoliberalist economic policy pursued by Britain and France, and, in fact, the European Community, Germany was fast dismantling the network of social security established in the prosperous 1960s. Hand in glove with this, '*Anschluß*'-type unification gave it the chance to dismantle democratic structures step by step, under the pretext of righting the wrong done under the GDR system.

An International Labour Organisation (ILO) report spoke of more than 120 million unemployed plus 700 million destitute in the world. In Latin America unprotected jobs had grown to 32 per cent of gainful employment.[4] The policy of state withdrawal from social security, free health and educational services imposed in Third World countries by the International Monetary Fund and the World Bank was leading to a situation recalling the dystopian visions of Orwell in *Nineteen Eighty-Four*.

While this policy is most blatantly practised in former colonialist and neocolonialist countries, it is also fast seeping into the First World. To provide employment for the nearly 17 million unemployed in the twelve states of the European Union in the wealthy North, a spokesman of the dominant political discourse, Jacques Delors, then President of the European Commission, in the white paper on 'Growth, Competitiveness, Employment' adopted by the European Council in Brussels in December 1993, suggested cuts in taxation for enterprises, in employers' contributions towards the social services and in the so-called 'supplementary costs' of wages and salaries.

Federal Association of German Industry (BDI) President Tyll Necker's pronouncement that 'the over-extensive social welfare network with its overwhelming costs should be adapted to the narrow financial margins'[5] revealed that German VIPs were in full agreement with Delors's policy on this.[6]

As yet, however, the political, economic and social conditions in the First World, notwithstanding the increasing polarisation between rich and poor, are still preferable to those in the rest of the world. To keep out the masses of those who can no longer exist in the impoverished South, or whose countries are involved in one or the other of the many genocidal wars, post-unification Germany was building up more powerful barriers than the Wall ever was. By modifying its constitutional provisions to keep refugees and poor immigrants off its doorstep it unwittingly encouraged the cruder racist interventions by neonazis. While Government spokespersons asserted that Germany was not being xenophobic, Kurdish refugees were ruthlessly sent back to Turkey where they face repression, and refugees from war-torn Yugoslavia and other immigrants were kept in overcrowded hostels and allotted food vouchers rather than money or work permits.

Even those the West German Government invited to come to fill the many vacancies for low-grade manual jobs in the 1950s and 1960s, and who had lived in the country for decades, their children and sometimes their grandchildren having been born there, were discriminated against. So were the Vietnamese, Cubans, Sudanese, Angolans and Mozambicans who were recruited by the GDR Government. Nothing was done officially to help German citizens understand what they owe to the exploitation of people in the Third World countries, increasingly also in Eastern Europe for the upkeep of their living standards. Foreign immigrants in Germany, in fact, contributed considerably to the German budget. In the decade from 1981 to 1991, immigrant workers produced an addition to the gross national product worth DM90 billion, and paid DM29 billion in taxes and contributions to social insurance, yet received but DM16 billion in social security.[7]

During the first decade of Herr Kohl's premiership, net unearned incomes rose by 43.1 per cent, whereas the incomes of the waged increased only by 6.1 per cent; the incomes of unemployed people and recipients of social assistance dropped by 0.6 per cent. The proportion of the net incomes of waged and salaried earners and of the net unearned incomes, 70.9 per cent and 29.1 per cent of the total West German income in 1982 respectively, had shifted by 1991 to 61.2 per cent for the gainfully employed and 38.8 per cent for unearned incomes.[8] Of the total amount of DM3,600 billion available in Germany in 1992, only one-twentieth belonged to the East German states. In the West the average household then owned DM119,000 although half the population had no or only a marginal share of this and one per cent of the population owned 13 per cent of it. East German households owned, on average, DM31,000; a sum which, however, was far more equitably distributed.[9]

Despite the recession, the banks had, in past years, enjoyed super profits. The German Bank, the Dresden bank, the Bavarian Banking Society, the Commerical Bank, and the Bavarian Mortgage and Exchange Bank had jointly made DM10.6 billion profit (annual increments: 15, 25, 32, 24, per cent respectively).[10] The German *Bundesbank*'s annual balance also revealed record profits, not their least source being the interest on the national debt. Liquid capital to the tune of DM700 billion has been accumulated which the banks could make available for investments in East Germany. They promised Chancellor Kohl to invest 1 billion when he pleaded with them in January 1993. Banks and savings banks were to take over viable East German enterprises at their own risk. The private banks committed themselves to invest DM400 million and so did the Federal State banks and savings banks, with cooperative banks adding another DM200 million. Yet by 15 February 1994, only two of the 214 enterprises offered to them for sale had actually been taken over under this 'pact of solidarity' between Herr Kohl and the banks.[11]

In any case, the German Government preferred to economise at the expense of the gainfully employed, the 3.66 million unemployed,[12] the old age pensioners and the recipients of social benefits,[13] to avail itself of the wealth of the banking establishment.

One of the many inaccuracies in *The Economist*'s survey on Germany of 21 May 1994 relates to the nursing-care scheme for the elderly, designated 'the biggest welfare reform of recent years ... [which] will widen, not narrow, welfare's scope', it being concluded that 'So far, there is little sign of either big party contemplating a radical overhaul of the welfare state.'[14] The nursing-care scheme has indeed initiated a new phase in the history of German social services inasmuch as it is the first infringement upon the principle of shared employer–worker costs of social/health insurance introduced under Chancellor Bismarck in 1883 in response to Social Democratic pressure. This new service, initiated early in 1995, is paid for entirely by employees. To fund the employers' contribution, workers now work on one of the official or their individual holidays.

Both the coalition parties, CDU/CSU and FDP, and even the SPD opposition have underwritten a budget which discriminates against the socially weak by cutting unemployment benefit and social security, by postponing the promised establishment of kindergartens, cutting expenses for education and research, culture and public health, etc., while giving advantages to the banks and big business in general.

Unification under the aegis of the present political class in Germany was geared to the international economic transformation process in which the German capitalists played a pioneer role in their determination not to allow newcomers in Asia to overtake them. The recession undermined the need to set a new pace in overcoming what *The Economist* calls 'The perils of cosy corporatism',[15] i.e. the relationship between unions and employers' federations designed to harmonise their relevant interests. The '*Anschluß*' policy, which fixed East German wages, salaries, unemployment benefits, social security and pensions considerably below those in the West (in 1994 the gap was between 20 and 40 per cent of the wages and over 50 per cent of pensions), had eroded the former happy marriage between the employers and the unions.

One of the most striking examples, which revealed the limitations of the former system and showed that trade union leadership was less and less able to look after the interests of all their members, was the closing down of the profitable and efficient potassium mine at Bischof-ferode in Thuringia. At the bidding of the West German competitor *Kali & Salz AG*, a daughter of the IG-Farben successor BASF (*Badische Anilin- and Soda-Fabrik*), the East German potassium industry was merged with the West German one in 1993. Both the SPD and officials of leading sections of the German trade unions supported the merger, which was ruthlessly enforced. As was to be expected, it put an end to practically the entire East German potassium industry, also the mine at Bischofferode. For more than a year the miners had fought a losing battle, with marches and hunger strikes. For a while they won broad grassroots and left-wing support, even from the odd rank-and-file trade unionist from the West, and it looked as if they might win. The German Anti-monopolisation Commission pronounced the merger an infringement of its legislation. The miners hoped for a veto to the merger by the EC. However, German Minister of Economy Günter Rexrodt, a former *Treuhand* manager (see below), went to Brussels and talked the Commission round. The miners were promised 700 replacement jobs by the central and state governments, but nothing came of this.

Measures were introduced to cope with the fierce competition, such as lean production, minimum expenses for wages and social supplements, production transfer to places where low wages yielded extra profits; and imports of cheap raw materials while subsidies to the steel and mining corporations continued to allow these to reorganise production on the required lean level at the expense of the taxpayer. The German Government gave unwavering support to big business and the banks.

The *Treuhandanstalt* – the Biggest Holding Company in the World

Under such circumstances, unification was bound to 'destroy all alter-native chances of retaining East German independence, its industry, culture and identity'.[16] If any institution can be said to have the lion's share of responsibility for this, it certainly is *Treuhand*. In the areas of culture and identity, the so-called Gauck-administration, the Federal Government's administration of the files of the former GDR Ministry of State Security, and the parliamentary commission to review GDR history were the major instruments of what amounted to a form of ideological colonisation.

The *Treuhandanstalt* was set up by the provisional GDR Government under Hans Modrow on 1 March 1990. It was designed to take in trust and administer faithfully the people's property.[17] The dissolution of the 'workers' and farmers' state' had called for new provisions for that state's nationalised property. Those employed in the enterprises, for the first and so far last time, felt that the enterprises belonged to them, and a lively debate took place on how to proceed with this property. The debate was exceedingly short-lived. The new, 'first freely elected GDR government,' which was also the last, hastened to change the purpose of the *Treuhandanstalt* from taking care of the national property to privatising and reorganising the national property. This revised law was passed by parliament on 17 June 1990 and heralded by a handful of perceptive critics (e.g. the former dissident writer Stefan Heym) as the sell-out and destruction of the people's property. Former Minister of Economy, Professor Christa Luft, called the new law one which changed the original *Treuhand* commission out of all recognition.[18]

After unification, the Federal Minister of Finances became the controller of the largest ever holding company in the world, with no parliamentary commission installed to control him. The first *Treuhand* president came from the West German railway company, a state-owned enterprise. When privatisation of the *Treuhand*-administered property was, increasingly, given priority by the Government, he was no longer the right man for the job and his place was taken by Detlev Karsten Rohwedder, a finance expert who had saved the Hoesch steel company and led the enterprise from impending ruin to new triumphs. A member of the SPD, Rohwedder's appointment stood for a policy of reorganising GDR enterprises in a way that would make them viable. Privatisation was, then, to take second place to restoration and development. On 31 March 1991 he told the *Frankfurter Allgemeine*: 'A pure, theoretically sound market economy without frills in East Germany' is impossible; '100 per cent privatisation is impossible. Many enterprises will have to be privatised with a high quota of state participation.' Herr Rohwedder feared that 'the West German monopolist firms would grab the cheap East German state enterprises and ignore the rights of the staff ... We should think about the effects on competition and on the social interests of the workers.'[19]

On 1 April 1991, Detlev Rohwedder was killed in his own home. He had been standing with his back to a window on the first floor when an expert marksman shot him from about 70 yards away. He died immediately. Journalists remarked on the inadequate investigations by the police, and that security measures in respect of the *Treuhand* manager had also been strangely defective.

The ultra-left terrorist organisation the Red Army Fraction (RAF) was immediately suspected of the crime, no one considering whether the murdered man might not have had enemies other than on the left. No trace was ever found of those responsible, but the moral indictment of the RAF hampered left-wing criticism of the *Treuhand* when its present director, Birgit Breuel, took over.[20]

Frau Breuel had a record of being a neoliberalist hardliner as Minister of Economy, and later Finances, in Lower Saxony from 1978 to 1990. Her appointment symbolised the victory of the rival majority 'privati-sation before rehabilitation' faction within the *Treuhand* management and put paid to any but the most ruthless privatisation strategy. Indeed, where her predecessor had taken seven months to privatise 600 of the total of 8,000 GDR enterprises and trusts, under her rule 300 were privatised in one month – a figure which escalated to 562 in June 1992. By the end of 1994, the date for winding up the institution, there were only about hundred enterprises left. Within less than three years, *Treuhand* destroyed or handed over to West German big business for next to nothing national property to the value of at least several hundred billion Deutschmarks. The value of this property (industrial enterprises only) was estimated in GDR terms at 1 to 1.3 billion GDR Marks; Rohwedder had valued it at DM600 to 650 billion whilst according to the so-called Deutschmark opening balance of 1990 it had been valued at 520 billion. The most likely figure is generally considered that suggested by Rohwedder.

While the West German purchasers of these firms at such generous prices were able to improve their position in international competition, the ordinary taxpayer will in the end have to pay for the nearly DM300 billion debt the institution heaped up. By the end of 1992 industrial production in East Germany sank to less than one-third of the 1989 figure, and, of the 4.1 million industrial jobs there had been, every second one was lost. By that date every fourth employable person in East Germany was out of a job, supplemented by those coerced into early retirement, or (particularly women) into accepting lower qualified employment. Mecklenburg-West Pomerania's former status as an investment site moved down to rank 240 after Sicily according to one EC statistic. Crime rose to 300 per cent of its previous level, and the suicide rate to 180 per cent; the birth rate sank to 55 per cent, the rate of marriages to 50 per cent. Women were particularly seriously affected, with their rate of unemployment at 65 per cent, only a little over 40 per cent being involved in temporary job-creation schemes.[21] Frau Breuel's top staff were encouraged by bonuses to speed up privatisations, cost what it may. In addition to making them virtual presents of the best bits of former GDR industrial enterprises, huge sums were handed to the big concerns and not a few shady adventurers for the purpose of clearing up former ecological damage, for new investments, and for compensating former staff for the loss of their jobs, etc. Against this practice of generosity at the expense of the former GDR citizens who had built up these enterprises, *Treuhand* policy towards the occasional management buy-out teams was mean. They had to pay high prices for their own enterprise and also cover the firm's 'old liabilities' – sham debts arising from financial transactions between national enterprises and the GDR state. It need only be added that they were not allocated any of the funds showered on the West German buyers.

The regular salaries of top personnel of *Treuhand* were more than generous and they were eligible for a pension after only one year's service.[22] Even these advantages, a level of remuneration far above that usual elsewhere, did not seem to satisfy the rapaciousness of the recipients. In fact, the system promoted fraudulent deals, encouraging embezzlement, bribery and corruption. The Minister of Finances, Herr Waigel, in a letter to Frau Breuel of 8 December 1992, admitted: 'As the legislator had provided *Treuhand* with a margin in respect of privatisation processes, an indictment for embezzlement will, as a rule, not be provable.'[23]

Liquidation procedures involving enterprises valued at many millions were entrusted to nine former top employees of *Treuhand* who took 15 per cent of the total fees allocated to the approximately 600 liquidation officers under the institution. The Munich-based lawyer Karl Tynek was put in charge of liquidations for which fees of DM27.5 million (£11 million) were charged – a sum corresponding to about 50 working years for one person. As the one man could, naturally, not perform this work on his own, he charged a further DM6 million for qualified assistants.[24]

Numerous *Treuhand* managers were indicted for corruption, the biggest fish among them being probably Herr Tränkner, the man in charge of the liquidation department. After most careful investigations undertaken by the German central office for the prosecution of crimes involving the Government and in connection with unification, Tränker was indicted for embezzlement. In one instance suspected of having cashed half a million too much,[25] he covered up for liquidators who charged excess payments, and was also charged with using criminal liquidation methods, e.g. coercing the profitable and ecological pioneer refrigerator firm, *Foron GmbH, Niederschmiedeberg*, into liquidation.

Though the Public Prosecution instituted extensive investigations, employing 150 public prosecutors and investigators fine-combing 51 premises, the camouflaging practices by the *Treuhand* management prevented sufficient evidence being found. Herr Tränkner was not sacked but left *Treuhand* of his own free will, with plans to open a rehabilitation company to serve the remaining *Treuhand* enterprises.[26]

Treuhand public relations officer Wolf Schöde stated that their own investigations had led to the conclusion that their representatives were innocent of indictable acts. The networks of secrecy, distortion, camouflage and spiriting away of evidence also turned the investigation by a parliamentary commission, only established in September 1993 under pressure from the opposition, into an ineffective sham. The Federal Government, accused of having gravely neglected its duty to control the Breuel institution, operated hand in glove with that institution, and blocked the commission's work by withholding 80 per cent of the evidence, classifying files as confidential as soon as the commission applied for them. Only when the SPD threatened to turn to the Constitutional Court was the commission allowed access to a fraction of the documents.[27]

Both the Minister of Finances and, of course, Frau Breuel and her representatives, claimed that their work has been spectacularly successful, despite some 'serious errors made'.[28] Their mistake, they insisted, had merely been to underestimate the difficulties due to the East German enterprises' uncompetitiveness and their former managers' 'closeness to the state'. In the introduction to the 560-page whitewash report on '*Treuhandanstalt* – Daring the Impossible', the public was asked 'not to judge *Treuhand*'s achievement only on the strength of mishaps, failures, and also criminal proceedings'.[29]

By March 1994, their assignment nearly concluded, *Treuhand* had privatised 13,800 industrial enterprises; a further 3,354 had been closed down. *Treuhand* admitted that the transactions had produced no assets, only liabilities to the tune of DM230 billion, to which some DM45 billion would have to be added to deal with what would be left by the end of 1994. These liabilities meant a national debt of nearly DM2,000 billion being placed on the German taxpayer. Nobody later mentioned the pious plans of 1990 which foresaw the allocation of bonds on GDR national property to be distributed to each East German citizen as their share of the expected eventual revenue from that property.

It was in fact perfectly legal for *Treuhand* to block redevelopment measures at many enterprises and thereby jeopardise their existence, which alone would have safeguarded the continued existence of entire regions, for example: the camera firm of *Pentacon*, the film producers *Orwo*, the computer works *Robotron* in Sömmerda, *Interflug* airport, Mansfeld mining company, almost the entire textile, leather and clothing trades, and the household goods industry, which employed 460,000 women in GDR times, some 90 per cent of whose enterprises went bankrupt.

This development had been preceded by changes in the conditions of payment for the entire GDR trade with the USSR, the GDR's major export customer. The inevitable result of switching over from GDR currency to the Deutschmark was that most of the big machine tool and other capital goods producers lost this trade and collapsed. Government guarantees (*Hermes-Bürgschaften*) only came into operation much later.

The profitable petrol refinery at Leuna was filleted, being handed over to a consortium comprising Elf Aquitaine, Thyssen and the DSB Commercial Union, the hydrogenation works at Zeitz and the GDR petrol station chain of Minol being added for good measure. When Elf Aquitaine demanded further profitable favours, these were granted. What the purchasers had no use for was dissolved.

For one Deutschmark, the former Premier of Lower Saxony and Breuel's one-time boss, Ernst Albrecht, acquired the iron and foundry works at Thale complete with the workers' holiday homes. He sold back a children's holiday home to the local community for the actual price these premises were worth. The billionaire Claus Wisser from Frankfurt bought the Teltow equipment and regulator works, another enterprise worth billions, also for the princely sum of one Deutschmark, and was also given the usual presents of millions for reconstruction. The Slovak iron works VSZ A.S. Kosice, being owned by an Eastern European foreigner, had to hand over DM1 million for the rolling mill at Finow. The Italian *Riva* concern was given the steel works at Hennigsdorf and Brandenburg, cutting it down to fit its own purposes. Having also signalled interest in the last major steel works of the GDR, EKO Eisenhütten-stadt, with an investment grant of DM800 million, *Riva* withdrew from the deal in May 1994.

On 2 June 1994 Otto Köhler, a well-known West German journalist and writer, in an interview on the Brandenburg broadcasting station ORB, said there ought to be a commission similar to that in Salzgitter, which, during the GDR period, collected evidence of instances of GDR government activities and crimes, to collect data on the crimes of *Treuhand*.

Whilst a considerable number of *Treuhand* managers were involved in shady deals and some of them were actually indicted for infringements of the law, most *Treuhand* activities were perfectly legal, however, undertaken in an officially authorised exercise of its mandate to wind up the GDR economy.

The Return of the *Junkers*

Among the most questionable trends since 1989 has been the revival, by the grace of the German Government and parliament, of the old German *Junkers*. This class of aristocratic landlords declined more than 100 years ago. Fear of their workers made the political spokesmen of the then up-and-coming German capitalists under Bismarck decide to ally themselves to these landed gentry. In the period of the Weimar Republic from 1918 to 1933, members of that class were generally conservative; one of their most prominent figureheads, General Field Marshal von Hindenburg, helped Hitler to take power.

In 1945, about 3.3 million hectares which belonged to major landlords, active nazis and war criminals, or which were state property, were expropriated without compensation and transferred to the agrarian reform fund, out of which 2.1 million hectares were given to poor farmers, agricultural labourers and refugees from formerly German territories in Eastern Europe. The remaining 1.2 million hectares became nationalised land administered by state farms and forestry enterprises. The bulk of these lands were situated in Mecklenburg-West Pomerania and Brandenburg, the sites of the East-Elbian *Junkers'* estates.

In post-1945 West Germany, the emigrés from the area east of the Elbe prospered on compensation and bank credits which allowed most of them to establish themselves in business. Since the '*Anschluß*', their lobby has become exeedingly powerful and has loudly clamoured for the 'reparation of the wrong they suffered from the land reform'.

Treuhand offered some 770,000 hectares of forest, much of it nature reserves, for sale, preferably to West German bidders, at particularly low prices, despite vehement protests by the Society for the Protection of Nature (NABU), the Union of German Forest Owners' Associations, and others.[30]

The Unification Treaty of 1990 stipulated that

land expropriated under occupation law or authority (1945 to 1949) was not to be restituted. The Governments of the Soviet Union and the German Democratic Republic saw no way to revise the measures then taken. The Government of the Federal Republic of Germany acknowledged this in view of the historical development. It felt that a future United German parliament would take a final decision regarding a possible compensation by the state in lieu of restitution. On 23 April 1991 the Federal Constitutional Court confirmed that these 'expropriations under occupation law or authority (1945 to 1949) in the former Soviet zone of occupation shall not be revised and are to be considered constitutional'.[31]

Notwithstanding this acknowledgement of the land reforms of 1945 to 1949, the *Bundestag*, on 20 May 1994, passed the Compensation and Conciliation Bill (EALG) which would have paved the way to their virtual repeal. In the debate on 13 May, Parliamentary Secretary of State Jürgen Echternach argued in support of the bill:

> For the victims of the agrarian reform the Federal Government provides, outside formal legislation, the opportunity of reacquiring land under the land acquisition and settlement scheme. Agrarian reform victims are given the chance to acquire expropriated land administered by the Federation at most favourable conditions.[32]

The bill roused great bitterness and indignation, particularly in the East German states most concerned. Brandenburg's Prime Minister Manfred Stolpe (SPD) called it a major assault on East German farm land which we must all resist as it would 'put an end to cooperative farming'. The parliament of Mecklenburg-West Pomerania in Schwerin also opposed the bill; even conservative Prime Minister Berndt Seite (CDU) called it unacceptable.[33] The farmers' association of Saxony (less concerned, since agrarian reform land plays a minor role there) appealed to parliament to vote against the bill as it would invalidate the agrarian reform of 1945 to 1949.

On 11 June 1994 the *Bundesrat*, the second German chamber of parliament with an SPD majority, rejected the bill. With the exception of Thuringia, ruled over by a West German CDU Premier, all the East German states, including conservative Mecklenburg-West Pomerania, voted against it. The latter state's Premier, Berndt Seite, asked for equal opportunities for all potential buyers of former land reform land. The Compensation and Reconciliation Bill went before an arbitration panel and a provisional compromise was found which was passed by the *Bundesrat* on 6 September 1994. It authorised the sale of *Treuhand*-administered land reform estates at very favourable conditions to former owners as well as to local farmers and cooperatives; the last-mentioned, however, no matter how many farmers belong to it, count as one buyer and are only allowed to acquire landed property totalling one-eighth of the amount they cultivate. The Constitutional Court announced a revision of the law in 1995 by which time the former owners expect to have won sufficient influence locally and nationally to finally do away with the land reform.[34]

Although the former land-owners were already compensated when they migrated to West Germany, a DM20 billion fund was established out of which DM14.6 billion was allocated to compensation and conciliation payments. Most of the land compensation fund was to come from the Federal budget, i.e. the taxpayer, and DM3 billion to be contributed by *Treuhand*, i.e. from former GDR property. Thus the citizens of the GDR were expected to finance or co-finance, as taxpayers and as the creators of the wealth in question, the return of the former major landlords or their heirs. It goes without saying that these free gifts were to be handed over tax-free.[35]

Land reform 'victims' were to be issued transferable debenture bonds by way of compensation for former property. They would also be allowed to purchase some of their former land at three times its 1935 value which amounted to some 40 per cent of its post-*Wende* value.[36] The local farmers and cooperatives had to take considerable bank loans and were often in such financial straits already that they were unlikely to avail themselves of their right to buy this relatively cheap land. Thus, the revised ruling also clearly favours the former owners.

The small East German family farmers will, as a rule, not survive anyway because they do not have sufficient free capital for the improvements needed to stand up to the fierce European competition; this is why the bulk of the former cooperators preferred to stay in cooperative farming even though the collective forms of enterprises were seriously handicapped by tax and quota discrimination.

No more than four years after unification, the defeat, in the Eastern third of the country, of German big business and landlords who had backed the nazis to the bitter end was in the process of being reversed, even providing their heirs with unexpected and certainly undeserved windfalls.

The likelihood is that the East German countryside will eventually again become what it was before the Allies won the war: the site of major land–owners and of landless, underprivileged labourers, local and seasonal imports from Poland who will work for a pittance.

Expelling East Germans from their Homes

The revision of property rights established on the basis of the provisions of the Potsdam Agreement of 1945 was, by no means, the only form of expropriatory revision. Next to mass unemployment, the greatest problem for East Germans arose from the threat to their established rights to their homes. There were three main ways in which they were disadvantaged to the benefit of West German claims.

First, there was the highly problematical 'restitution before compensation' provision of the Unification Treaty, which gave every former owner of land or premises the right to reclaim their property. All property belonging to people who left the GDR at whatever period, for whatever reasons, and no matter whether they received GDR compensation or were expropriated without compensation, was administered by the GDR. The administration rented the housing property, often a piece of land with some form of building on it, to new tenants desirous of building a house. In rare instances, it even sold the land to them. As most land was public property and available at nominal rents, it never worried most of the new users that they were then in most instances unable to buy the site. They built houses and otherwise improved the property, paying the taxes and rents or rates.

After unification, a total of 2.17 million claims for restitution of property rights were filed under the above-mentioned regulation. The existing users of that property had no claim to the homes they might have spent most of their lives improving. The law to regulate property conflicts allowed 'honest owners', i.e. people who had bought the property of reclaimants before 18 October 1989, the date of Erich Honecker's fall, to keep it. The reclaimants then only had a claim to compensation. The new expropriation threat led to such mass protests by those under threat that the Government was obliged to amend the law. The amendment of 22 July 1992 extended the group of 'honest owners' to persons who bought the property after the stipulated date but arranged to purchase it before, or to people who could prove that the improvements they made before the stipulated deadline were worth at least half the value of the property.

Moreover, East Germans who built their houses on land being reclaimed, this affecting half a million sites, could be given notice to quit the site by the reclaimants. The fear of a 'German–German housing war'[37] induced the *Bundestag* to pass a regulation allowing the owners of housing property on reclaimed sites to either buy the site at half the actual price (which, due to the price explosion for landed property since the *Wende* resulting from unbridled speculation, the ordinary East German could hardly afford to do) or rent it as a permanent tenancy (*Erbpacht*). The rent would amount to a quarter of the charge usual in the West and rise within nine years to the 'normal' level. The unemployed, elderly, or the house-owners with large families among those affected would not even be able to pay the reduced, never mind the 'normal', rent as the following characteristic example from the 20,000 involved in East Berlin alone shows.

A couple with their two children, he a former construction engineer, she a one-time dispensary assistant, moved to a ramshackle house for which they paid more than 3,000 GDR Marks and another 3,200 Marks for the land, which was a lot of money for them at that time. However, as their ownership of the property was not then registered in the land register, they had no legal claim to the site. They took up a 42,000 Marks loan and turned the derelict shack into a comfortable home. If they now wanted to buy the site (again), it would cost them DM190,000. The wife was in retraining, the husband, after a long spell of unemployment, trying to establish himself in business. His prospective earnings in the immediate future would not exceed DM24,000 per annum. Purchasing their own property was therefore out of the question. *Erbpacht*, the permanent tenancy, would cost them DM158 per month for the first year, rising to DM633 by the ninth year, added to which would be maintenance costs of DM600 plus some DM20,000–30,000 for the impending modernisation of the sewerage system planned by the local council. If they sold the house for DM200,000, this sum would be insufficient to buy an adequate replacement flat.[38]

A further way of robbing East Germans of their homes arose from the mistakenly termed 'debt write-off' schemes. Housing in the GDR was almost entirely nationalised. Building residential estates was financed by state loans available to local councils, enterprises and cooperatives at nominal interest rates. In the case of rented housing property, the rents for the flats (the most usual form) were paid into the (state) banks by the housing estate administrations and, in return, these were allocated funds for maintenance. People who owned their houses or lived in housing cooperatives repaid the cheap loans cum nominal interest charges in monthly instalments amounting to no more than the very low average rent. After the 'monetary reform', assets and liabilities of the GDR state bank were taken over by the *Bundesbank* and the cheap loans transformed into normal West German bank loans with the customary high rates of interest. Housing property thus became burdened with liabilities owed to West German finance which had in reality not provided the funds in the first place.

To relieve the housing estate administrations and private house-owners of these sham 'liabilities', the West German Government instituted a 'debt write-off fund'. The 'liabilities' on housing property could be remitted if the price for 15 per cent of the property sold to private buyers before the end of 1993 was paid into that fund. At later dates, more property would have to be sold to get the benefit of the debt remission arrangement to repay the mounting interest on the 'liabilities'. As the bulk of East German tenants were unable to buy their rented flats or houses, many housing administrations rushed madly to sell 15 per cent of the property to West German buyers before the end of 1993. First-rate housing property was thus sold cheaply to banks and other financially well-off buyers. Choice bits of East Berlin real estate thereby changed into West German hands. Although the tenancy contracts in these houses are officially inviolate, the chances are that when large-scale modernisation is carried out by the new owners, the rents will escalate to a level which the present tenants are unable to pay.

Stasi Files: Chief Weapon to Remove the Ex-GDR Intelligentsia

In that last year of the GDR, the former Ministry of State Security was dissolved. Its most important and fateful legacy was tons of files and miles of tape-recordings. These meticulous records, often available in duplicate or triplicate, listed everyone who had ever worked for this institution in whatever capacity. These included the growing army of unpaid informants, and whatever activities this 'shield and sword of the party' had engaged in both at home and abroad, in espionage and in observing the ever-increasing number of suspects and potential suspects in the country. The documents comprised each and every one of the reports handed in by full-time and unofficial agents.

In 1990 civil rights groups had stopped their destruction. After unification, this ambivalent heritage was entrusted to the Rev. Joachim Gauck, a conservative dissident from Mecklenburg-West Pomerania, who became the Federal German Agent for the administration of these documents, generously supplied with funds, staff and extensive premises.

Since then, these documents, uncritically taken at their face value, have spelled the end of thousands of careers – sometimes even leading to the suicide of those incriminated.

Many of the former leading dissidents allowed themselves to be instrumentalised as professional avengers helping to turn GDR history into a list of criminal acts laid at the door of the nomenklatura, and of crimes allegedly perpetrated by every one of the over 80,000 paid officers of the State Security and their hundreds of thousands of unpaid informants.

The material administered by Herr Gauck did not lead to the rightful indictment of people guilty in law of infringements of civil or human rights. Nor was it instrumental in removing those from public office who had committed grave moral offences, such as the clandestine denunciation of colleagues. The Gauck administration became primarily a weapon to remove politically undesirable university staff, school teachers, medical practitioners, practising lawyers and civil servants. Political vetting by the Gauck administration meant that if the person's name was registered in the often inconclusive documents, it was assumed that he or she had acted as an 'unofficial informant'. Without further investigation to clarify whether the person had, indeed, committed him/herself to this activity, or under what circumstances, for what motives and with what effects (if any) on others, he or she would be instantly dismissed. Thus a professor at one of the East German universities was forced to give in his notice because he had signed an agreement to act as an 'IM' (unofficial informant). Some 20 years earlier, he had been blackmailed by *Stasi* officers into signing in return for being allowed to adopt his niece, the small daughter of his sister who had illegally left the country. He did not write a single report and therefore never harmed anybody. In the case of the former reforming chancellor of Humboldt University in 1989/90, the professor of theology Heinrich Fink, who had himself been observed by the *Stasi*, some ambiguous record in the files sufficed to give him the sack. Rehabilitated in a first court trial, the Senate of Berlin instituted a second in which two *Stasi* officers acting as his witnesses, who confirmed that he had never been their agent, were considered unreliable, and his dismissal was found legitimate on the strength of the ambivalent entry in the file.

While a shadow of a doubt is enough to deprive a teacher, engineer or post office worker of his or her living with no chance of ever finding work in his or her profession or trade again, a multiparty commission was installed working for more than a year to investigate the pros and cons of the *Stasi* connections of Brandenburg's Prime Minister Manfred

Stolpe. The former lawyer in the service of the Protestant Church had frequently negotiated with the *Stasi* in order to promote the Church's demands for more democracy and human rights, for which he was subjected to an increasing campaign of vilification by sections of the media, and by certain groups of former dissidents from GDR days. The Ministry of State Security was thus turned into a myth of unmitigated evil. This has also so far circumvented the indictment, never mind the punishment, of those guilty of real infringements of human rights. Thus the abuse of authority, for which members of various party apparatuses, and by no means only or chiefly the *Stasi*, were responsible, which led to long-term imprisonment, loss of positions or other discrimination for many individuals, has remained unrevenged. Thus those who, in GDR days, eliminated such political opponents as Rudolf Herrnstedt, one-time chief editor of *Neues Deutschland*, Robert Havemann, victim of nazi and Stalinist oppression, who lost his professorship and was detained in his house until his death, the late writer and publisher Walter Janka, the economist and ecologist Rudolf Bahro, one-time Minister of State Security Wilhelm Zaisser, communist activists and antifascists like Paul Merker, Leo Bauer and Bruno Goldhammer, the two last-mentioned kept for some years in Soviet detention, all of whom were loyal citizens who only wanted a more democratic socialism, got off scot-free. It only remains to recall that in West Germany ex-nazi and war criminals mostly had no problems achieving high and even highest office.

Investigation into GDR History

The *Bundestag* established a committee of inquiry to investigate the history of the GDR. Where there might have been some justification in carrying out an investigation of the cold war policies of both German states, the chief aim of the findings of this committee seemed to be to prove the GDR to have been an 'unlawful state' ('*Unrechtsstaat*'), this, in turn, substantiating the equation of the GDR with the nazi system. Although 'the GDR had not prepared a war of aggression' and 'racism and antisemitism were alien to the ruling ideology', the difference between the systems, the inquiry concluded, was merely 'one of the degree of criminal inhumanity'.[39]

This approach led the former dissident, Professor Wolfgang Harich, himself imprisoned in GDR times, to establish an alternative inquiry commission whose meetings were public and exceedingly well attended. He and his friends tried to establish a more balanced picture of the past. The official evaluation of the GDR gives that country no credit for not having, as the nazis did, officially legitimised the murder of political adversaries and genocidal 'ethnic purges'. Those who supported and served the nazis were never prosecuted in West Germany unless they were actually found guilty of a specific crime, and frequently not even then. Unconvicted, high-ranking nazis continued in their jobs, and, later, drew generous pensions, their families being eligible to claim dependants' pensions. Not so in the case of those who were now considered to have been 'close to the (GDR) state'. 'In the past three years more scholars were dismissed for political reasons than in more than 40 years of GDR existence', wrote Professor Kiel from Halle in June 1994, calling for their rehabilitation. While in GDR times, most of those politically discriminated against were not promoted, were handicapped in their academic progress, had their right to publish their findings restricted, etc., the new victims of political discrimination were deprived of their entire academic existence.[40]

Even the pensions of people considered to have been 'close to the state', i.e. all professional people (teachers, doctors, academics), civil servants, as well as anybody who ever worked in whatever capacity (be it but a cook or typist) for the police, armed forces or, of course, the State Security, were drastically reduced. Professional people's supplementary state pensions were frozen at the 1989 level, amounting to at most half the pension of a West German of corresponding rank, with the likelihood of the older pensioners never living long enough to ever get an increase.

Further Radical Changes

No doubt, the changed property relations described above constitute the most radical aspect of East Germany's transformation. Nevertheless, the changes in the social status of the East Germans in general and of the intelligentsia in particular, as well as the changes affecting the entire science, culture, literature and art of the country, affected people no less. West German legislation completely replaced GDR law. The united German legislation privileged property owners and discriminated against tenants, wage-earners and the needy in general, the handicapped, single parents, unmarried couples, foreigners and children. It favoured men before women in marriage, divorce, and in respect of pensions. The GDR laws providing for a legal claim to a job and a home, to paid leave of one year for either parent, or the grandmother, to look after a first and second child, and 18 months for every subsequent child, extensive paid leave for children's sickness, and other similar social amenities went altogether or were replaced by the much less generous arrangements provided by the former West Germany. Formerly self-evident rights, e.g. free or very cheap services for the handicapped and elderly, child-care institutions and youth clubs, holiday camps, etc., were no longer available, or were very expensive. On the other hand, new opportunities to buy on credit inveigled many an unsuspecting consumer into a mountain of debt, a contributory factor, for instance, in the increase in homelessness.[41]

The policy of appropriating such GDR industrial property as could be fitted into the 'capitalist revolution' and destroying what could not, of aiding and abetting the return of the former land-owning class, and the expulsion of thousands of East Germans from their homes was complemented by the transformation of the workplace, where the former atmosphere of cooperation and solidarity among the staff faded fast. In industry and the services, this came about through the polarisation of the former relatively equal level of wages and salaries. Thus the living standards of those employed in one and the same firm, within one branch of industry or area, between workers at more profitable workplaces (banks, insurance companies) and less profitable ones, between the upper and lower ranks of the gainfully employed, between men and women, between those in and those out of work and, last but not least, between West and East differed widely. The fear of not being kept on in a situation where finding a new job was almost impossible undermined resistance and made people put up with cuts in wages and greater demands on their time and strength. Confidence in their trade unions became brittle as the latter accepted compromise agreements. Furthermore, the hierarchic union structures tended to reflect those in society: top officers' incomes being those of top managers in industry, with increments from their insider knowledge as members of the boards of big monopoly firms. All of this increasingly isolated the staff from one another, who felt there was no one to protect them. Even the status of shop stewards became more vulnerable.

Reducing staff to lean production level therefore roused little protest. Only where the very existence of a large number of people was simultaneously jeopardised would they move – as in the case of the Bischofferode miners, the 130 staff members of the Belfa battery works in Berlin, the 400 sit-in strikers at the long-established hunting and sports weapons workshop at Suhl in Thuringia, the strikers at the steel works at Eisenhüttenstadt and elsewhere in East Germany – all these being industrial actions in the period 1992/93. Subsequent activities were less spontaneous protests of workers against their workplaces being destroyed than token strikes called by the unions when the rights of workers and employees in the whole of Germany were jeopardised. A case in point was the industrial struggle involving post office workers, who feared massive deterioration of working conditions following the privatisation of the postal services.

Under the pretext of righting the wrong done under the GDR system and of aligning it to the West German system, first the cream of the East German intelligentsia was ousted from public office, then the middle strata in universities and such other academic institutions as were allowed to survive became a prey to the policy of 'economising at public expense'.

The onslaught upon GDR culture, the replacement of the comprehensive school system by a class-divided one, the closure of academies and colleges, sports, senior citizens' and youth clubs, the replacement of the national health service by a very much more expensive and less popular commercial one, the lack of sufficient vocational training places, the likelihood of ending up in unpaid idleness after graduating from training or university, the cuts in the subsidies for theatres, orchestras, ballet groups, amateur music and theatrical activities, the blatant commercialisation of entertainment, the new availability, even to school children, of drugs, the cheeseparing down of funds for women's, children's and other social and academic projects, all had profound effects on the mood of the people. While the response to these changes differed widely between those who welcomed the chance to get to grips with this new reality and those who gave up, the bulk of East Germans meanwhile became very critical of the present social system.

The East German Response to Steamroller Unification

The moral and ethical values and the life styles in the country derived not from Stalinist rule but from the non-capitalist structures, as reflected in the discourses which could still be distinguished from the 'West' German ones, did not seem to be disappearing as fast as was expected. On the contrary, while individuals might hesitate to stick their necks out in face of encroachments on their rights at work, the rigorous steamrolling of East German culture in the wider sense of the word actually created what the former GDR rulers never achieved: an East German identity.

This was seen by a West German author in an article on the reconstruction of East Germany as 'indigenous factors of East German identity, which constitute an obstacle to the East German upswing' and he mentioned the 'trends frequently to be observed ... of a hierarchically oriented personality, intrinsically geared to being briefed, ... related to persons, closely internalised but subject to outside guidance, conformist', as against the West German personality, described by the author as 'market-oriented, negotiable, open to conflict, competition-oriented, expressive and open, individualist.'

He described an incident he considered typical of the East German mentality in the post-1989 period of adaptation when production often collapsed:

> Zero working hours were necessary in an East German enterprise. The management thereupon also took their 'fair' share in this arrangement. They did not mind that thereby the entire enterprise was paralysed. The avoidance of bad feelings among the workers which would have arisen had the burden of adapting the enterprise to Western conditions not been shared equally was considered of superior importance.[42]

The author never even asked himself what activities the management could pursue under the circumstances which forced the firm (presumably at the injunction of *Treuhand*) into inactivity. Neither did he consider that this was probably the only way in which the entire firm could express its protest.

In an opinion poll of December 1992 in East Berlin and Saxony-Anhalt, 48 per cent considered social security the best thing about the GDR, 14.4 per cent a safe job. Regarding the GDR's worst feature, 23 per cent felt this to be the lack of freedom to travel, while only 7.8 per cent nominated the State Security. Only 0.7 per cent found the GDR wholly good, and only 1 per cent wholly bad.[43] Another opinion poll found that 58.3 per cent of those interviewed felt excluded, at present, from political decision-taking, and 72.9 per cent wanted a new constitution. Only 9.4 per cent shared the official view that the GDR was an 'unlawful state' while 65.2 per cent consider it the failed attempt to build a just society.[44]

A difference from the early post-*Wende* period, when East Germans set about trying out the new Western commodities, was that East

German products made a comeback. The weekly *Das Parlament* devoted a whole page to the 'surprising revival of East German commodities', evaluating this 'turning of the people back to "their own" Eastern products since 1992 as a deliberate act of self-preservation – individually and socially ... amounting to a vote by means of the shopping basket.'[45]

The lack of success of some West German periodicals among readers of the former GDR was a constant matter of contention, wrote the *Frankfurter Allgemeine*,[46] while the same paper explained away the continued, or rather the new, popularity in East Germany of the left-wing daily *Neues Deutschland* by telling its readers that it was the paper 'of a fallen ruling caste'.[47] They thereby ignored the change of composition of both readers and contributors, the latter now also including prominent former dissidents. High listening/viewing figures in the East were recorded where GDR actors, producers, etc., appeared in television features, or where day-to-day East German problems were critically commented upon.

Defiance and Resistance

The defiant mood, which became very general in East Germany, revealed many contradictory features. The illusion that unification would bring the East Germans freedom and wealth faded and was replaced by an awareness that they were now part of a system even less just than the one they wiped off the face of the earth. The people realized that their present rulers, the established parties' top echelons, were neither less corrupt nor more philanthropic. Quite a number of people, women overproportionally represented among them, became aware that they had been robbed of social benefits they ought to have fought to retain. Most of those who, for a brief historical moment in October/November 1989 felt they could get things really moving now again felt there was nothing they could do about it all. They returned to their niches, glad if they had been allowed to keep their jobs or find another one, even though gainful employment had been totally stripped of the rather cosy neighbourly qualities of GDR times and was becoming more and more of a rat race. If they were in work, and even if not, they could take advantage of and rejoice in the plentiful supplies of commodities in the shops, in the cheap holidays to the many places they could not visit before, in many new and exciting leisure pursuits.

Quite a number of those who were politically active in 1989 now kept out of politics and instead committed themselves to some project in line with their political position or outlook, e.g. women's studies, or work among the refugees. Or, particularly if unemployed or in enforced retirement, they went in for autonomous schemes of political education, for historical, sociological, Marxist and other studies. At the same time there was no hard and fast demarcation line between this majority and the articulate, sometimes even vociferous, minority who were making use of the democratic rights they had been deprived of in the GDR, and who opposed the politics of the new regime. There were such factions in all the political parties, prominent among them in this respect being the non-hardliners in the Party of Democratic Socialism (PDS; the reformed successor party to the SED), who formed the majority of that party's activists and, without giving way to nostalgia, opposed the unbridled discrimination meted out to the East. These, often young, people wanted a united Germany which would be a true home for all who lived there, a place where they could earn their living, bring up their children and enjoy their lives in a world no longer torn by wars, where natural resources were respected and the ever-growing division between rich and poor, North and South, was at least reduced.

There were many independent associations in the tradition of the GDR civil rights groups, e.g. the Independent Women's Federation, or groups of professionals, pensioners, senior citizens, school and university students, tenants, parents, etc., and clubs organising the protest of those whose jobs, research and other scholarly ventures, pensions, homes, summer cottages, child-care facilities, schools, clubs, etc., were jeopardised. Others might rally to oppose the excessive charges for installing, for instance, new sewerage. There were antifascists who opposed the ruthless deleting of names of streets recalling communist and socialist resistance fighters murdered by the nazis, or the plans to raze to the ground memorials to antifascists as the Berlin Senate would like to do to the Thälmann memorial in the district of Prenzlauer Berg and had already done to the Lenin memorial. There were those who carried on a deeply committed struggle against the erosion of democratic rights, among them the right of refugees from any oppression to find shelter in Germany. Patients of medical specialists ousted from their posts rallied in protest meetings, and letters of protest were showered on those responsible for sacking popular university professors. Many expressed their outrage against the dismissal of a popular scholar, artist or teacher at meetings or in letters to the press.

The discrimination against people who had merely been loyal to their government without having committed any offence in law, among them prominent physicians, scientists, artists, sportspeople, actors, writers, increasingly roused public indignation as opposed to consensus.

No New 1933

Although the daily violence against refugees and the increase of racist and antisemitic acts including arson and murder seem to point towards a German renazification, this would be the wrong conclusion to draw. It was true that a growing number of young and even very young people were becoming the prey of extreme right-wing and fascist demagogues, but these neofascist elements both in East and West were but a small minority. They were, however, supported by right-wing and conservative politicians, and by some policemen and judges. They were, moreover, encouraged by the implicitly nationalistic positions underwritten both by the government and by the opposition towards 'our foreign co-citizens', notwithstanding constant professions of profound friendship towards and sympathy for them.

Following the Inglorious Unification, Where Do We Go Now?

This book provides selected information on what its authors consider focal issues characterising the nature of German unification. Chapter 2 surveys the political scene, providing the reader with information on the character and record of the political parties in East Germany. They all shared the reality of having evolved from the GDR past, and their integration into the West German parliamentary system reveals essential facts about the political situation in contemporary Germany. The transformation of the 'planned economy', discussed in Chapter 3, under the auspices outlined above will suggest to readers that the option taken has proved to be against the interests of the broad majority not only of the people of the former GDR but of the whole of Germany. It can even be said to have tipped the balance to the disadvantage of the European nations. Both this Chapter and Chapter 4 outlining the specifics of the agricultural transformation make clear that other options would have also been possible in establishing a market economy.

Chapters 1 to 4 surveying the political and economic transformation are followed by Chapter 5 which puts the case of the women, that largest section of losers from '*Anschluß*'-type unification. Again, their losses remain not without ill-effects for the hard-won advances of the German and global women's movements in the 1970s.

The history of the growth of neonazi activities in a country otherwise boasting of its antifascist nature, and the East–West connections of this right-wing extremist faction, is discussed in Chapter 7, complementing Chapter 2 on the political parties.

Chapter 6 outlines the policy pursued by the German 'victors' vis-à-vis GDR science and culture. In this Chapter, perhaps even more than in the others, many aspects of the subject had to be completely neglected or could only be barely touched upon, just as it was also not possible to do justice to it in this introduction. The fate of GDR dramatic art, film and television productions, of sport, at one time so highly appreciated, of the writers, to mention just a few of these subjects, would deserve another book. The authors have based their evaluation of the subject matter they dealt with on their professional competence. These assessments do not tally in every respect with those of the editor.

As is shown in this book, East Germany, undergoing a painful transformation, is affecting the whole of 'Greater Germany' in more ways than the West Germans are as yet aware of. East Germany's lot is a characteristic instance of processes also going on elsewhere.

The whole of Europe, indeed the entire world, is at a crossroads. Humankind will only survive if people everywhere realise what is at stake: is the option exemplified by the present destruction of what made up the former GDR to become the general principle guiding the dealings of the powerful with the rest of the world? Will the world in the future be a place worth living in only for a shrinking élite who will pursue a policy geared to keeping up their lifestyle, wealth and power at the price of the segregation, impoverishment or even genocidal annihilation of those not needed, and therefore unwanted? Our other option has yet to take shape. Its strategies need still to be elaborated – by the people affected when they realise that they, and only they, can do this: globally.

Notes

1. The events of October 1989 which swept away the undemocratic system under Honecker and broke down the Berlin Wall.
2. *Junge Welt*, 1 June 1994. Already on 11 January 1994 Minister of Economy Günter Rexrodt announced his plans for an enhance-

ment of cooperation between German and foreign arms manufacturers. General export permits granted to the cooperating firms
were to replace the checks on each export consignment to safeguard
'a minimal number of orders for the firms and the minimal
equipment of the *Bundeswehr* and the other allied armed forces'
(*Berliner Zeitung*,11 January 1994).
3. Gregor Gysi, 'Zur politischen Situation und zum Programm der
PDS' [On the political situation and the programme of the PDS],
Disput 3/4 (1993: Parteivorstand der PDS, Berlin), p. 18.
4. Quoted from *Neues Deutschland*, 30 May 1994.
5. Quoted from *Junge Welt*, 1 June 1994. Herr Rexrodt, too, believed
that the wages in East Germany had risen too fast and that the supplementary liabilities of firms in respect of social benefits which
the law and wage agreements prescribe needed correcting because
'employment opportunities are curbed since the nature and scope
of the social benefits exceed the possibilities of our market society'
(*Neues Deutschland,* 11 December 1993).
6. These sentiments were echoed by John Parker in *The Economist*'s
survey of Germany of 21 May 1994.
7. Gysi, 'Zur politischen Situation', p. 22.
8. Ibid., p. 19.
9. Uwe Witt, 'Die Schere öffnet sich immer weiter' [The gap widens],
Junge Welt, 8 June 1994.
10. Uwe Witt, 'Die Banken sind immer und überall die Gewinner'
[The banks are the winners – always and everywhere] *Junge Welt*,
28 April 1994.
11. Petra Wache, 'Die Milliarde – bisher ein Flop' [The billion – a
flop so far], *Berliner Zeitung*, 15 February 1994.
12. The optimistic May 1994 report by the *Bundesanstalt für Arbeit* which
shows a seasonal decrease of the winter figures. Quoted from
Neues Deutschland, 8 June 1994.
13. Gysi, 'Zur politischen Situation', p. 19.
14. John Parker, 'Model Vision: Germany', *The Economist*, 21 May 1994,
p. 7. Among other howlers, Parker makes 'wage inflexibility'
responsible for 'huge government subsidies to bankrupt industries
such as coal and steel' when their market is destroyed by imported
Polish dumping of priced coal and Polish and Russian steel mined
and forged by workers existing at Third World living standards. It
is not the wages which are subsidised. In 1993 1,300 jobs were lost
each month at the West German Rheinhausen steel works; the East
German counterpart at Schwedt suffered job cuts from 2,000 to

500, quite apart from the job losses in other East German steel and mining enterprises. Mr Parker's contention that the 35 hours working week is the culprit which prevents the redundant (miners and steelworkers?) getting jobs in the servicing trades is no less ludicrous. Already neither shop assistants, nor railway or bus drivers, nor postal workers enjoy a 35-hour week. Their proper working week is between 38 and 40 hours, not counting unpaid or badly paid overtime (teachers, child-care and health workers get no overtime payments). None of this has prevented mass unemployment – on the contrary. As for the author's reference to the debt write-offs, I refer to Chapter 3 below on the economy. His references to the restoration of 'stolen property', particularly the assertion that former owner's compensation amounted to only 20 per cent of the actual value of their property, bear no resemblance to reality. The matter is discussed in Chapter 3 and in Chapter 4 below on agriculture.

15. Parker, 'Model Vision', p. 8.
16. Gysi, 'Zur politischen Situation', p. 18.
17. Christa Luft, *Treuhandreport*, (1992: Aufbauverlag, Berlin), p. 40, writes: 'Also on 1 March 1990 the Council of Ministers decided to transform the national trusts, enterprises, and institutions into structures in conformity with a market economy, i.e. into joint-stock companies.'
18. Ibid., p. 66.
19. Gerhard Wisnewski, Wolfgang Landgraeber and Ekkehard Sieker, *Das RAF-Phantom* [The RAF phantom] (1992 Knaur, Munich), pp. 230–3.
20. Ibid., pp. 243–59; see also Otto Köhler, *Die große Enteignung* [The great expropriation] (1994: Knaur, Munich), pp. 228–9.
21. Gysi, 'Zur politischen Situation', pp. 19–21.
22. 'Breuel-Behörde guckt nicht auf die Mark' [Breuel institution not cheeseparing], *Berliner Zeitung,* 5 March 1994.
23. Otto Köhler, 'Treuhand-Geschichte', *Junge Welt,* 8 June 1994.
24. 'Vorwürfe gegen Bereich Abwicklung der Treuhand' [*Treuhand* liquidation department censured], *Berliner Zeitung,* 9 May 1994.
25. 'Treuhand-Ermittlungen – Eine Million Mark Schaden' [*Treuhand* investigations: Spoils of one million Marks], *Berliner Zeitung,* 19 April 1994.
26. Dietmar Koschmieder, 'Solidarität mit Treuhand-Direktor Tränkner' [Solidarity with *Treuhand* director Tränkner], *Junge Welt,* 30 April 1994. A rehabilitation company is a firm which handles the recon-

struction considered necessary (in view of the totally changed market conditions) prior to selling the enterprise to a private bidder.

27. *Berliner Zeitung,* 4 February 1994; *Junge Welt,* 12 March 1994 . State Secretary of Finances Joachim Grünewald (CDU) retaliated, on 14 April in the *Bundestag*'s question time, that the commission's demands for documents were excessive. The commission cost the taxpayers DM6–8 million per annum. The Government and *Treuhand* had handed over as much as 139,000 sheets of material (*Berliner Zeitung,* 15 April 1994).

28. 'Breuel: "Eklatante Fehler"' [Breuel: 'Serious errors were made'], *Berliner Zeitung,* 8 March 1994.

29. Hans-Werner Oertel, 'Außer Geburtsfehlern war eigentlich alles optimal' [Apart from congenital deficits everything was fine], *Neues Deutschland,* 13 February 1993.

30. Heidrun Braun, 'Tafelsilber wird verscherbelt' [Our treasures are squandered away], *Junge Welt,* 20 April 1994.

31. Quoted from *Neues Deutschland,* 10 May 1994, p. 3.

32. Ibid.

33. '"Infame" Entschädigung' ['Disgraceful' compensation], *Berliner Zeitung,* 20 May 1994.

34. *Neues Deutschland,* 8 September 1994, also points out that only a few of the former owners are likely to cultivate the land. Most of them will just collect the rents, thus depriving the national, regional and local budgets of dearly needed revenue.

35. '18 Milliarden Mark im Entschädigungsfonds' [18 billions compensation fund], *Neues Deutschland,* 20 May 1994.

36. 'Die Junker kommen zurück' [The *Junkers* are returning], *Junge Welt,* 20 May 1994.

37. 'Gefahr des "Häuserkriegs" eingedämmt' [Danger of a housing war mitigated], *Berliner Zeitung,* 29 April 1994.

38. Sabine Deckwerth, 'Wir haben uns als Eigentümer gefühlt' [We thought we owned the place], *Berliner Zeitung,* 9 March 1994.

39. *Berliner Zeitung,* 5 May 1994.

40. Siegmund Kiel, 'Das Prinzip "Aschenputtel"' [The 'Cinderella' principle], *Neues Deutschland,* 10 June 1994.

41. Heinrich Stein, 'Obdachlosigkeit nimmt im Osten immer mehr zu' [Homelessness on the increase in the East], *Junge Welt,* 25 November 1993.

42. F. Klinger, 'Aufbau und Erneuerung: Über die institutionellen Bedingungen der Standortentwicklung in Deutschland' [Recon-

struction and renovation: On the institutional conditions of developing industrial sites in Germany], *Aus Politik und Zeitgeschichte*, supplement of *Das Parlament*, 12 April 1994, B17/94, pp. 6ff.
43. *Berliner Zeitung*, 10/11 July 1993.
44. *Neues Deutschland*, 4 May 1994, quoting Ident-Projekt, PF345, 13003 Berlin.
45. *Das Parlament*, 28 January/4 February 1994.
46. *Frankfurter Allgemeine*, 25 March 1993.
47. *Frankfurter Allgemeine*, 17 March 1993.

2   East German Political Parties and Movements Before and After the Fall of the GDR

Manfred Behrend

Five years after German unification, East German political parties and organisations are still very different from those in West Germany.

The history of the former started with Order No. 2 of the Soviet Military Administration in Germany, dated 10 June 1945, which admitted the establishment and activities of antifascist parties, free trade unions and organisations acting in the interests of the working people. Based on this order, the Communist Party of Germany (KPD), the Social Democratic Party of Germany (SPD), the Christian Democratic Union (CDU), the Liberal Democratic Party of Germany (LDPD), and political organisations like the Free German Trade Union Council (FDGB), the Free German Youth (FDJ), the Democratic Women's Federation (DFD), etc., registered in the Soviet occupation zone and Berlin in mid-1945. Similar to the organisations then established in the West, they intended, until the 1960s, to expand throughout Germany and not only in one occupation zone. It was, above all, essential to eliminate the fascist heritage and to guide the war-damaged country along the road to reconstruction. The decision of the East German political parties to join forces and form an antifascist bloc was not only the wish of the Soviet side, but also stemmed from the awareness of the job to be done.

Emergence and Subsequent Stagnation of the East German Political System

The concepts of the individual political parties differed in accordance with the interests of the different classes and strata of society they represented. There was unanimity that, as the Communists first put it, 'it would be wrong to force the Soviet system on to Germany'. 'The decisive interests of the German people in the current situation dictate ... the setting up of an antifascist, democratic regime, a parliamentary-democratic republic with all rights and liberties for the people'.[1] Although this awareness did not ensure a lasting consensus, the representatives of all parties and organisations still saw it as their duty to set up an antifascist, democratic state by establishing new legislative and executive bodies needed for a democratic society, by implementing land reform and expropriating the big trusts which had collaborated with Hitler, and by reforming the educational system. In fact these steps were more in line with the Allied decisions of Yalta and Potsdam than the actions taken by politicians in the Western occupation zones.

The merger of the Communist and Social Democratic parties was an important step towards a democratic and possible later socialist development. The Social Democrats had been the first to urge the merger at a time when the Communist leaders still held back.[2] This changed in November 1945 when the Communist parties in Hungary and Austria suffered serious election defeats. Now it was the Communist Party of Germany who wanted the merger. A number of SPD leaders, especially Kurt Schumacher operating from the British zone, fiercely opposed this move. Repressive measures in the Soviet zone to force hostile Social Democrats to cooperate strengthened the position of the anti-Communist group of Social Democrats in the West. In the East, most Communists and Social Democrats joined forces voluntarily and founded the Socialist Unity Party of Germany (SED) in Berlin on 21–2 April 1946. Their motives for merging lay in the lessons they had learnt from the fate of their two parties under the nazis.

Although life generally in the Soviet occupation zone (the later GDR) ran smoothly, certain authoritarian trends, like those under Stalin's rule in the Soviet Union, had exceedingly negative effects. The way they 'settled' differences of opinion with leaders of the Christian Democrats and the Liberals, the other two parties of the power bloc, was to put pressure on them or even clap their leaders in jail. Furthermore, two new political parties were formed in the first half of 1948, led by former Communists and in direct competition with the Liberal and Christian Democratic parties – the Democratic Farmers' Party of Germany (DBD) and the National Democratic Party of Germany (NDPD). Then, in the summer of 1948, the transition of the Socialist Unity Party into a 'party of a new type' began, aimed at organising it along the lines of Stalin's Communist Party of the Soviet Union. Under the guise of 'democratic centralism', the rank and file were to implement orders from 'above'. Opponents, former Social Democrats as well as Communists, were attacked as 'enemies of the party', expelled and marginalised. The 'mass organisations', e.g. trade unions and the youth organisation, were degraded to a kind of 'transmission belt' in the service of the SED executive, this being also in line with the Soviet model. The youth organisation, the FDJ, was seen as the 'reserve of the party'.

The Stalinisation of the system brought about the break from the parliamentarian and democratic objectives of 1945. Since the defeat of the Socialist Unity Party at the district and Federal State elections of 20 October 1946 and the failure of the 'People's Congress Movement for Unity and Just Peace', initiated by the SED at the 3rd People's Congress on 15–16 May 1949, free and universal elections on the Western pattern were banned. Subsequently, there was to be only one unified list of the National Front (*Nationale Front*) candidates.[3] In this manner those in power guarded against any unpleasant surprises. By eliminating genuine elections as a means of monitoring the mood of the population, and by also bringing the media into line, thereby eliminating any plurality of political views, they opened the way for bureaucracy and arbitrary decisions. The bond between party leadership and the membership, politicians and the people, imperative for democracy and socialism, was seriously impaired. Opponents of the regime, inside and outside the country, focused on precisely this lack of democracy in their criticism of the regime.

Throughout the history of the GDR and the SED, many attempts were made to reverse this development. Notable examples were in 1953, 1956 and in 1968 in the wake of the invasion of Czechoslovakia on the instigation of the Soviet Union. Somehow the SED leadership always managed to stay in power. Fear of losing their hold motivated the SED bureaucracy to thwart most reform plans, even those put forward in the upper echelons of the SED itself. In the 1960s, for instance, Walter Ulbricht, General Secretary, personally supported the 'new economic system of planning and management'. But that did not save it from being prematurely broken off.

Meanwhile, the GDR party system stagnated more and more. At the helm was the SED, i.e. its leadership and apparatus. In 1968, they set out their own hegemonic claim, of exercising what they misnamed the 'leading role of the working class and its Marxist–Leninist party', as Article 1 of the GDR Constitution.[4] The SED was entitled to nominate the head of state and the Prime Minister and to appoint the main ministers. According to a carefully worked out scheme, the SED in the *Volkskammer* (the GDR parliament) was entitled to 127 (25.4 per cent) of the 500 seats. However, as the majority of the deputies elected by the trade unions

(FDGB), the Free German Youth, the Democratic Women's Federation, the Cultural Association (*Kulturbund*) and, since 1986, the Farmers' Mutual Aid Association (*Vereinigung der Gegenseitigen Bauernhilfe*; VdgB) were also SED members, the SED actually held more than 50 per cent of all seats in parliament. Moreover, it also called the tune in what was called the democratic bloc of parties and mass organisations which had emerged from the antifascist bloc of 1945, now called the National Front.

All decisions not the prerogative of the Soviet occupation forces were taken by the political bureau. This meant in practice by the General or First Secretary of the Central Committee, who also chaired the Politburo, and by his closest advisors. It was a situation actually in contravention of the Constitution, but none of the SED's 'friends in the democratic bloc' dared oppose it. Those taking decisions at the top of the SED hierarchy were, in turn, guided by the apparatus.

The political parties allied to the SED (CDU, LDPD, DBD and NDPD) held 52 seats in the *Volkskammer* each (10.4 per cent), regardless of their actual significance and influence in society. Their leaders were at the same time deputy chairmen of the State Council, a body formally elected by the *Volkskammer*. In 1960 a few more ministers' posts were handed over to the top people of the other political parties, but they had no real share in decision-taking. The SED Politburo and the Secretariat of the Central Committee of the SED checked all important documents and party congress speeches of the 'friends in the democratic bloc' before these were published. The SED even manipulated the membership figures of these parties.[5] Nevertheless, the leadership and apparatus of these satellite parties did wield a certain amount of power in the sense that, in implementing the 'correct' political line laid down by the SED, some acted in an even more authoritarian way than the SED itself.

The political parties in the GDR, especially the SED, owned holiday and political education centres, they had money and other assets, and sizeable real estate. They held highly paid positions and were subsidised by the state right up to the end. Not only the existence, but also the possibilities of a political opposition in the GDR were denied to the very last. The phraseology of the semi-official small political dictionary (*Kleines politisches Wörterbuch*) reads,

> There is no objective social and political basis for an opposition in the socialist countries, because the working class – in an alliance with all gainfully employed – is the ruling class and at the same time the main productive power in society, whose fundamental interests are

as a matter of principle in accordance with those of the other classes and strata of society.[6]

In reality, 'the working class' wielded no power in any 'socialist' country at any point. Power meant the authority of a small group of political bureaucrats far removed from the workers. Not that there was any shortage of causes for an opposition. But though opposition was often voiced, it was usually refused media coverage. 'Opposition', by the way, meant less the extreme right-wing[7] than forces from the left and partly the centre of society. Until near the end, however, opposition groups were not sufficiently strong to bring about political changes under GDR conditions.

GDR Opposition until 1989

The history of opposition in the GDR can only be broadly outlined here. The first to resist against the regime, which promised socialism and democracy but destroyed the prerequisites for either, were actually SED members. Among them were: Rudolf Herrnstadt, editor-in-chief of the SED's main daily newspaper, *Neues Deutschland*; Minister for State Security (*Stasi*) Wilhelm Zaisser; some years later the philosopher Wolfgang Harich; Karl Schirdewan, the man responsible for the policy relating to SED cadres; and the physicist and analytical chemist Professor Robert Havemann. Tens of thousands of ordinary members and officials of the party protested on various issues against the party leadership. Mostly they were on their own, could expect no help from capitalist West Germany, and often paid dearly for their opposition. The contradiction between their socialist ideals and Marxist world views, on the one hand, and political reality, on the other, time and again roused people to protest.

In the 1970s, protests came from intellectual circles, most of whom were party members. For instance, they protested especially against the expatriation of the poet Wolf Biermann from the GDR and against the slandering of novelist Stefan Heym, both harsh critics of the official course. In 1981, a more or less stable group evolved around Robert Havemann, who had been expelled from the party in the mid-1960s after his attacks on the dogmatism in GDR science and on the SED Politburo. He was dismissed from Humboldt University (Berlin) and lost his membership of the Academy of Sciences, and was eventually placed under house arrest at his home in Grünheide, near Berlin. Some of his supporters were socialists, others conservatives like the Rev. Rainer Eppelmann, then an active pacifist. Despite constant surveillance by the *Stasi*, Robert Havemann and his friends managed to establish and maintain contacts across the borders with Western newspapers and publishers, radio and TV. The latter made it possible for their voices to be also heard in the GDR. Differing from official GDR policy, their peace appeals called for disarmament not only of NATO but also in the East. In April 1986, after Robert Havemann's death, his group and other dissidents came out in the open as an autonomous peace movement. They wrote to Erich Honecker criticising the curtailing of civil rights and the economic and environmental policies of the GDR. They also warned against the rise of neofascism in the country.[8]

The Initiative for Peace and Human Rights (*Initiative für Frieden und Menschenrechte*; IFM) was formed at the beginning of 1986 under the wing of the Protestant Church. Its argument was that human rights and peace were inseparable. Where official GDR policy advocated disarmament and détente only, it also demanded civil rights and democratisation. It was a very heterogeneous group, including Bärbel Bohley, Ibrahim Böhme, Thomas Klein, Gerd and Ulrike Poppe and Wolfgang Templin. For a time they formed a kind of general staff of the civil rights movement. Supported by the Environmental Library, established in one of the adjacent buildings to Berlin's Church of Zion, they published 600 copies of a dissident journal by the name of *Grenzfall* (Borderline Case).

A pressure group called Rejection of the Practice and Principle of Segregation (*Absage an Praxis und Prinzip der Abgrenzung*) had been active within the Church since 1986/7. Living up to its name, it opposed an important principle of government policy, namely the rejection of any rapprochement with Western democracy. The group turned to Protestant Church congregations to support its demands for GDR citizens to have freedom of travel to the West and for the dismantling of ideological barriers. As the state crisis of the GDR worsened, this group became more radical. Backed by the writer Christa Wolf and the Consistorial President of the Berlin–Brandenburg Protestant Church, Manfred Stolpe,[9] it drew up an 'appeal for intervention on our own behalf' on 12 September 1989, which led to the foundation of the civil rights movement Democracy Now *(Demokratie Jetzt*; DJ). In their appeal, the authors called for 'an acceptable socialist alternative to Western consumer-oriented capitalism', and also stated: 'We want the socialist revolution, which came to a standstill with nationalisation, to be continued and thus be given a chance in the future.'[10] Among the initiators of Democracy Now were the physicist Hans-Jürgen Fischbeck, the conservative film director Konrad Weiß, the theology professor Wolfgang Ullmann and also Ulrike Poppe, former member of the IFM. All such groups and other civil rights campaigners were under surveillance by the *Stasi*. Some suffered repressive measures, the most serious being directed against the IFM, their journal *Grenzfall* and the Environmental Library on 25/6 November 1987. Action was also taken against groups which had planned a protest against the suppression of free speech at the annual demonstration in honour of Karl Liebknecht and Rosa Luxemburg in Berlin on 17 January 1988. The demonstrators had been taken into custody when they tried to unfurl banners with Rosa Luxemburg's words 'Freedom is always freedom of the dissenter'. However, in comparison to earlier periods, the reaction of the authorities was moderate, suggesting that the leadership had become uncertain how to deal with such forms of opposition. The civil rights campaigners detained in November 1987 were soon set free. Those arrested in January 1988, among them Bärbel Bohley, Wolfgang Templin and Vera Wollenberger, co-founder of the grassroots Church (*Kirche von unten*), were charged with 'riotous assembly'. They were released on condition they left the country for West Germany or Britain, some for good, others temporarily.

The decisive year 1989 saw growing economic difficulties, aggravated political and social contradictions and increasing hostility towards the regime among large parts of the population. The party leadership and government in the second half of the 1980s prevented reforms similar to the Soviet *perestroika*, which had at first been aimed at more socialist democracy. The GDR leaders thwarted truthful reporting in the media, and would not permit GDR citizens to travel freely to the West.

To present to the world a picture of unity of purpose between the leadership and the people, the local elections results of 7 May 1989 were faked, for which Politburo member Egon Krenz was responsible. Even long-standing SED members were indignant about such procedures. On every 7th of the succeeding months, young people, loudly blowing their whistles, marched through the city of East Berlin to remind people of the fraudulent election and demanded punishment of those responsible. In the summer of 1989 the mass exodus of GDR citizens to West Germany started via other 'socialist' countries, especially Hungary. At the same time activities of the opposition in the country increased.

On 9–10 September 1989 the largest oppositional group, Awakening 1989 – New Forum (*Aufbruch 89 – Neues Forum*), was established in Grünheide near Berlin. Among its founders were the painter Bärbel

Bohley, a former IFM member, the lawyer Rolf Henrich, who had been expelled from the SED because of his critical book *Der vormundschaftliche Staat*, (The paternalistic state) and Hans-Jochen Tschiche, principal of Magdeburg Protestant Academy, who had also been active in Robert Havemann's circle. A feature of this new group was that instead of a programme it presented a questionnaire and called for a broad and open discussion of the questions. New Forum became the most popular of the civil rights organisations and participated in demonstrations and meetings, collecting some 200,000 signatures in support of its foundation appeal within only two months.

In September 1989 two more groups sprang up, one more left-wing, the other one more right-wing than the earlier movements. The first calling itself United Left (*Vereinigte Linke*, VL), adopted the 'Böhlen document' (*Böhlener Plattform*) on 3 September. Its aim was 'real socialism' achieved by 'real socialisation' of the national enterprises, self-government by the producers and the elimination of bureaucratic rule by establishing a truly planned economy. Among its initiators were Marxists who had been active in the IFM, like Thomas Klein, and Christian socialists like Marion and Roland Seelig.

The conservative group Democratic Awakening (*Demokratischer Aufbruch*; DA) was introduced to the public through an interview given by one of the founders, the Rev. Edelbert Richter, a clergyman from Erfurt, in a West Berlin newspaper in mid-September.[11] It formally organised itself as a political association on 29 October 1989 in Berlin, and formed a political party on 16/17 December in Leipzig. At both functions, the Rostock lawyer Wolfgang Schnur, who had been introduced by the Rev. Rainer Eppelmann of the Robert Havemann circle in East Berlin, took the chair. Another leading DA figure, the Rev. Friedrich Schorlemmer from Wittenberg, said on 24 October that they were concerned 'with the development of democracy and socialism in our country'.[12] Only a few days later, the basic policy statement of the DA was published, advocating a 'high-performance industrial society of an ecological and social, but not socialist orientation'.[13]

Two years after East German supporters of the Social Democrats had adopted a programme called 'Movement for a Democratic Socialism' (*Bewegung für einen demokratischen Sozialismus*), on 7 October 1989, they founded the Social Democratic Party of the GDR (SDP), in Schwante near Berlin. Their leadership comprised chairman Ibrahim Böhme (a former IFM member) and Angelika Barbe, Stephan Hilsberg and the Rev. Markus Meckel. The party advocated an 'ecologically oriented market economy', but, at the same time, recognition for the continued existence of the two German states. In its inauguration document it stated its readiness to 'cooperate with all democratic initiatives, groups and people in our country, regardless of their structure, their political, religious or social allegiance'.[14]

By then, the situation in the GDR had become explosive. 'We are the people' chanted tens of thousands of participants in the illegal Monday demonstrations in Leipzig, challenging the regime, which regarded itself the sole legitimate representative of the people. Erich Honecker was meanwhile preparing the usual pageant for the occasion of the fortieth anniversary of the GDR's foundation on 7 October 1989. It was to be an historical climax and living proof of the stability of the regime under his leadership. But pressure was growing. By closing the last open GDR border to Czechoslovakia at the beginning of October, the mass exodus of GDR citizens to West Germany via 'friendly states' was interrupted. Growing discontent with the regime in all strata of the population made the regime fear that there would also be demonstrations against them in East Berlin. Expressions of sympathy for victims of the Chinese Tiananmen Square massacre on 3 June 1989 by high-ranking representatives of the regime increased general anxiety, because no one knew whether the regime in the GDR might not resort to similar repressive measures. The brutal attacks on demonstrators by members of a task force and State Security on 4 October in Dresden and 7 October in Berlin indicated that these fears had a real basis.

The fact that they never materialised was due to the Soviet Union renouncing the so-called 'Brezhnev doctrine',[15] stating that it would no longer interfere in domestic issues on behalf of allied regimes. The GDR opposition warded off attacks by demonstrating increasing unanimity and strictly refraining from violence, so as not to give the regime a pretext for retaliating. The broad membership of the SED made it clear that they would not support any repressive measures. The armed forces were not united enough for a large-scale military action to save the isolated Honecker regime, which finally collapsed like a house of cards.

A *putsch* by a group of politbureaucrats around Egon Krenz and Günter Schabowski, leading to the fall of Erich Honecker on 18 October 1989, was only the prologue of events to come. On 4 November 1989, more than 500,000 people demonstrated in Berlin, among them civil rights campaigners and many SED members, for an independent and democratic development of their country. On 8 November 1989, 50,000 Berlin SED party members rallied in front of the Central Committee building, calling on their leadership to account for their disastrous policy. On 1 December, the *Volkskammer* deleted the 'leading role of the SED' from the Constitution. On 3 December 1989, Egon Krenz, the Politburo and the SED Central Committee resigned under the pressure of the party rank and file.

In recollecting these positive events, one of a totally different nature must be added: on 9 November 1989, a significant day in German history,[16] the SED Central Committee opened the GDR borders to the West. They did so to ease the pressure in the country and to win popular support against the critics in their own ranks. Neither of these expectations were realised. The opening of the border seriously jeopardised the chances of an independent democratic development in the GDR and threatened the very existence of the state.

Parties and Movements in the Last Year of the GDR

In late autumn of 1989, and to some extent right up to the end of that year, there was still a chance to transform the German Democratic Republic into a democratic and socialist country. Reformers were to be found among the socialist opposition in the SED, which was then undergoing a process of transformation. Similarly minded people were also to be found in the civil rights movements, to which were added in November/December 1989 the Initiative for a Green League and Green Party (*Initiative für eine Grüne Liga und Grüne Partei*) and the Independent Women's Association (*Unabhängiger Frauenverband*; UFV). There were also reform elements in the mass organisations and the former satellite parties, which were leaving the democratic bloc. Reformers became active especially in the Liberal Democratic Party. Since 1987, its party leader, Manfred Gerlach, had come out for more civil liberties. In 1989, the LDPD handed to the SED proposals for a democratisation, but these were turned down by the SED leadership, which claimed that they would only serve the enemy.[17] In contrast to the NDPD, certain members of the Democratic Farmers' Party were also in favour of reforms, as were a minority of the Christian Democrats. SED members from Thuringia published, in September 1989, the 'Weimar Letter', which sparked off political changes in that area.

In the late autumn of 1989, representatives of all these organisations expressed their determination to find a way to restructure the GDR so as not to let the country be swallowed up by the Federal Republic. The meeting of 500,000 people in Berlin on 4 November 1989 mirrored the mood of the people, just as did the Monday demonstrations in Leipzig that same month. No slogan at that time called for the renunciation of the socialist ideal or for a speedy merger with West Germany.

However, in December 1989 the atmosphere began to change. A nationalist and antisocialist trend set in. Sections of the population who had up until then not been active took to the streets with the German flag, the GDR emblem torn out, chanting 'We are one people': The inference was allegiance to the Federal Republic. They were encouraged in this and in their attacks on pro-GDR demonstrators by West German 'political tourists' who came across the border with large consignments of leaflets and posters from the extreme right wing. Intellectuals from various political backgrounds tried to stem this development by the appeal 'For our country' (*Für unser Land*). The appeal was eventually signed by almost 1.7 million GDR citizens, which, however, means that not even every other SED party member signed it.

Generally speaking the political development was still very heartening. The media ceased to operate as mouthpiece of the party apparatus and were taken over by mostly young journalists. They established pluralism of opinion. The intelligent and witty journalism they presented to the public had a new quality. *Volkskammer* deputies who had before been abused as mere voting machines, agreeing unanimously to previously prepared resolutions, carried on lively debates genuinely striving for political solutions. Hundreds of thousands of viewers watched the *Volkskammer* sessions on TV and radio, and responded in demonstrations, at meetings and by writing letters of protest to the papers.

A new political institution was invented – the Central Round Table – at which Government spokespersons debated major current issues with the political parties, mass organisations and civil rights campaigners. The sessions were chaired by Church dignitaries. From 7 December 1989 to 12 March 1990, the participants discussed fundamental and current issues of GDR development. Sixteen meetings were held lasting approximately ten hours each. They drafted more than 100 bills, including an electoral law and one on the rights of political parties, a social charter and the most democratic constitution in German post-war history.[18]

The new Provisional Government under Hans Modrow, in office since mid-November 1989, also put forward reforms. However, at first their relations with the Round Table were strained. The government feared the Round Table's competition and commissioned incompetent or uncooperative representatives to attend the sessions. Opinions differed widely, especially on the Ministry of State Security and its future. In view of the growing instability in the country, the Prime Minister himself decided to attend the Round Table session at Bonhoeffer-Haus on 15

January 1990. He asked for the Table's support for his efforts to stabilise the situation and admitted civil rights campaigners as ministers without portfolio into his cabinet. At about the same time, the Christian Democrats left the Government, urged by their big brothers in Bonn. A cabinet made up of GDR reformers had already been suggested by Social Democratic circles in the West in December 1989. The Lord Mayor of Berlin then in office, Walter Momper (SPD), advised GDR civil rights campaigners and the Social Democrats to form either a government solely from their ranks or together with Hans Modrow, Gregor Gysi and Christa Wolf.[19] Although the West German Social Democrats were not then bent on speedy unification, this initiative was never pursued.

There were three main reasons why the many reform projects were never implemented in the forty-first year of the GDR.

First, the necessary reconstruction would only have been possible in cooperation with the other 'socialist' countries. But from Prague to Budapest, these countries were undergoing changes in the opposite direction. The Soviet Union, under Mikhail Gorbachev, seemed to have given up trying to bring about a socialist reform in favour of alignment with the capitalist West, under the illusion that they would be rewarded by adequate financial aid. At the turn of the year 1989/90, Moscow more or less dropped the GDR, a step which they had been considering on several occasions since Stalin's death.

Second, West Germany had become the strongest economic, political and conventional military power on the European continent. The Christian Democratic leader, Helmut Kohl, a Federal Chancellor who had not previously in any way promoted German unification, seized his chance. Supported by a strong group within the ruling class and despite initial resistance at home and abroad, he pushed through unification by what amounted to an '*Anschluß*' of the GDR to the Federal Republic. The main instrument to influence the East Germans was the Deutschmark, i.e. the economic power of West Germany. This enabled Herr Kohl to beguile millions of GDR citizens into following him and his CDU. Many of them had not been able to travel to the West before. They were dazzled by the splendour of a fully developed consumer's paradise. The Deutschmark was at the same time a weapon with which to blackmail the East German state. Helmut Kohl offered economic aid, cooperation and an agreement in exchange for 'a binding decision that a fundamental change of the political and economic system of the GDR be irreversibly set in motion'.[20] Although this was effected, he did not keep his word but dangled the carrot from a bit further away.

When the next GDR government took office subsequent to the first 'free elections', Kohl dictated the speedy introduction of the Deutschmark, and then the merger with West Germany. The Federal Government and the West German political parties, including the neo-fascists, operated freely in East Germany and helped to destabilise it politically. At the same time, the large West German trade chains started to take over GDR retail trade, helped by collaborators from the GDR wholesale business.

Third, the GDR reformers proved to be weak, naive and disunited. Sadly, Prime Minister Hans Modrow was one of the first to give in. On his return from Moscow, having visited Mikhail Gorbachev, he tabled the concept 'Germany, a united Fatherland', which was applauded immediately by the conservative demonstrators in Leipzig. It goes without saying that neither Hans Modrow nor Minister of Economy Christa Luft, who was undertaking to restructure GDR enterprises for their survival under market economic conditions, wanted to sell off the GDR. But the Modrow concept was abused in order to achieve precisely this. The United Left left the GDR Government at that point. They continued to advocate independence, even though the chances for such a development were dwindling fast.

Even before the *Volkskammer* elections on 18 March 1990, most political parties of the GDR had given up their course of socialist independence and, bowing to pressure from Bonn, had adopted the idea of merging with the Federal Republic. At their special party congress of 15/16 December 1989, the Christian Democrats replaced their former slogan of 'advocating a humane socialism' with a demand for an 'ecological and social market economy'.[21] Democratic Awakening also dropped the term 'socialism' from its programme. Under Wolfgang Schnur it vehemently supported the surrender of the GDR to West Germany and adopted a clearly conservative course; as a result, Friedrich Schorlemmer, Edelbert Richter and other DA co-founders left the party. Some of them joined the Social Democrats, others Democracy Now, although they were no better off there, as these organisations were also undergoing a process of re-orientation. With the support of the arch-conservative Bavarian Christian Social Union (CSU), twelve conservative splinter groups founded the German Social Union (DSU) in Leipzig on 20 January 1990. They became temporarily an East German CSU branch adopting more or less the entire CSU programme, which was even printed at that party's headquarters.[22]

Contrary to his earlier statements, Manfred Gerlach, acting State Council Chairman and leader of the Liberal Democratic Party, caused surprise by declaring that his party would tolerate no form of socialism.[23]

In cooperation with the West German Free Democratic Party (FDP), the LDPD established an Alliance of Free Democrats – the Liberals (*Bund Freier Demokraten – Die Liberalen*; BFD) together with two other newly founded liberal groups.

Sections of the NDPD, among them four district chairmen, collaborated with the West German neofascist National Democratic Party of Germany (*Nationaldemokratische Partei Deutschlands*; NPD).[24] The first stage of the 14th NDPD Party Congress in Berlin, on 21 January 1990, ended with the new party chairman, Wolfgang Glaeser, calling for an 'aggressive election campaign on all fronts', primarily directed against the SED–PDS. But the time was not yet ripe for such a policy, and Wolfgang Glaeser had to step down as chairman two days later.[25]

All the civil rights movements, the Initiative for Peace and Human Rights, Democracy Now and New Forum (NF), as well as the election alliance Green Party/Independent Women's Association still called for a democratisation of the GDR in their election programmes for the 18 March *Volkskammer* elections. Democracy Now called for a 'socially and ecologically oriented market economy',[26] although without favouring immediate unification by merger of the two German states.[27]

The case was different with New Forum. At its Berlin conference on 27/8 January 1990, the majority advocated speedy unification. Among them was the lawyer Rolf Henrich, who hoped for economic aid from the West and the transition of the GDR on that basis into a thriving country.[28] New Forum passed a policy statement on 10 February 1990 which made the process of unification of the two German states conditional on the dissolution of NATO and the Warsaw Treaty[29] at the Vienna disarmament negotiations. Had that happened, it would of course have slowed down the process of unification considerably.

The Social Democrats at first wanted to ally themselves with their friends in the civil rights movement and entered an election alliance with them, but this was dissolved again. The West German Social Democrats expected a resounding SPD success at the *Volkskammer* elections with a similar triumph to follow in the West, and, therefore, thought their East German comrades needed no such alliances. The latter, on the other hand, did not envisage a speedy merger of the two German states at that stage. Their party executive stated on 4 December 1989 that

> The Social Democrats of the GDR advocate unity of the German nation ... We are about to become equal partners in bringing about this unity. A speedy re-unification in the sense of an *Anschluß* to the

Federal Republic of Germany would endanger precisely this aim. The population of this country would have to bear an unjustifiable social and political burden.[30]

At their first national conference on 13 January 1990, the 100,000 East German Social Democrats' declared aim was, as it remained, to drive the SED–PDS from power.[31] The election congress in February 1990 in Leipzig produced a unanimous 'Yes' to German unification and at the same time 'No' to both a 'market-oriented planned economy' or a 'socialist market economy'.[32]

The campaigns for the 18 March 1990 *Volkskammer* elections were fought on the territory of the GDR, formally still sovereign. Not that this worried the established parties of the other German state. On the contrary, they took over the management of the election campaigns in the East and sponsored their junior partners there by providing speakers, funds – the latter also from public revenue – and printing facilities. The CDU and their Chancellor Helmut Kohl, already seeing himself as 'Chancellor of all the Germans', were especially active during that period. Under his patronage the three conservative GDR parties, Democratic Awakening, German Social Union, and the East German Christian Democrats joined forces in an Alliance for Germany. They adopted the slogan 'Freedom and prosperity – instead of socialism' and called for immediate German unification according to the provisions of the West German Constitution. This in effect heralded an '*Anschluß*'. They also demanded the immediate introduction of Federal German social market economy and the Deutschmark.[33] Helmut Kohl promised GDR citizens that the new German Federal States would have achieved prosperity within three to four years.[34] The conservative election campaign was especially targeted against the PDS, but also against the SPD and the civil rights campaigners. The DSU even employed gangs of thugs in its campaign. SPD executive member, Egon Bahr, said that these were the dirtiest elections he had ever witnessed.[35]

On 18 March 1990, election day, the Conservative Alliance for Germany triumphed. The East German Christian Democrats, under Lothar de Maizière, won the lion's share of 40.59 per cent of the vote and 163 seats. The DSU won 6.2 per cent and 25 seats. The DA, initially favoured by Helmut Kohl, rapidly lost popularity when its chairman Wolfgang Schnur was revealed to have been a collaborator of the East German Ministry of State Security, a so-called 'unofficial informant' (IM).[36] The DA only won four seats and 0.93 per cent of the votes.

In contrast to many predictions, including their own, the GDR Social Democrats did not win the expected land-slide victory. In fact, only 21.76 per cent voted for them, which gave them 88 seats in the *Volkskammer*. The Alliance of Free Democrats – the Liberals won 5.28 per cent and 21 seats. The Green Party and the Independent Women's Association (UFV) got 1.96 per cent and six seats. The candidates of the UFV, however, were left out in the cold when their allies, the Green Party, refused to let them have a share of their seats. The DBD, the farmers' party, won 2.17 per cent of the votes and nine seats. They merged with the Democratic Women's Federation, the reformed former GDR women's organisation (0.33 per cent and one seat). The NDPD achieved 1.96 per cent of the voters, giving them six seats.

In their election campaigns nearly all other political parties had attacked the PDS. Nevertheless, that party emerged third strongest with 16.32 per cent of the votes and 66 seats. The United Left/the Carnations won 0.18 per cent and one seat. All other candidates did not get into parliament. Right-wing extremists had been excluded from the elections.

These results proved decisive for the final stage of GDR history. Victory for the alliance under the flag of the East German Christian Democrats meant in practice a victory for the West German Christian Democrats. The Alliance of Free Democrats – the Liberals and the East German Social Democrats joined Lothar de Maizière's government, which meant that the West German Liberals and Social Democrats also had a say in the affairs of the GDR. What emerged was an East Germany dependent on the Bonn government and strengthened by the support of the Social Democrats.

After the *Volkskammer* elections the NDPD joined the Alliance of Free Democrats – the Liberals and the Democratic Farmers' Party and Democratic Awakening merged with the East German Christian Democrats. These decisions were mostly taken exclusively by the executives without the consent of the membership. As a result, many people left. Only some 10 per cent of the 120,000 DBD members joined the Christian Democrats. The party of Helmut Kohl and the liberal FDP under Count Lambsdorff were the main winners of these mergers. The West German Christian Democrats inherited the second strongest and second richest party of the GDR, and in addition the DA and DBD. The West German liberal FDP did likewise, incorporating not only the established East German LDPD but also the NDPD and the two new liberal parties, the FDP-East and the German Forum Party. The Social

Democrats did not gain in this way from the '*Anschluß*' as they did not inherit any of the established GDR satellite parties. From February to October 1990, they also experienced a severe drop in membership, from 100,000 to 20,000, a direct result of the disappointment at the policy of the party. The SPD treasurer in Bonn was obliged to finance the apparatus of the East German Social Democrats almost single-handedly. But the SDP received, among other things, DM75 million in cash for the assets it lost in the merger with the Communist Party in 1946.

In many instances the victorious West German parties treated their East German fellow-members very shabbily. Of the 4,100 full-time officers of the LDPD and NDPD, 3,300 were dismissed at short notice; many became unemployed. Former party staff lost the pensions they had contributed towards and been promised. When the Liberals from East and West merged in Hanover in August 1990, there were more members from the East (137,000) than the West (67,000). As the Western partners did not want the Easterners to monopolise the party they decided not to allow branches to send delegates according to the number of party members, as is usual, but rather according to the number of voters. This way the West German FDP with 3.5 million voters was clearly superior while the Eastern alliance could only muster 600,000. At the merger congress, the West German Liberals were therefore represented by 402 and the East German faction by 260 delegates.

For the conservative Bavarian-based CSU, German unification proved a loss. The death of its long-standing chairman, Franz Josef Strauß, and the emergence of the neofascist Republican Party had been severe blows. German unification decreased its relative weight vis-à-vis the other established political parties. The CSU tried to compensate for this by sponsoring the German Social Union in the East. However, this party became increasingly insignificant, polling, as we have seen, only 6.2 per cent at the *Volkskammer* elections. At the local elections of 6 May 1990, it only mustered 3.4 per cent, and at the elections to the Federal State parliaments on 14 October 1990 only 2.1 per cent. Nevertheless, the DSU wanted to expand to the West. This, however, made it a competitor not only for the CSU but also for Helmut Kohl's CDU. The CSU feared the CDU would respond by extending its sphere of influence to Bavaria, thereby jeopardising the CSU monopoly there. The CSU, therefore, hastened to break off all relations with the DSU when that party decided, in April 1993, to officially extend its activities to West Germany.

The Mad Rush to German Unity

Their own dissolution after unification was the declared objective of the last GDR government under de Maizière. The Prime Minister proclaimed that this was to be conducted with dignity,[37] but there was little chance of this as the GDR had already more or less surrendered its identity. The main policy decisions were taken in Bonn and merely implemented by the East German aides in Berlin. Because everything had to happen very quickly, unification was something of a plunge into the unknown.

Integration into the West German currency system by adopting the Deutschmark followed a suggestion put forward to the *Bundestag* on 17 January 1990 by Frau Ingrid Matthäus-Maier, Social Democratic financial expert. The treaty on establishing a monetary, economic and social union was agreed between West German finance minister Theo Waigel (CSU) and his GDR colleague, the Social Democrat Walter Romberg, i.e. Theo Waigel dictated the terms. Switching over to the Deutschmark on 1 July 1990 meant the collapse of large sections of the GDR economy, as they were suddenly exposed to the more powerful West German competition.[38] At the same time the vital commercial links of the GDR with the East and South East European markets were severed.

Klaus Reichenbach, formerly of the CDU and Minister at the Office of the GDR Prime Minister, was one of those who prepared the political ground for this '*Anschluß*'-type unification. In good time he eliminated the GDR social science research institutes, a thorn in Bonn's side. Of the industrial enterprises, he said, 'just throw overboard everything unfit for survival under the new conditions'.[39] This concept of destruction was later perfected by the *Treuhandanstalt* at a time when the Modrow government was still hoping to adjust the state enterprises to market economic conditions while also handing out shares to the GDR citizens. The *Treuhand* approach resulted in the squandering of assets, mass unemployment and enormous debts instead of a surplus.[40]

Herr Reichenbach was not the only East German gravedigger of the GDR. Another East German Christian Democrat, Günter Krause, Parliamentary State Secretary to the GDR Prime Minister, negotiated the Unification Treaty with Bonn's Minister of the Interior, Wolfgang Schäuble. Krause was quick to learn and both Wolfgang Schäuble and Helmut Kohl were full of praise for him. He was a clever demagogue. He surrendered essential social and political rights of the GDR citizens in negotiations with Bonn, and helped to draft the legal provisions which allowed many thousands of West Germans and West Berliners to claim property which had been rightfully maintained by East Germans for decades. While claiming to be upholding the interests of the GDR citizens and their property rights, including those stemming from the land reform after 1945,[41] the State Secretary sold his countrymen and women down the river.

The first freely elected *Volkskammer* found itself unable to do more than give its consent to decisions already drafted in Bonn, including legislative projects which could not even be leafed through in the short time available, let alone debated. The German Social Union (DSU), close to the Bavarian CSU, whipped up emotions before and after the elections with slogans like 'We have to crush the red seeds which are beginning to bud again'[42] or by likening Gregor Gysi[43] to nazi propaganda minister Goebbels. On 31 May 1990, the DSU moved in the *Volkskammer* that all GDR emblems be removed from public buildings and an independent commission be set up under the auspices of the Prime Minister to take over the trusteeship of the assets of all GDR political parties and mass organisations. In August the DSU tabled a draft for the expropriation, without compensation, of all real estate and other assets which had been bought by the GDR parties since 1945. The West German CDU/CSU/FDP coalition and the West German Social Democrats approved of this proposal[44] – designed to deal a severe blow to the PDS. DSU parliamentary party leader Joachim Walther also proposed that the SED be declared a 'criminal organisation', thereby opening the way to the prosecution of left-wingers.[45]

It was also a DSU Member who first proposed that the GDR should apply to join the Federal Republic of Germany.[46] This motion did not meet with the necessary support at the time, as the domestic and international conditions were not ready for such a move. But in July 1990, the Alliance of Free Democrats – the Liberals and the East German Social Democrats, supported by their West German senior partners, as well as the MPs Wolfgang Ullmann and Konrad Weiß of Alliance 90/the Greens (*Bündnis 90/Die Grünen*) advocated a speedy accession. A change in the leadership in the East German Social Democratic Party had made this change of policy possible. Party leader Ibrahim Böhme was ousted from office suspected of having worked for the GDR secret service, and Wolfgang Thierse, who had only become a party member in January 1990, was elected his successor. He even attacked Prime Minister de Maizière when the latter wished to delay the immediate merger of the two German states on the ground that there were still loose ends to be tied up.[47] In contrast to the Christian Democrats, the liberal Alliance of Free Democrats – the Liberals and the Social Democrats urged speedy unification so that the general elections already due in the West could be extended to the East.

According to West German electoral law, political parties require a minimum national vote of 5 per cent to get into the *Bundestag*. Under those conditions neither the PDS nor the civil rights movement would have stood a chance at such elections. After de Maizière changed his mind, at the end of July 1990, in favour of speedy unity, an electoral law was agreed including most of the proposals of the Social Democrats and Liberals. It also included a proviso allowing the DSU candidates to stand for parliament on a joint list with the Bavarian CSU. However, on 29 September 1990 the Federal Constitutional Court rejected the bill and ruled that in the forthcoming elections the East would still vote according to its own law, i.e. without the 5 per cent hurdle.[48]

The PDS, whose development will be dealt with at the end of this chapter, and the civil rights movement stood up to the pressure from Bonn. Commenting on the monetary union, a representative of New Forum, part of the civil rights movement, remarked: 'Renouncing all sovereignty, the GDR Government has bowed to the dictate of the victors in Bonn. By making sure of its future supremacy, Germany has walked roughshod over the dignity and the interests of the GDR people.'[49] Jens Reich, one of the founders of New Forum, described the document as a 'semi-colonial treaty'.[50] Wolfgang Templin of the Initiative for Peace and Human Rights called the signing of the treaty a near criminal manoeuvre.[51] The draft constitution drawn up by the Round Table of the GDR was swept aside in the *Volkskammer* without debate, and, instead, constitutional principles suggested by Bonn for adjusting the GDR Constitution to West German conditions were adopted. This move was severely censured by Wolfgang Ullmann (Democracy Now) as unconstitutional, since the GDR Constitution could only be changed by amending its own text. Federal Chancellor Helmut Kohl favoured accession of the GDR to the Federal Republic according to Article 23 of the West German Constitution. This was opposed by Wolfgang Ullmann, among others, who assessed it as

not an accession on democratically negotiated terms, but rather an *Anschluß* and a take-over, camouflaged by Article 23 of the Constitution – which is the objective of the Germany policy pursued by the Bonn Government coalition and their alliance lobby here in the GDR.[52]

After the *Volkskammer* elections of 18 March 1990, the GDR civil rights campaigners had, in general, stood by their progressive positions. The only exceptions were the pleas by Wolfgang Ullmann and Konrad Weiß for a speedy merger, the acceptance by Konrad Weiß of the Unification Treaty, and also his leading role in baiting the PDS. On 5 August 1990, the GDR civil rights movement and the Greens in both German states agreed to cooperate and coordinate their election programmes for the approaching *Bundestag* elections. They adopted the policy proposed by Konrad Weiß, which was primarily targeted against the PDS.

In September civil rights campaigners of various political shades and the songwriter Wolf Biermann seized the building of the former Ministry for State Security at Ruschestraße in Berlin. They wanted to prevent *Stasi* files being moved to ensure that they would remain accessible. Some of those who took part in this action were aware of the fact that the knowledge contained in these files could well be instrumentalised against the interests of GDR citizens.

From 1 to 2 October 1990 the Christian Democrats in East and West merged at their congress in Hamburg. Lothar de Maizière was elected deputy party leader. On 3 October 1990 German unification was achieved by formal accession of the GDR to the Federal Republic of Germany. In contrast to the fall of the Wall in 1989, this event did not spark off any great emotions. Helmut Kohl promised the GDR citizens, 'Nobody will be worse off, but many better off!'[53]

The number of East Germans unemployed at that point stood at half a million. It was to increase dramatically.

The Established Parties after the Merger

The first united German *Bundestag* elections on 2 December 1990 mirrored the political mood at the time. The results also illuminate the East–West problems. In the whole of Germany 77.8 (in the East 74.7) per cent of the voters went to the polls. Of these 36.7 per cent gave their decisive second vote[54] to the Christian Democrats (41.8 per cent in the East), 7.1 per cent for the CSU (0.0) and 0.2 (1.0) per cent for the DSU. The liberal FDP won 11.0 (12.9) per cent, the Social Democrats 33.5 (24.3) per cent of the second votes. The PDS vote was 2.4 per cent in the West (11.1 in the East) and Alliance 90/the Greens won 1.2 (6.0) per cent, as compared to 3.8 per cent for the West German Greens, while the neo-fascist Republicans got 2.1 (1.3) per cent. The 5 per cent minimum clause in West Germany meant that the West

German Greens did not get into the *Bundestag* even though their vote was higher than that of Alliance 90 (including the East German Greens). The PDS and the DSU did get into the all–German Parliament, thanks to the Federal Constitutional Court ruling on waiving the 5 per cent clause for East Germany.

The Christian Democrats remained the determining political factor in East Germany. Under Helmut Kohl the CDU became the party which steered the course from then on, causing devastation in the East. It destroyed more than half of the 9.6 million jobs which had existed in 1989, almost completely eliminated the sciences, culture and the arts in the GDR and marginalised East German academics.[55] The other established parties – CSU, FDP and SPD – also contributed to this destructive policy, a development which led to the shrinking of support for those parties in East Germany. Their influence there, and to some extent also in West Germany, was also diminished when the world economic crisis, temporarily delayed by unification, overwhelmed the Federal Republic. The national debt rose steeply. Modelled on the policies of Margaret Thatcher, the CDU/CSU and the liberal FDP called for more and more cuts in social expenditure, most of which were implemented. The East was worst hit by this policy of axing social benefits.

East German CDU membership figures sank quickly from 200,000 in October 1990 to between 80,00 and 100,000. According to an opinion poll in spring 1994, the number of CDU voters declined in Saxony from 53.8 to 38 per cent, in Thuringia from 45.4 to 29 per cent, in Saxony-Anhalt from 39 to 20 per cent, in Mecklenburg-West Pomerania from 38.3 to 17 per cent and in Brandenburg from 29.4 to 16 per cent.[56] On the other hand, the West German Christian Democrats also suffered severe losses in elections at this time – in Baden Württemberg, Schleswig-Holstein and Hamburg. And their ally, the CSU, lost some influence in Bavaria. In fact the position of the governing CDU/CSU twin parties was shaken just four years after their greatest victory since 1949.

Factors conditioning the diminishing influence of the right in East Germany were the disappointment of some of their supporters at the dismantling of the social welfare state, the breach of their election promises, and also the many political scandals in the East in which imported or indigenous conservative politicians were involved and which gave rise to repeated changes of cabinets and ministers. Such goings on were considered evidence of the corruption, lust for power, and greed of the rulers.

On 2 July 1991 the first Saxony-Anhalt government under Christian Democrat Gerd Gies came to grief. The Prime Minister's fall had been preceded by a public campaign in which he and several of his closest political friends were accused of having gained their Federal State parliament seats, and thus their public offices, by spreading the false report that some of their fellow-Christian Democrats had been in the pay of the *Stasi*. But the new government of Saxony-Anhalt did not last either. It fell on 28 November 1993 when it became known that Premier Werner Münch and other cabinet members brought in from the West had been unlawfully lining their pockets. They had not only secured for themselves the highest possible West German salaries, but also continued to take their former parliamentary allowances to which they were no longer entitled.

Christian Democrat Günter Krause, the co-drafter of the Unification Treaty, had meanwhile risen to be Federal Transport Minister. Federal Chancellor Helmut Kohl had saved him from the consequences of many earlier exercises in personal enrichment, but on 6 May 1993 moving house at the taxpayer's expense cost him his office and the chairmanship of his party in Mecklenburg-West Pomerania.

Further resignations of individuals and entire cabinets were initiated by the West German CDU apparatus and its General Secretary Volker Rühe, who blamed the East German party officers for the dwindling backing the party had in the former GDR.[57] Some East German up-and-coming Christian Democrats even applauded this move in the hope it would improve their prospects of earlier promotion. Others were convinced that not only the SED but also the CDU was responsible for what went wrong in the GDR and should be made to pay the price.[58]

Former GDR Prime Minister Lothar de Maizière was an early victim of attacks from the CDU party apparatus. On 6 September 1991 he had to resign from his posts as deputy national chairman of the Christian Democratic Union, chairman of the party's policy commission, and as leader of the Brandenburg party organisation. He, too, had earlier temporarily withdrawn from political office when he was accused of having been an unofficial informer of the *Stasi*.[59] This time it was final.

As deputy national chairman of the Christian Democrats he was replaced by the East German Angela Merkel, Minister of Women and Young People. In June 1993, she also took over Günter Krause's post of chairperson of the Mecklenburg-West Pomeranian CDU.

The Prime Minister of Thuringia, Josef Duchac, was another who fared badly. He had to resign on 23 January 1992 when a 'reformist group' within the Christian Democratic Party attacked him on account of his GDR past and his incompetence. He, too, was succeeded by a West German, the Christian Democrat Bernhard Vogel, who had lost his office as Prime Minister in the Rhineland-Palatinate when he was defeated in elections there. Just one Eastern federal state, Saxony, was safely CDU, namely in the hands of the West German professor Kurt Biedenkopf, an old opponent of Kohl's. The one remaining conservative East German Prime Minister, Alfred Gomolka, who had ruled Mecklenburg-West Pomerania since 1990, had to go on 14 March 1992 following a dispute relating to the privatisation of former GDR ship-building yards. He had, unfortunately, also publicly criticised Federal policy vis-à-vis the GDR, and thus Helmut Kohl.[60]

The 63 East German conservative MPs complained that their political influence was insignificant. Their status in the parliamentary CDU/CSU was inferior. CSU members in particular often rudely stopped their requests to speak by telling them: 'You've got the Deutschmark, so shut up now.'[61] The continuing decline in the East alarmed the East German MPs, who were worried about their image in the eyes of their electorate. Therefore they drafted a twelve-point plan for the reconstruction of East Germany, and this was adopted in Erfurt in August 1992. They demanded investments in East German industry, funds for establishing new enterprises and for housing, as well as a transfer of 25 per cent of the West German gross national product over a period of 15 years. Federal Chancellor Helmut Kohl and Parliamentary Party Leader Wolfgang Schäuble considered this plan, the outcome of which was a proposal for an additional investment loan for the East. Though carried by a majority vote of the CDU executive, not even this watered-down plan was ever actually implemented. The liberal FDP, the Bavarian CSU and sections of the CDU objected that higher income groups in the West would have had to pay for this loan.[62]

Meanwhile the Federal Republic drifted more and more to the right. Trade union autonomy in negotiating wages was restricted, social benefits cut, the constitutional right to political asylum eliminated and German military action outside NATO sanctioned. In 1994, Helmut Kohl supported the candidature of his East German party friend, the Saxon Minister of Justice Steffen Heitmann, as Federal President and the successor to Richard von Weizsäcker, whose period of office terminated that year. This also corresponded with the general trend towards the right, and Heitmann was duly nominated by the CDU and CSU. However, he aired such reactionary views, especially with regard to women and foreign citizens in Germany,[63] that even prominent Christian Democrats turned him down. Under strong public pressure, he was encouraged to withdraw his candidacy on 25 November 1993, which was a defeat for Helmut Kohl. The CDU/CSU candidate to replace him, and present holder of the office, was Roman Herzog, judge at the supreme court, while the Social Democrats put up Johannes Rau, the Prime Minister of Northrhine-Westphalia. The only other East German candidate was the civil rights activist Jens Reich, who was put up by a number of men and women prominent in public life ranging from the civil rights party to the moderately conservative. However, he never had the slightest chance of being elected by the *Bundestag*.

Attempts by the East German Christian Democrats to achieve more democracy were regularly thwarted by their West German friends in the party. Indeed, in response to an East German motion at the Hamburg CDU congress in February 1994, the party's legal expert and former Minister of Defence, Rupert Scholz, claimed that demands for sovereignty of the people were only useful for destabilising 'socialist' states. The slogan of 'We are the people' was suitable under a totalitarian regime, but, he said, 'in a democracy it would discredit our parliamentarian system'.[64]

Some CDU politicians moved even farther to the right. At the beginning of December 1992, some 200 of them set up the so-called 'Germany Forum'. The most prominent member, Heinrich Lummer MP, came out in favour of coalition negotiations with the neofascist Republicans.[65] Another spokesman of the Forum, Rudolf Krause, MP, from Saxony-Anhalt, publicly aired militant xenophobic and pro-fascist views.[66] Censured in parliament, he left his party and since then has represented the neofascist Republicans in Bonn.

The liberal FDP was also directly involved in Bonn's destructive policy towards East Germany. The Liberal Günter Rexrodt served on the board of *Treuhandanstalt* before he became Federal German Minister of Economy. His colleague, Frau Irmgard Schwaetzer, Minister of Housing, was responsible for rent increases well above the margin laid down in the Unification Treaty. Long-standing party leader Count Otto Lambsdorff (at one time convicted of bribery) and other FDP politicians were in favour of keeping East German wages well below the West German level and of cutting job-creation schemes. The FDP threw overboard what was left of their progressive liberal traditions. They, too, advocated the dismantling of the constitutional right to political asylum and an extension of the *Bundeswehr* army mandate for military action outside NATO. At party congresses in Bremen, Jena and Münster, a majority refused to break off relations with the right-wing extremist chairman of the Austrian Freedom Party, Jörg Haider, or to censure the right-wing positions which were making themselves felt in the party, or even the arson committed against the homes of foreign citizens in Germany.[67] Two women in leading positions tried to counteract this trend – Minister of Justice Sabine Leutheusser-Schnarrenberger and the unsuccessful FDP candidate for the Federal presidency, Hildegard Hamm-Brücher.

Taking advantage of the scandals involving leading officers of the so-called 'Elbe Circle', right-wing liberals, by forcing them to resign, foiled their project for maintaining jobs and modernising industry in the East.

As a result of right-wing liberal policies, party membership in the East quickly dropped by half to 70,000, equalling the figure for West Germany. In local and federal state elections, the party lost all its seats, as it didn't manage to win the necessary 5 per cent, a trend which continued. Consequently the Liberals failed in the 1994 elections to get into the state parliaments in Saxony-Anhalt, Brandenburg, Saxony and Bavaria.

The Social Democrats, at their National Party Congress in Berlin in December 1989, adopted a programme which declared as its objectives 'democracy and socialism, political self-determination and a say in shaping the world of work' as means to overcome class society. Their programmes also included the stipulation that 'shelter for the politically persecuted should remain an unrestricted basic right'.[68] But instead of fighting for the implementation of this programme in a united Germany, the Social Democrats helped to bring about the '*Anschluß*' of the GDR to West Germany in 1990, thus surrendering all East German social and political achievements. Under the chairmanship of Björn Engholm (1991) and Rudolf Scharping (1993) the party drifted further and further away from the principles of its Berlin Programme. The Social Democrats broke their promise to fight for the maintenance of the basic right to political asylum, voted in favour of worldwide military action of the *Bundeswehr* under UN command and even gave their consent to large-scale wire-tapping operations, which would provide the German State Security and police with *Stasi*-like privileges of monitoring people's activities. The SPD also favoured financing the new scheme for the care of the elderly entirely by the gainfully employed themselves, even though the Social Democratic expert in this field, Rudolf Dreßler, described this as a 'flagrant breach of the principles of our social insurance'.[69]

On various occasions the party tabled a package of proposals for the economic development of East Germany. These included relieving East German enterprises, under the trusteeship of the *Treuhandanstalt*, of their 'debts', creating jobs by means of funds for structural reform, funds for repairs of environmental damage and promoting local community and cooperative housing schemes. Brandenburg party leader Steffen Reiche, in cooperation with other East German SPD party organisations, tenants' organisations and trade unions, planned to organise mass demonstrations in support of these aims in 1992. However, he received no support from the party executive or from the executive of the German Trade Union Council (DGB), which is close to the SPD, and the demonstrations therefore did not take place.[70]

Deputy SPD leader Wolfgang Thierse played an ambivalent role in these conflicts. On the one hand, acting as the 'mouthpiece of the East Germans', he asked his East German compatriots to stand up and rally to the streets in protest, calling for the radical redistribution of financial means from West to East Germany.[71] On the other hand, he did nothing to support the demonstrations planned by Steffen Reiche, intended to implement what he himself had asked for. Thierse was also the first politician from the former GDR to advocate the so-called 'opening clauses' in East German wage agreements, which would enable employers to undercut East German wages, already well below those in the West.[72] His colleague on the Social Democratic Party Executive, Oskar Lafontaine, the Prime Minister of Saarland, also demanded a slower adjustment of East German wages and pensions to the Western level. And for this he was criticised by his own party rank and file. But not so Wolfgang Thierse.[73] Just like the Christian Democrats and the Liberals, the Social Democratic leaders came out in favour of attracting capital to the East by lowering the labour costs there, coupled with tax remission, so as to encourage investors to make a profit by putting their capital into industry rather than into money transactions.

Time and again, blue- and white-collar workers were let down by the SPD. When Brandenburg's Minister of Employment and Social Affairs, Regine Hildebrandt, one of the most popular East German politicians, promised the potash miners at Bischofferode, who were on hunger strike, support for the struggle to save the mine, she was let down by SPD leader Rudolf Scharping, who refused any help, saying that there was no other way but to close the pit.[74]

The Social Democratic Party, too, was affected by its dwindling reputation and falling membership figures. There were vehement reactions in the SPD after the Brandenburg local elections of 5 December 1993. The Party of Democratic Socialism (PDS) emerged as the second strongest party. This proved to be but a forerunner of that party's successes at local elections in all the other East German states, in the

European parliamentary elections of 12 June 1994 and at the East German state elections in Brandenburg and Saxony.

The established parties and former civil rights campaigners were horrified at the election results in Brandenburg's capital Potsdam, where the SPD candidate for Lord Mayor, Horst Gramlich, got only 30 per cent, whereas the PDS candidate, Rolf Kutzmutz won 43.5 per cent of the vote. The latter had been exposed as an informal *Stasi* agent only three days before the elections. Thereupon Kutzmutz made public his *Stasi* file, which proved that he had not been guilty of any crimes. Horst Gramlich, formerly a lecturer in the political economics of socialism at the College for Civil Service and Legislation at Potsdam-Babelsberg, with a record no less close to the GDR state, needed an anti-PDS alliance to win the final ballot of 19 December 1993. (The alliance of all parties opposed to the PDS candiate won a total of 54.93 per cent, whereas Herr Kutzmutz's polled 45.07 per cent of the vote.)

The Potsdam State President, Helmut Przybilski (SPD), who had made known the *Stasi* file of Kutzmutz, lost his office to a PDS candidate in January 1994.

Brandenburg's SPD chairman, Steffen Reiche, who had slandered the PDS before the elections as an 'inflated therapy group for old Stalinists',[75] was so impressed by its election success that he was moved to say: 'We will have to open our party to former SED members, also to those who might have borne responsibility in the GDR before 1989. We must throw overboard the methods of the Holy Inquisition.'[76] The Prime Minister of Brandenburg, Manfred Stolpe (SPD), advocated cooperation in certain matters with the PDS, where the PDS positions were close to the Social Democratic point of view.[77] Wolfgang Birthler, chairman of the Brandenburg Parliamentary Social Democratic Party, repudiated the 'policy of marginalisation' against the PDS.[78] Both Wolfgang Birthler and Manfred Stolpe were harshly attacked for this by the top echelons of all the established parties and the former civil rights organisations. This, however, did not prevent Stolpe's overwhelming triumph at the Brandenburg elections in September 1994.

CDU General Secretary Peter Hintze even demanded a statement on the matter from SPD chairman Rudolf Scharping, who dutifully announced an 'offensive against the PDS'. Deputy chairman Wolfgang Thierse followed suit by rejecting any form of cooperation with this party.[79] East German SPD leaders tried to convince their potential voters that a vote cast in favour of the PDS would prevent the change-over to a Social Democratic government.[80]

The Federal Association of Young Socialists, consisting of 140,000 young Social Democrats from West and East, distanced itself on this issue from their mother party. On the other hand, it did not respond to the Social Democratic approval of the policy of dismantling the right to political asylum by leaving the party, as it had threatened to do, or by putting up rival candidates to all those SPD Bundestag candidates who had voted in favour of this fundamental constitutional change. The Young Socialists did, however, insist on a separate, more militant election programme of their own, demanding, for instance, a speedy abandonment of nuclear energy. In opposition to the bulk of the SPD leadership, they also advocated cooperation with the Alliance 90/the Greens.[81] From 1993, the Young Socialists declared themselves open to non-SPD party members.

East German Civil Rights Activists and the Greens in the United Germany

Many former GDR civil rights campaigners were dissatisfied with the outcome of German unification. The number of supporters of New Forum, which once had had a following of 200,000, sank below 3,500. They were often busy fighting each other. In 1991, Democracy Now could only muster 650 active members and the Initiative for Peace and Human Rights 200. The reputation and influence of the once proud civil rights movements faded. With the end of the GDR, the civil rights campaigners had lost their former purpose of opposing the state. Most of their leaders were not prepared to continue the struggle against oppression and injustice in 'Greater Germany' with the same vigour as under the GDR regime. There were, however, a few steps in this direction: the grassroots Round Table, dealing with social issues; the movement for a more democratic constitution for the whole of Germany; the campaign to abolish all secret services; and the struggle against the discrimination of women, disabled and foreign citizens. However, these activities were not pursued vigorously enough to build up a new opposition, and therefore generally failed.

In any case, most of the former civil rights campaigners did not consider the struggle against Bonn's destructive and colonialist policy and the discrimination of millions of East Germans to be a priority. Instead, they kept up the battles of yesterday, chiefly directed against the SED and *Stasi*. They continued attacking the once mighty but no longer existing GDR party and the Ministry of State Security, dissolved years before. For many of them, the PDS, but also the former Consistorial President of the Protestant Church and re-elected Prime Minister of Brandenburg, Manfred Stolpe (SPD), were the arch-enemies, to be politically eliminated. Their campaigns only served the ruling government parties, who had every reason to be keen on diverting attention from the negative consequences of their own policy.

One of New Forum's regional anti-*Stasi* activities was the publication in the weekly *die andere* in 1991, of the salary records listing the names of the relatively well-paid full-time members of the Ministry of State Security in Berlin and of thousands of informal *Stasi* agents in the region of Halle. To have done this contradicted the most elementary rules of the Data Protection Act. Both actions were enough of a sensation to provide the initiators with short-term publicity and led to a short rise in the circulation of *die andere*. Law suits filed for slander by the indicted resulted in claims for compensation which exceeded the periodical's financial means. The downfall of *die andere*, the last publication close to New Forum, was hastened by the publication of these lists.

Bärbel Bohley, Reinhardt Schult, Wolfgang Templin and others stubbornly tried to discredit Brandenburg's Prime Minister, alleging that he had been an informal agent of the *Stasi* who harmed civil rights campaigners in the GDR. They claimed that instead of acting on behalf of the Church in his dealings with the state, he had worked for the GDR regime within the Church. In spring 1994, Günter Nooke, leader of the Alliance 90 parliamentary party in Brandenburg, called Manfred Stolpe a liar.[82] While the escalation of the dispute didn't bring about Stolpe's fall, Günter Nooke's party broke up and both his splinter group and the bulk of the Alliance 90 party failed to get into state parliament at the September 1994 elections.

Other champions in the battle against the former SED were Konrad Weiß and Wolfgang Ullmann, both members of the *Bundestag*. They demanded that the SED and the *Stasi* be declared criminal organisations and their leaders brought to trial, as prominent nazi war criminals had been at the Nuremberg Trial.[83] Konrad Weiß even proposed that the Government should send German commandos, a GSG9 unit, to Moscow to take Erich Honecker, in exile there at the time, back to Germany for trial on charges of murder at the Wall, the sale of GDR citizens and the illegal detention of millions.[84] Such a step would have been an infringement of international law. In his loathing of the GDR, Weiß claimed to see many similarities between it and Hitler's fascist Germany. Although there were no gas chambers in the GDR, he said, there had been 'this terrible Wall'.[85]

These two MPs ignored the fact that the Party of Democratic Socialism was not the old Honecker party. Konrad Weiß in particular refused any cooperation with the PDS. Berlin's Alliance 90 parliamentarians who opposed this view were labelled traitors by him and accused of cheating their voters.[86] He denounced the PDS as the '*Stasi* party'; he called its election victories a disaster and denounced the internationally renowned GDR dissident Stefan Heym as a 'pervert', because he had agreed to be nominated as candidate for the PDS open list for the 1994 *Bundestag* elections.[87] For the same reason former GDR civil rights campaigner Vera Wollenberger maligned the writer as a 'PR puppet of the PDS'.[88]

In 1992 their blind anticommunism led former civil rights activists to attack the Committees for Justice and their initiators. This also reflected their concern that this new civic movement might become the successor of the old movements represented by them.[89]

Their anticommunism was often linked to other retrogressive attitudes. Konrad Weiß, for instance, attacked a bill on abortion which had been supported by his own fellow-MPs, aimed at legalizing unconditionally the right of women to terminate a pregnancy (as had been the practice in the GDR). Weiß even went as far as to demand of *Bundestag* President Rita Süssmuth (CDU), that the bill be repudiated as an infringement of basic moral and ethical values.[90]

In the debate on the atrocities perpetrated in Bosnia, a minority of the West German Greens and of Alliance 90 demanded a break with pacifism. Their *Bundestag* party supported 'peace-keeping operations' by UN troops in favour of the Bosnian Muslims. The Alliance's Council of Speakers appealed to the peace movement in an open letter to supplement the principle of non-violence by that of intervention.[91] *Bundestag* members Gerd Poppe, Werner Schulz and Vera Wollenberger demanded military action against the Serb army and arms consignments for the Muslims. However, they and their political friends were not able to get a majority for this motion at their extraordinary party congress held on 9 October 1993 in Bonn, and thus the pacifist principles of the party were retained.[92]

Some former civil rights campaigners even appear to be drifting off into right-wing extremism. Wolfgang Templin gave an interview to *Junge Freiheit* (Young Freedom), a periodical close to the neofascist Republicans, in which he demanded, 'Above all, Germany must act as a member of the Western community of states of equal status'.[93] In the summer of 1990, the periodical had praised Konrad Weiß's 'national qualities'. Jens Reich gave an interview to the monthly *MUT* (Courage), which had moved to a conservative stance.[94]

Whereas New Forum, the Independent Women's Federation and the United Left continued to exist in a small way, the Green Party of the ex-GDR with its 5,000 members merged with the 41,000 West German Greens on 3 December 1990. The East–West relationship was not harmonious in this organisation either. In 1992, leading East German representatives of the merged party argued, 'Vested interests and election arithmetic are particularly well developed among the Greens; there is the danger of the party copying the Federal German colonisation model.'[95] Christine Weiske (East), co-speaker with Ludger Volmer (West), resigned from her post in 1991 for this reason.[96]

In a subsequent merger, the Greens fused with Alliance 90, which comprised most sections of the East German civil rights movement. This merger took a long time to negotiate because Alliance 90 and representatives like Konrad Weiß insisted on parity in the executive bodies, a clear approval of the market economy society, and the rejection of any 'socialist experiments'. The Greens stuck to their position that state intervention in the economy was indispensable.[97] To begin with, Alliance 90 seemed successful in getting most of their ideas accepted.[98] At the first national assembly of the new party Alliance 90/the Greens in Leipzig, from 14 to 16 May 1993, Ludger Volmer and the former Brandenburg Minister of Education, Marianne Birthler, were elected Federal spokespersons. The 5th Federal Assembly in Mannheim, in February 1994, voted in favour of dissolving NATO and the *Bundeswehr* and for the abandonment of nuclear energy within a period of two years. This was seriously criticised by the established parties and provoked a decided 'No' to a potential coalition with that party on the part of the Social Democrats.[99]

The Green–Alternative Youth Alliance, founded on 15 January 1994, declared its openness towards cooperation with other parties, including the PDS, against the advice of Marianne Birthler and to the annoyance of Konrad Weiß.[100]

In Brandenburg the civil rights alliance set up under the leadership of Günter Nooke, who had stayed out of the merger of Alliance 90/the Greens, has moved to the right and worked for the economic interests of medium-sized businesses.

The Road Taken by the PDS

Before the *Wende*, the leading Socialist Unity Party of Germany (SED) numbered 2.3 million members. Its annual membership fee income was 700 million Marks. Members came from all classes and strata of society, with academics having a disproportionately high share of the membership. Motivations for joining this party were diverse and ranged from a belief in socialist ideals and confidence that socialism would be built up under that party's guidance to pure careerism. Behind the monolithic exterior of Marxism-Leninism, the most diverse views were held by party members: communist and socialist but also social democratic, liberal, conservative and even dyed-in-the-wool reactionary. The SED was hierarchically structured, and dominated by a group of politbureaucrats. Real power was not wielded by the elected representatives of the membership but rather by the top echelon of the apparatus and by officers appointed by a select circle.

The history of the SED is also one of heretics and heresy. Time and again, communist and socialist members, in some instances also from the top ranks, criticised the course of the party and suggested a different, a more democratic road. These heresies were stamped out. Only after Gorbachev initiated his course of *perestroika* and *glasnost* in the Soviet Union did a broader discussion start in the SED concerning the political situation and the reforms needed.[101]

The chief contribution by SED rank and file members to the overthrow of the regime in 1989 was their abstention from defending their leadership. The latter, for this reason, did not dare to resort to violence when the rank and file protested sharply at the police brutality shown towards demonstrators early in October. After Erich Honecker's fall, the grassroots membership made sure that the old system with slightly modified methods was not continued under the new leader, Egon Krenz. Members from the WF enterprise for television sets, from Humboldt University, and from the two Berlin Academies, for Sciences and Social Sciences, were instrumental in forcing the Politburo and the Central Committee to resign and in convening an extraordinary party congress.

This party congress, the last one under the name of the SED, took place in Berlin from 8/9 and from 16/17 December 1989. Campaigners for a reform of the party succeeded in bringing about the election of the opposition lawyer Gregor Gysi, who had formerly been the defending counsel of dissidents. He became chairman of the party. They introduced independent platforms and workshops within the common framework of the party. Supporters of the old course, by threatening to leave the party, then prevented the much-needed profound analysis and discussion of the past. The new name adopted later was the Party of Democratic Socialism (PDS).

The core of the apparatus was at first left unmolested, which handicapped cooperation with other left-wing elements. At its instigation,

the party branches at enterprise level were dissolved and the party educational centres closed. This happened at a time when links of party
members with other working people were vital, and when the political
and theoretical discussion among the party members was indispensable.
The apparatus administered the party assets in real estate and cash, which
was more than generally assumed and in some cases acquired in questionable ways. While the party executive transferred more than 3
billion GDR Marks to the Government and stated their readiness to
hand over the bulk of the holiday homes, enterprises and real estate,
treasurer Wolfgang Pohl and financial director Wolfgang Langnitschke
pursued a different policy: they could have made good use of the
party's assets in politically responsible ways by financing non-party
left-wing journals, publishers, research institutes, educational centres
and other important projects of the left-wing movement, while this
was still possible. Instead, they assisted certain members to establish
themselves in business by handing to them billions of GDR Marks in
interest-free loans. They also transferred abroad DM107 million to a
party banking account.

The loans to private individuals were legal but disreputable; the
money transfers were downright illegal and in defiance of the Amendment
to the Political Parties Act of 31 May 1990, the law which strictly ruled
that all assets of political organisations had to be handed over to the Independent Commission for Vetting the Assets of All GDR Parties and
Mass Organisations. The West German secret service (*Bundesnachrich-
tendienst*), knew of the illegal transfer of millions. By uncovering these
deals, both the Commission and the *Treuhandanstalt* were placed in an
ideal position to institute proceedings designed to drain the PDS and
other left-wing groups and institutions of their financial means, thus
putting them under pressure and even causing them to close down. For
many party members, the disclosure of these shady transfers came as a
shock. It contributed to a drastic drop in membership from 1.7 million
at the extraordinary party congress in December 1989 to less than
300,000 at the time of the '*Anschluß*'.

Subsequently, the PDS tried to represent the interests of the East
Germans. Their programme of 25 February 1990 was oriented towards
preserving the new democratic rights introduced during that last year
of the GDR and the social accomplishments of the old GDR in the
united Germany.[102] At meetings, demonstrations and in *Volkskammer*
debates, the PDS canvassed for the constitution drafted by the Round
Table, for adopting a new and democratic trade union law, for safeguards
against social decline and unemployment, and for bringing about

German unity – not through an *'Anschluß'* in line with Article 23 of the West German Constitution, but rather through a fusion of equal partners. They were for an exchange rate for the GDR currency of DM1:1 and proposals were made for the protection of GDR industry and agriculture as well as the GDR's arts, culture and health service. Most of these objectives were not achieved. Any motions of this nature were rejected by the *Volkskammer* majority, made up of Conservatives, Liberals and Social Democrats. Such lack of success along with the general propaganda against the PDS by the other parties who indiscriminately heaped all the blame for the wrong done during the GDR period on the 'SED successor party' caused the number of PDS voters to decline steadily. It dropped from 16.32 per cent at the *Volkskammer* elections on 18 March 1990, to 14.59 per cent at the local elections of 6 May 1990, 11.63 per cent at the Federal State elections on 14 October 1990 and to 11.1 per cent at the *Bundestag* elections on 2 December 1990.

Since then, the PDS has developed into a totally different party from the SED. Apart from the radically changed political framework, the party, due to financial straits, has drastically reduced its apparatus from its former 44,000 to less than 150 paid staff.

The PDS also dealt with its historical roots more thoroughly and with greater determination than any other political group in Germany ever did. In GDR times, the errors and crimes for which the SED was responsible or other 'skeletons in the cupboard' of the communist movement were taboo. After the reform, the party leadership and large sections of the membership debated the past endlessly, sometimes almost to the exclusion of all else. A prominent issue in these debates was the part played by the former Ministry of State Security of the GDR. Yielding to public pressure, the PDS often sacrificed perfectly sound people who had never harmed anybody and had done no more than sign on as informal agents of the *Stasi*.

Within the party, different factions developed. The most prominent was a social reform group. The communist strand within the party continued to claim that a better social order than the capitalist one could only be achieved by a socialist revolution and socialisation of the chief means of production. The few thousand members of the Communist Platform (KPF) of the PDS considered that socialism required nationalisation of the means of production. According to the hardliners of that group, Stalin's system, established in the Soviet Union and transferred to other countries later, was the only way socialism could survive. This thesis was vehemently contradicted by critical Marxists within and outside the PDS, and also by some within the ranks of the Communist Platform.[103]

The leadership of the party advocated a 'step-by-step transformation of capitalist society towards overcoming capitalism'.[104] This strand, while going further than the social reformists did, was still closer to them than to the communist faction. However, Gregor Gysi pointed out that the PDS would make itself redundant 'if it did not go further than classic social democracy'.[105] Both Gregor Gysi and the current party chairman, Lothar Bisky, have always been adamantly anti-Stalinist.[106]

In consequence of the general witch-hunt against left-wing movements, and also Germany's accelerated move to the right, the PDS suffered further setbacks and met with ostracism in the course of 1991–92. In nearly all East German regional parliaments and in Bonn, PDS speakers were often ignored. PDS motions were frequently rejected only because that party proposed them, indeed identical motions were sometimes tabled successfully later by other parties. Some East German media joined in the baiting campaign, although the West German media mostly ignored the PDS. When PDS speakers took the floor at *Bundestag* debates, television cameras would stop filming. The only exceptions were talk-shows and other events with Gregor Gysi, who was much sought after, also in the West, as a brilliant speaker and quick-witted interviewee.

In 1993 the attitude towards the PDS changed in East Germany. In their favour was the evident breach of election promises made by the ruling CDU/CSU/FDP coalition but also policies articulated by leading, generally West German, Social Democrats which were felt likewise to be against the interests of the East Germans. In contrast to the coalition parties and some Social Democratic leaders, the PDS sided with the demonstrators and strikers in many disputes. The steamrolling destruction of the GDR gradually undermined the propaganda that all evil had come from the SED and from its successor party, the PDS. Sympathy grew for the only authentic East German party, whose parliamentarians and other members took up the problems and worries of those who were discriminated against in the former GDR. As the antipathy of considerable sections of East Germans against the arrogant West German representatives, felt to be acting like colonialists, and their local collaborators increased, the anti-*Stasi* campaign lost its appeal, too. Time and again, allegations by members of the former civil rights movement and the 'expert reports' from the *Stasi* files issued by the Gauck administration were shown to be exaggerated, irrelevant or just plain incorrect.

Though the PDS also hoped for a breakthrough in West Germany, this was not achieved. The number of its West German party members is still an insignificant 1,180.

At the local elections held in the state of Brandenburg on 5 December 1993, however, the PDS not only reversed the downward trend but increased its poll compared with the results of the *Volkskammer* elections of 1990. This trend continued at the 1994 European and the state elections in Brandenburg and Saxony when the success of its top candidate for Potsdam, Rolf Kutzmutz, caused a sensation.

Worried by this success in the Brandenburg local elections and by the subsequent successes, harsher actions against the PDS were demanded by the authorities in several Federal German states, where the secret service was commissioned to observe the party, or at least its Communist Platform and its Young Comrades Association. The Bavarian Minister of the Interior, Günter Beckstein, tried, so far in vain, to ban the PDS; his plan was not supported by the coalition parties or the Federal Chancellor.[107] Social Democratic leader Rudolf Scharping claimed that, for his party, the PDS was no less an enemy than the neofascist Republicans.[108]

The established parties, including also former civil rights campaigners from Alliance 90/the Greens, were particularly concerned when the PDS won prominent, non-party candidates for its open list for the 1994 Bundestag elections.

At a third Federal party congress of the PDS, held in three stages – in January and June 1993 and in March 1994 in Berlin[109] – a new Federal executive was elected and a basic programme adopted. Despite the party's considerable losses in membership since 1990, the PDS, with 131,406 members, is still the largest East German party. Gregor Gysi remained the leader of the parliamentary party in the *Bundestag*, but was replaced as national chairman by media expert Lothar Bisky, formerly at the helm of the PDS in Brandenburg.

The new 'Basic Programme' of the PDS proclaimed the need for unity. There was unanimity among the ranks of the party in respect of the need to overcome political rule in the interest of the big capitalists, and to maintain and protect the humanitarian and democratic traditions of the socialist movement. But in respect of private property as an economic factor, opinions differed. PDS political objectives ranged from the democratisation of society to averting global threats to humankind, all being designed to bring about a socially just, but not necessarily socialist, society. The party professed openness towards 'those people who want to fight against capitalist society, which they reject, on principle, as well as to people who believe the present social system can be changed gradually and overcome in that way'. While the PDS was keen to get into parliament, it considered the struggle outside parliament to be just as decisive.[110]

Four and a half years of restructuring and reforming the party towards a pluralist and democratic approach, and of opening itself up to a range of communist and socialist ideas and traditions, were beginning to bear fruit. At local and state elections in several of the new Federal States in 1994 the PDS increased its polling results spectacularly. It achieved remarkable results in some East German and East Berlin constituencies. At the elections to the European parliament held in June 1994 the PDS only barely missed getting in.

This showed that there was room for a new party to the left of social democracy. As the German Social Democratic Party was felt by some to be surrendering even liberal positions, having already abandoned social reformist ideas, there was a growing area of viewpoints and ideas no longer its prerogative.

The Elections of 1994

The year 1994 abounded in elections. The Germans elected various local, regional and state parliaments; they went to the polls to vote for the European Parliament and they elected the 13th *Deutsche Bundestag*, their Federal parliament, on 16 October. The SPD was able to win votes and mandates. The CDU and the CSU recorded losses everywhere except in Saxony. There Saxony's Premier, Kurt Biedenkopf, won the state elections and his party remained in its top position also at the general elections. The FDP disappeared in the state and regional/local parliaments. Backed by the CDU it did get into the *Bundestag*, though by the skin of its teeth. Alliance 90/the Greens also managed to return to Federal parliament by virtue of gains in the West which offset the losses in the East where it disappeared in a number of state and regional/local parliaments. The PDS was successful in East Germany in all the 1994 elections and was even able to improve its poor polling results in the West. At the general elections it failed to overcome the 5 per cent barrier (its all-German vote was 4.4 per cent as against around 20 per cent in the East) but did get into the new *Bundestag* thanks to the four direct mandates it was to win in Berlin. These were won by the head of the PDS parliamentary group Gregor Gysi, former minister of the economy Christa Luft, the novelist and former GDR dissident Stefan Heym and the trade union officer Manfred Müller, incidentally a West German.

If a party standing for parliamentary elections wins three or more direct mandates, the 5 per cent clause is waived and all the votes are counted. The PDS was, therefore, returned to the *Bundestag* with a total number of 30 deputies.

Months of baiting that party by all other political contenders had not been able to prevent this. The CSU parliamentary party, its chairman Wolfgang Schäuble and Helmut Kohl, the party's national chairman, had called the membership of the PDS 'fascists painted red'.[111] They claimed this expression to have been a quotation from a statement made by the late Kurt Schumacher, one-time leader of the Social Democratic Party, and urged that party to stick to the extremely anticommunist course Schumacher had pursued. Thereupon Social Democratic attacks on the PDS gained in vigour. SPD chairman Rudolf Scharping even rejected the option of being elected Federal Chancellor with the votes of that party.[112] He appealed, though in vain, to Chancellor Kohl to support an appeal to the electorate to give their first vote to candidates of the SPD to prevent PDS candidates from winning direct mandates.[113] The resolution taken by the SPD in Saxony-Anhalt subsequent to the state parliamentary elections proved of great political significance. The party rejected the option of forming a coalition government with the CDU and established a minority government together with Alliance 90/the Greens. To rule the country, this government required the support, from time to time, of the PDS. The CDU and CSU violently opposed this so-called 'Magdeburg option' (called after the capital of Saxony-Anhalt). The SPD and Alliance 90/the Greens, on the other hand, hoped thereby 'to strengthen the self-confidence of the people who grew up in the East' and 'to return to the roots of the "peaceful revolution" of 1989 in the GDR'.[114]

The 1994 marathon election year revealed that about half the German electorate desired a change of policy. The other half – the majority of them residents in the West – had been persuaded by the media that changes would spell a 'red alliance' and rob them of their comforts. They are slowly beginning to realise that the continuation of conservative policy also undermines their living standards, emptying their pockets and depriving them, bit by bit, of their hard-won rights.

Notes

1. 'Gründungsaufruf der KPD' [Inauguration Address of the Communist Party of Germany], dated 11 June 1945, in Lothar

Berthold and Ernst Diehl (eds), *Revolutionäre deutsche Parteiprogramme: Vom Kommmunistischen Manifest bis zum Programm de Sozialismus* [Revolutionary German party programmes: From the Communist Manifesto to the programme of socialism] (1964: Dietz, Berlin), p.196.

2. Hermann Weber, *Geschichte der DDR* [History of the GDR], 2nd edition (1986: Deutscher Taschenbuchverlag, Munich), pp. 116ff.

3. *Nationale Front* was an umbrella organisation for the political parties and other organisations in the GDR; it helped the Socialist Unity Party to control these bodies.

4. Karl G. Tempel, *Die Parteien in der Bundesrepublik Deutschland und die Rolle der Parteien in der DDR* [The political parties in the Federal Republic of Germany and the role of the political parties in the GDR] (1987: Landeszentrale für Politische Bildung, Berlin), pp. 218ff.

5. Interview with Günter Maleuda, leader of the Democratic Farmers' Party from 1987 to 1990, in *Junge Welt*, Berlin,13 June 1992.

6. *Kleines politisches Wörterbuch*, 4th edition (1983: Dietz Verlag, Berlin), p. 695.

7. See Chapter 7 below.

8. *Der Tagesspiegel*, 13 June 1992.

9. Helmut Müller-Enbergs, Marianne Schulz and Jan Wielgohs (eds), *Von der Illegalität ins Parlament: Werdegang und Konzept der neuen Bürgerbewegungen* [From the undergound into parliament: Development and concept of the new civil rights movements] (1991: Links Druck Verlag, Berlin), p.113.

10. *Frankfurter Rundschau*, 3 October 1989.

11. *Der Tagesspiegel*, 15 September 1989.

12. Siegfried Prokop (ed.), *Die kurze Zeit der Utopie: Die 'zweite' DDR im vergessenen Jahr 1989/90* [The brief period of utopia: The 'second' GDR in the forgotten year of 1989/90] (1994: Elefanten Press, Berlin).

13. *Frankfurter Rundschau*, 31 October 1989.

14. *Frankfurter Rundschau*, 9 October 1989.

15. According to this doctrine, the countries of the 'community of socialist states' were not entitled to leave the community. Should a member state intend to do so, the allied countries, especially the Soviet Union, would intervene, by military force if the need arose.

16. On 9 November 1848 in Vienna the counter-revolution murdered Robert Blum, left-wing member of the German National Assembly

at Frankfurt. On 9 November 1918 the November Revolution triumphed in Berlin. On 9 November 1923 Hitler and General Ludendorff instigated a *putsch* in Munich against the Weimar Republic, which had emerged in the wake of the November Revolution. On 9 November 1938 the biggest Nazi progrom against the Jews in the whole of Germany was launched by attacks on synagogues and Jewish shops.

17. *Frankfurter Rundschau*, 23 October 1989.
18. Helmut Herles and Ewald Rose, *Vom Runden Tisch zum Parlament* [From the Round Table to parliament] (1990: Bouvier, Bonn), pp. 3ff.
19. Editor-in-chief Klaus Wolfram in *die andere*, 2 October 1991; Rainer Eppelmann in an interview for *Junge Welt*, 9/10 December 1989.
20. Helmut Kohl, 'Zehn-Punkte Programm zur Überwindung der Teilung Deutschlands und Europas' [Ten-point programme to overcome the division of Germany and Europe], speech delivered on 28 November 1989 at the German *Bundestag*, in *Frieden und Einheit*, (n.d.: Bonn), pp. 47ff., quoted from Prokop (ed.), *Die kurze Zeit*, p. 228.
21. 'Programm der CDU (draft)', in *CDU-extra* (March 1990: CDU Headquarters, Berlin).
22. *Grundsatzprogramm der Deutschen Sozialen Union* [Basic Programme of the German Social Union] (January 1990: CSU, Munich).
23. *Berliner Zeitung*, 16/17 December 1989.
24. *Die Zeit*, 26 January 1990.
25. *National Zeitung*, 23 January 1990; *Neues Deutschland*, 24 and 25 January 1990.
26. Policy Statement of Democracy Now (DJ) in *die andere*, 8 March 1990.
27. *Junge Welt*, 22 January 1990.
28. *Neues Deutschland*, Berlin, 9 February 1990.
29. *die andere*, 1 March 1990.
30. Declaration of the Social Democratic Party of East Germany on the German Question, in *Wir sind das Volk* [We are the people], part 3: *Die Bewegung: November/Dezember 1989* [The movement in November/December 1989] (1990: Mitteldeutscher Verlag, Halle/Leipzig).
31. *ExtraBlatt* (January 1990: SPD executive, Berlin).
32. *Berliner Zeitung*, 20 September 1990.
33. *Frankfurter Rundschau*, 2 March 1990.

34. Helmut Kohl, Deutschland wächst zusammen [Germany is becoming one], in Helmut Kohl, *Bilanzen und Perspektiven*, (n.d.: Bonn), quoted from Prokop (ed.), *Die kurze Zeit*, p.288
35. *Neues Deutschland*, 20 March 1990.
36. Informal agents were unpaid people who provided information, either having signed on or being tapped without their knowledge. Since 1990, politicians and the established political parties, former GDR civil rights campaigners and some of the media have misused the files on 'informal members' for political slander, often aimed against people innocent of offences in law and in many cases based on misleading or faked data. See Chapter 1, pp. 20–22.
37. Government Policy Statement by the Prime Minister of the GDR in *Neues Deutschland*, 20 April 1990.
38. See Chapter 3 below.
39. *Die Welt*, 7 June 1990.
40. See Chapter 3 below.
41. *Neues Deutschland*, 10 August 1990.
42. Party leader, the Rev. Ebeling, quoted according to *Neues Deutschland*, 13 March 1990.
43. Hubertus Nowack (DSU) in a *Volkskammer* debate on 20 April 1990.
44. On 26 August 1990 in Bonn.
45. *Neues Deutschland*, 29 and 30 August 1990.
46. Jürgen Schwarz, MP, in the presence of the Federal Chancellor in the *Volkskammer* on 17 June 1990.
47. On 21 July 1990 in the *Volkskammer*.
48. *Neues Deutschland*, 1 October 1990.
49. *Neues Deutschland*, 19/29 May 1990.
50. *Junge Welt*, 21 June 1990.
51. *tageszeitung*, 23 May 1990.
52. *Volkszeitung*, 22 June 1990.
53. See Chapters 3 and 6 below.
54. The second vote went to a political party, whereas the first vote was for an individual candidate.
55. See Chapters 3 and 6 below.
56. EMNID poll, quoted according to *Der Spiegel*, 21 February 1994.
57. *Der Spiegel*, 19 August 1991; *Neues Deutschland* 31 August and 1 September 1991.
58. *Berliner Zeitung*, 2 September 1991. Interview with Arnold Vaatz, head of the Saxon State Council.

59. From an interview with Lothar de Maizière in *Die Welt*, 12 September 1991.
60. *Junge Welt*, 18 December 1991.
61. *Berliner Zeitung*, 18 December 1992.
62. *Junge Welt*, 26 August and 10 September 1992.
63. *Dresdner Neueste Nachrichten*, 18–20 April; *Berliner Zeitung*, 8 September 1992; *Süddeutsche Zeitung*, 18 September 1993; *Neues Deutschland*, 4 October 1993.
64. *Neues Deutschland*, 24 February 1994.
65. *Junge Welt*, 8 February 1993.
66. Rudolf Krause, *Denkschrift zu nationalen deutschen Fragen*, [Memorandum on national German issues] (23 November 1992: Bonn).
67. *Neues Deutschland*, 5 October 1992, 9 March and 14 June 1993.
68. *Grundsatzprogramm der Sozialdemokratischen Partei Deutschlands* [Basic Policy Programme of the Social Democratic Party of Germany], adopted at the Programme Congress of 20 December 1989, in Berlin, pp. 6, 21 and 22.
69. *Junge Welt*, 12 March 1994.
70. *Neues Deutschland*, 2 July 1992; *Junge Welt*, 10 July 1992.
71. *Neues Deutschland*, 25 February 1991; *Junge Welt*, 27 May 1991.
72. *Junge Welt* and *Berliner Zeitung*, 25 September 1992.
73. *Neues Deutschland*, 11 and 18 October 1993.
74. *Berliner Zeitung*, 28 September 1993.
75. *Neues Deutschland*, 17 December 1993.
76. *Berliner Zeitung*, 20 December 1993.
77. *Berliner Zeitung*, 29 December 1993.
78. *Berliner Zeitung*, 19 April 1994.
79. *Neues Deutschland*, 30 December 1993; *Berliner Zeitung*, 31 December 1993.
80. *Neues Deutschland*, 28 April 1994.
81. *Junge Welt* and *Neues Deutschland*, 21 March 1994.
82. *Berliner Zeitung*, 15 and 16 March 1994.
83. *Junge Welt*, 11 September 1991 and 27 February 1992; *Freitag*, 13 September 1991.
84. *Berliner Zeitung*, 25 and 26 April 1992.
85. *Neues Deutschland*, 18 April 1994.
86. *Frankfurter Rundschau*, 26 February 1992.
87. *Neues Deutschland*, 19 October 1990, 7 December 1993 and 10 February 1994.
88. *Welt am Sonntag*, 13 February 1994.

89. *Junge Welt*, 15 August 1992.
90. *Berliner Zeitung*, 17 October 1991.
91. *Plädoyer für eine Erneuerung: Offener Brief des Bündnis 90 an die Friedens-bewegung* [Pleading for reform: Open letter of Alliance 90 to the peace movement] (24 August 1992: Berlin).
92. *Junge Welt*, 11 October 1993.
93. *Junge Freiheit*, 25 February 1994.
94. *Neues Deutschland*, 10 March 1994.
95. *Neues Deutschland*, 11 August 1992.
96. *Neues Deutschland*, 18 January 1993.
97. *Junge Welt*, 4 May 1992; *Berliner Zeitung*, 18 May 1992.
98. *Junge Welt*, 18 January 1993; *Freitag*, 21 January 1993.
99. *Junge Welt* and *Berliner Zeitung*, 28 February 1994.
100. *Neues Deutschland*, 21 February 1994.
101. The following passage is based to a large extent on the article 'Niedergang und Chance: Zum Weg der PDS' [Decline and chances: The path of the PDS], *Arbeiterstimme* July 1992: pp. 11–19.
102. Partei des Demokratischen Sozialismus, *Programme and Statuten* [Programmes and statutes] (1990: Berlin), pp. 7ff.
103. Sahra Wagenknecht, 'Marxism und Opportunismus: Kämpfe in der sozialistischen Bewegung gestern und heute' [Marxism and opportunism: Struggles in the socialist movement of yesterday and today] in *Weißenseer Blätter* (Vol. 4/1992: Hanfried Müller, Berlin); Günter Grenzroth, 'Der falsche Weg: Ehrenretter des Stalinismus und ihr Geschichtsbild' [The wrong road: Restorers of Stalin's honour and their picture of history], in *Hintergrund*, Vol. IV, 1992; Eberhard Czichon and Heinz Marohn, 'Marxismus und Dogmatismus: Zur Verteidigung des revolutionären Marxismus' [Marxism and dogmatism: Defending revolutionary Marxism], unpublished ms, Berlin, 1993.
104. *Arbeiterstimme*, June 1994, p. 17.
105. *Junge Welt*, 1 February 1994.
106. *Disput*, Vol. 3/4, 1993 special edition: 'Der dritte Parteitag' [The Third Party Congress], pp. 25 and 59.
107. *Neues Deutschland*, 13, 14 and 17 December 1993.
108. *Neues Deutschland*, 7 April 1994.
109. *Disput*, Vol. 3/4 and 13/14, 1993, special edition: 'Der dritte Parteitag' [The Third Party Congress], and *PDS-Pressedienst*, No. 11/12, 1994, 'Der Wahlparteitag der PDS' [The Election Congress of the PDS].

110. 'Programm der Partei des Demokratischen Sozialismus', [Programme of the Party of Democratic Socialism] *Disput*, Vol. 3/4, 1993, pp. 36ff.
111. Press release by the CSU parliamentary party, 14 July 1994; Schäuble to the members of the CDU parliamentary party, quoted from *Neues Deutschland*, 1 August 1994; Kohl's statement according to *Berliner Zeitung* of 26 August 1994 and *Neues Deutschland* of 26 September 1994.
112. *Neues Deutschland*, 11 August 1994.
113. *Berliner Zeitung*, 28 September 1994.
114. *Neues Deutschland*, 18 July 1994.

3 An Unparalleled Destruction and Squandering of Economic Assets

Harry Nick

Unification – A Contradictory Experience

Over the years from 1989 the population of East Germany simultaneously witnessed, acted in and was affected by a process without parallel in history, whose main component was the transition from a planned to a market economy.

East Germans experienced this radical change as a sudden overturning, literally 'overnight', of their situation as consumers. During the weekend preceding monetary union on 1 July 1990,[1] not only the shop-windows but also the shops were completely cleared of GDR goods following a closing-down sale: these were then replaced by 'Western goods'.

This was not only the fulfilment of what large sections of the population had longed for, it was also a convincing performance demonstrating market economic efficiency, a masterpiece of economic logistics. With regard to the areas close to the consumer – the retail outlets, banks, savings banks, insurance offices, distribution systems – East Germans experienced the arrival of Western capital as a steamroller onslaught which crushed all existing structures.

In the spheres of production and the commercial services, the working people of East Germany experienced the transition to a market economy as an economic disaster. Whereas in the month before monetary union (June 1990) industrial production was still 86.5 per cent of what it had been the same month a year earlier, it was down to 48.1 per cent of the year before in August 1990, one month after monetary union. The summer of 1990 saw a sudden collapse, a halving of production from one month to the next.

The number of people employed in East Germany dropped from 9.5 million in the first quarter of 1990 to 6.1 million in the second quarter of 1993. The industrial employment figure per 1,000 inhabitants sank from 132 in 1990 to 47 in 1993. The number of researchers in industry sank from 86,000 at the end of 1989 to 16,000 at the end of 1993. In agriculture, too, employment dropped by four-fifths.

Doubtless economic and social difficulties and setbacks were unavoidable in this first phase of transition from a centrally run to a market economy, as it was a process representing a profound change in the property structures of an entire economy, its material structures as well as the totally different character of its links with the global economy. It was a switch-over to completely changed means of controlling the economy for which there was neither the necessary prior knowledge nor the ingrained behavioural patterns necessary.

Furthermore, this economic transition was connected with thoroughgoing changes in the political, intellectual and cultural fields, transforming the way of life and the psycho-social state of the people.

Yet at the end the question remains whether this historically unparalleled transition really had to entail such a devastating economic collapse. Was the de-industrialisation and widespread destruction of agricultural production it brought with it so inevitable?

Causes of the Economic Decline

Some authors contradict the assertion made especially by the Federal Government, namely that the former 'mismanaged' economy of the GDR was exclusively to blame for the economic decline in East Germany. They argue that the collision of three strands of causes precipitated the economic decline:

- the state of the GDR economy at the time of unification, its low degree of competitiveness under world market conditions;
- the sudden introduction of the Deutschmark, which exposed the economy from one day to the next to the competition of the world markets without affording it any protection from the effects;
- the official economic policies of the state, as pursued especially by the Federal Government, which believed it could do without a special economic strategy for this transition and put its trust solely in market forces.[2]

The decline of the East German economy can only be explained by a combination of these three causes. Had the East German economy been competitive, it wouldn't have collapsed; had monetary union not taken place at the start rather than the end of a process of restructuring, the disaster wouldn't have been so overwhelming. Despite the weaknesses in economic structure and efficiency in the former GDR, an active structural, industrial and employment policy on the part of the government could have cushioned the effects of the overnight monetary exchange much more effectively than in practice happened.

The GDR Economy and Free World Market Competition

At the time of the *'Anschluß'*, the GDR economy was characterised by the following conditions:

- GDR industrial productivity was only 35 to 40 per cent of West Germany's; this being due not only to the generally lower technological level but also, possibly to quite a considerable degree, to a lower level of work intensity (slower pace of work, interruptions due to lack of supplies etc.).
- Compared with the West German situation, the capital assets of GDR industry were very much out-dated. The average age of production plant in GDR industry was 18 years as compared to eight years in the Federal Republic; at the end of the 1980s the proportion of equipment of GDR industry under ten years old and therefore still in full operating use stood at 49 per cent as against 70 per cent in the West.
- The economic development caused increasing damage to the natural environment, especially on account of the large volume of soft-coal mined mostly for the purpose of producing electricity (the top mining yield was 320 million tons p. a.).
- Two-thirds of East German industrial exports went to the Soviet or East European markets, which functioned more or less separately from those of the industrialised capitalist countries. On this market, sheltered from free competition, the GDR held a dominating position in some areas.
- Politically overambitious attempts at going it alone in important technological fields put a growing strain on the overall economic performance of the GDR. This increased the disproportion between the innovative potential based on research and development, on the one hand, and the investment resources, on the other. The innovation deficits of the economy were, therefore, not primarily due to insuf-

ficiently productive technological ideas so much as to their delayed practical implementation, and especially their slow dissemination.

- The centralist management of the economy, unrestrained right up to the very end and resulting in conflicts of vested interests between the state and the enterprises, caused a permanent shortage in all spheres of the economy, including commodity supplies. This factor in turn hampered both ability and readiness for innovation in the economy and paralysed its social driving forces.

- In formulating targets for social and economic development, the SED party leadership and government of the GDR increasingly ignored objective economic conditions, i.e. the reality of the decline in the economy. They tried to maintain a drive towards more consumer goods at the expense of the economic substance and the environment and thus to the detriment of future generations. They evaded the need to face up to the growing contradictions and refused to draw the necessary conclusions.

- In industry and in cultural development, major projects were undertaken which broke into the funds needed for the maintenance and modernisation of the existing economic foundations, running them down far below the critical minimum and overtaxing the economic potential of the GDR. This increased the deficitary situation of the entire economy.

Thus, in the end the SED party and state leadership had manoeuvred itself into a situation in which, quite apart from its unwillingness to undertake reforms, the objective possibilities for reforming the country were sharply reduced.

The necessary economic leeway was impeded not so much by the extent of the debts, which were actually not excessive relative to the economic potential of the GDR or compared with other countries, but rather by the scarcity of hard currency, this in turn resulting from the general deficits and from the terms of payment of the loans taken out by the GDR, which were mostly short term, while the credits handed out by the GDR were long term. Under these circumstances a very strong central administration was indispensable to ward off disaster.

Facile attempts to explain away everything by referring only to the mismanaged economy of the GDR ignore the following factors:

- Whilst the GDR did not belong to the ten leading industrial states of the world, it was a developed industrial country, and not derelict. The standard of living of the East Germans exceeded by far that of the population in market economies such as those in Southern Europe (Turkey, Greece, Southern Italy, Spain, Portugal). The standard of living in the GDR was also considerably higher than that of the other socialist countries.

- The isolation of GDR foreign trade from the Western industrial countries, especially in the technological field, was by no means deliberate GDR policy, but had rather been forced upon East Germany by Western embargo politics, using mechanisms which even increased in sophistication in the mid-1980s when the focus was on high technology. The West German Ministry of Economy described this using the slogan 'higher fences to shut out more products'. Ultimately the Western countries cut off the socialist countries completely from the international division of labour in the field of high technology, with the result that whatever these countries were not able to produce by themselves, they did not have. With regard to consumer goods, this was marked by a lack of high-tech spin-offs, so that GDR consumers, for instance, could not buy video recorders, video cameras, personal computers, etc. One may smile now at the efforts made by the GDR to establish itself all on its own in the field of microelectronics, but chips were very hard to come by from both the West and the East, while the range of products which depended on them grew steadily.

- The claim that GDR products generally did not come up to quality standards allowing them to compete on the world market cannot be sustained. Certain GDR enterprises in the field of investment goods, for example, exported a large proportion of their production to Western countries and were very well established there until recently. Just how many West German trade chains ordered huge amounts of consumer goods in the GDR – not only the wood carvings from the Erzgebirge mountains but also furniture, watches and textiles, etc. – is not known because tags revealing the GDR origin of the commodities were not attached or removed, in contrast with the practice with imports from other countries.

The weakness of GDR enterprises did not primarily relate to the quality of their products but to the costs. These were definitely too high and corresponded less and less to world market prices. From the early 1980s, the terms of trade for GDR machine tool exports therefore declined, a factor also due to inadequate maintenance servicing, and to what were publicly known as 'compulsory export prices'. Sales at dumping prices were as a rule the result not of inferior quality, but simply of the fact that GDR firms selling machines with parameters identical to those of their Western competitors had to accept a very much lower price on the world market, sometimes only half.

At the beginning of the 1990s, more differentiated assessments of GDR industrial competitiveness were made. These assessments showed that a large proportion of industry was hopelessly outdated or would have to be shut down for environmental reasons. Other areas of the investment goods industry, e.g. steel construction, machine tools, electrotechnical equipment for generating and distributing power, measurement and control technology, were, on the other hand, considered efficient and had good prospects for the future.[3] However, those areas also collapsed.

Pilot schemes evolved for the economic development of East Germany contend 'that the non-competitive section of the assets which would, therefore, have to be eliminated made up 30 per cent of the stock re-evaluated at the time of monetary union'.[4] But after that point in time industrial production in East Germany dropped to 30 per cent, which meant that some 40 per cent of the 70 per cent of industrial potential which could have been saved had gone.

Thus the state of the GDR economy was not exclusively responsible for its subsequent collapse. In any case, even if the lag in labour productivity had not been 60 to 65 per cent, but only, say, 20 per cent, the hasty monetary union and the more or less non-existent structural policy would have led to the same result, particularly as, under the relentless conditions of international competition, a lag of even 10 per cent can already be fatal.

To blame the economic decline solely on the mismanagement by SED party apparatus follows populist judgements according to which a low level of effectiveness equates with a run-down economy, brought about solely by the failings of a burnt-out political leadership. If this were true, most parts of the world could be considered run-down.

The Promised 'Thriving Lands' in the East

At the turn of 1989, most East Germans still favoured a German Confederation and a thorough reform of the GDR. But then public opinion changed dramatically, with hopes raised by the forthcoming monetary union which was to bring about a second German economic miracle, similar to the one which followed the 1948 monetary reform in West Germany. People were told to expect a speedy modernisation of the East German economy based on Western capital flooding in and boosting a dramatic rise in activity on the part of the enterprises and their workforce. In his speech of 1 July 1990, the day of monetary union, Federal Chancellor Helmut Kohl made that famous but wrong forecast that has been held against him ever since:

> Nobody will be worse off, but many better off. Only monetary, economic and social union offers the chance, indeed the guarantee, that living conditions shall change rapidly and improve thoroughly. By our joint efforts we will soon turn Mecklenburg-West Pomerania and Saxony-Anhalt, Saxony and Thuringia into thriving lands agreeable to live and work in.

There were lively and controversial discussions, especially in the first half of 1990, on whether a speedy introduction of market economics or a long-term transformation making possible a process of adjustment would be the better scheme; and whether monetary union should take place at the beginning or the end of such a process.

The following reasons were put forward in favour of a speedy monetary union:

• The present was the most favourable moment, offering the optimal macro-economic constellation for a monetary union: the Federal Republic was in an excellent economic shape, its surplus on current account in 1989 was DM150 billion. In contrast there had been a deficit on current account in West Germany at the time of the 1948 monetary reform. Also the economic forecast was positive at that time, particularly because of the foreseeable economic effects of West European integration.

• Access to the Deutschmark and thus to Western commodities and services would quickly increase work motivation on the part of the people and the enterprises.

• The exodus particularly of young people, skilled workers, technical engineers and medical practitioners to West Germany could not be stopped in any other way.

• The rapid elimination of shortages of investment goods as well as commodities and raw materials would very quickly overcome all obstacles in the way of increasing productivity.

• For Western capital investors and those starting up new firms all convertibility and transfer problems would immediately vanish. This would bring about a rapid and generous flow of Western capital, stimulated also by the fact that East German net wages stood at only half the Western level at that time.

- The traditionally close economic relations between the GDR and the Soviet Union as well as the other Eastern European states would secure East Germany important advantages in competition as compared to West German and Western European companies, and thus also promote economic prosperity on a long-term basis.
- Particularly high hopes were attached to the speedy development of medium-sized firms, indeed, a real boom in setting up new companies was expected, which would create at least half a million jobs in a short time, according to a pronouncement made by the Federal German Ministry of Economy.

The most optimistic forecast related to the rapid modernisation of the former GDR economy would even give it privileges in competition with West Germany within a relatively short period of time, as it would then boast more up-to-date means of production, fewer 'technological hangovers' and more modern economic structures. The idea was that the GDR with its 'new market economy would take up the challenge with vigorous programmes and get to grips with its many encrusted structures, such as we, in the Federal Republic, cannot overcome'.[5] This spirit of broad economic optimism was vividly and extensively articulated in February 1990 by Ingrid Matthäus-Maier, deputy leader of the Social Democratic parliamentary party of the Bonn parliament. 'The introduction of the Deutschmark', she said, could be 'the starting signal for an economic miracle in the GDR'. Commenting on the possible risks and dangers, she added that 'problems of adjustment would arise anyway, with or without monetary union'.[6]

Of course the risks were also mentioned, but the problems of adjustment and transition were generally greatly underestimated. They were passed off as negligible and the possibilities of overcoming them were usually assessed positively.

The results are inescapable. All predictions came true which forecast the collapse of some 50 per cent of all enterprises in view of the East German economic lag in efficiency and that this would be accompanied by an extremely high rate of unemployment. The President of the German Economics Institute, Lutz Hoffmann, was right in predicting:

> The conclusion to be drawn from these considerations is that it is in the interest of the economy and the working people of the GDR as well as of the economy and the labour market of the Federal Republic to maintain two separate economic spheres until the difference in productivity has been reduced to a minimum.[7]

An Unjustifiable Analogy

The frequent talk of the 'invisible wand' of spontaneous market forces which would make everything turn out all right often referred back to the 1948 monetary reform in the West. Like the monetary reform then, it was claimed that the monetary union of 1990 would lead to a new economic miracle in the East. But this analogy was wrong on decisive points.

Apart from the fact that the monetary reform of 1948 was not linked, as in 1990, with a transformation of the socio-economic fundamentals of society, i.e. its property relations, West Germany in 1948 was in comparison in a better economic state than the GDR at the time of the monetary union of 1990.

Firstly, before the 1948 monetary reform the West German economy had held back in anticipation of the boom to come; commodity supplies and production capacities were ready to thrust ahead in production to meet demand, and thus speedily gave a powerful stimulus to the entire economic development.

The East German economy of 1990 was in quite a different position. It was nowhere ready for a new start; on the contrary, it was rendered helpless by the sudden avalanche-like invasion of goods from regions economically much superior. Furthermore, West Germany had profited from the export boom following the Korean War (1950–3), which had tied down US economic forces, then superior to the German.

Secondly, West Germany 'entered the post-war period with remarkably extensive and relatively modern capital assets'.[8] Though some 17.4 per cent of the fixed capital assets (1936 = 100) had been destroyed during the war, investments from 1936 to 1945 increased by 75 per cent. Thus, in 1948 the gross fixed assets of West German industry amounted to 111.1 per cent of the 1936 figure, even taking into account the dismantling of equipment and plant after the war by the Allies (4.4 per cent). Out of the fixed assets in 1948, 16 per cent were no older than five years and 50 per cent were under ten years old. GDR industry was far less well equipped than that in 1989.[9]

Thirdly, market economics were not introduced in West Germany overnight after the 1948 monetary reform:

• Major areas of the economy were subsidised in the Federal Republic for decades and protected by import taxes: mining, the steel industry, shipbuilding and especially agriculture (even at the end of the 1980s, some 30 per cent of West German farmers' incomes came from government subsidies). Added to that, there were considerable subsidies for economically disadvantaged regions such as the areas bordering on the GDR and for West Berlin.

- After monetary reform, price regulations remained in force for large sectors of the economy, i.e. coal, coke, electricity, gas, water, rolling mill and forged iron products, washing powder and many foods. Ceilings were introduced for rents; the strict control of rent development was only loosened in the 1960s and dispensed with as late as the 1970s.

- Foreign trade in its entirety was firmly controlled for many years after monetary reform. When in 1950 West Germany was threatened with insolvency, import permits were newly regulated (16 October 1950) to provide an effective protection against flooding West Germany with imports. Import permits were only issued against deposits of 50 per cent of the foreign currency earnings in Deutschmarks, which were remitted on arrival of the goods. This 'cash deposit' curbed the influx of imports considerably. At the same time the volume of imports was restricted and import taxes imposed which increased with the rising level of processing of the imports.

- The convertibility of the Deutschmark was not introduced with the monetary reform either but more than ten years later (on 31 December 1958), when the results of the economic reform had become transparent and, above all, manageable. In the state of Saarland, the Deutschmark was only introduced three years after that state's incorporation into the Federal Republic in 1957, even though no change in the economic structures was involved. A transitional period of three years was agreed with France in which the French franc remained legal tender.

Had monetary parity between the GDR Mark and the West German Deutschmark been introduced step by step, as the economic performance of the East German economy increased, an economic collapse would have been averted or, at least, mitigated. In fact it would have been very helpful to take note of the conditions for the rise in West German economic prosperity after the 1948 monetary reform and to apply the conclusions.

As an article in a German business journal in 1992 remarked,

If the Federal Republic of Germany had entered into an economic and monetary union with the United States in 1948, at an exchange rate of DM1:1 to US Dollar, which is what happened in the GDR in respect of the transfer to Deutschmark, then the Morgenthau Plan envisaging the devastation of Germany would have become reality.[10]

Had the Federal German Government really taken account of the West German experience with the 1948 monetary reform, it would have arrived at diametrically opposed conclusions with regard to economic policies concerning the development of East Germany.

No notice was taken either of the experience of the European Community. The EC developed protective measures and transitionary regulations for economically weaker member countries, and envisaged a joint currency in 1999 at the earliest, when the process of balancing and adjustment would have progressed further.

This prompts the question: Would a longer transitional phase of adjustment for the East German economy have been at all possible?

Though the discussion of this question bears the mark of speculation, it has its uses in view of the argument that the government had no other choice but to embark on a speedy monetary union. The main argument put forward is the fact that the majority of the East German population did indeed clamour for the 'hard Deutschmark'. They also connected access to this currency with the idea of true freedom of travel, leaving behind an economy characterized by shortages, and of enjoying a much better supply of goods and services.

Of course it is difficult to say how, under the conditions of an open border and two different currencies side by side for a certain period of time, fruitful economic cooperation, a modernisation of the GDR economy and, last but not least, a limited access of the population to the Deutschmark could have been implemented. But answers to such questions were sought and many suggestions were made as to how these problems might have been solved. As these suggestions were never verified in practice, an analysis of the concrete suggestions is futile.

Lutz Hoffmann still believes 'the claim that there were no alternatives is unacceptable'.[11] He points to the fact that in the past political mergers also happened without monetary unions (in the Commonwealth) or with contractual agreements concerning a later unification (e.g. relating to Hong Kong). Import taxes and trade restrictions, as applied in the 1950s and 1960s in West Germany, might have protected the East German economy for a certain time of transition. A free trade zone, a price relation of East and West German products of 1:3 or 1:4 would not necessarily have entailed inflation. The pressure exercised by the imports would have introduced an element of healthy competition for the East German economy.

However, such considerations were brushed aside.

Why West German Capital Didn't Come

East Germany did not become a thriving land but a de-industrialised zone. This is the outcome of the '*Anschluß*' policy. Lutz Hoffmann and like-minded people proved right with their predictions which foresaw the ruin of the enterprises in the country and an escalating rate of unemployment.

Those who expected that after monetary union both West German and foreign capital would readily flow into the East German economy, especially into the processing industry, were disappointed. The new German economic miracle, this time in the East, failed to materialise. Federal Chancellor Helmut Kohl repeatedly showed his surprise and disappointment at the low degree of commitment of West German investors in East Germany and tried to induce them to change their minds. This lack of interest seemed all the harder to understand as every investor was promised an additional Mark in subsidies for every mark of their own capital invested, and East German companies could often be bought up for a song.

Western capital was indeed very hesitant in its approach to the East German processing industry. Writing in 1993, Lutz Hoffmann argued that:

> The main reason for this will have been that any extension of capacities at West German locations would generally have been simpler, less expensive and better to calculate. New branches cause higher costs at the initial stage, especially in a new environment, and apart from that there is considerable uneasiness with regard to the long-term development of the East German market. Thus it would always be more rational to expand existing plants in West Germany or increase output by minor investments.[12]

Thus the main reasons for the hesitant flow of West German capital into the processing industry of East Germany were oversupply, typical of a free market economy, as well as long-term overcapacities. That is to say, the production capacities not being used by West German firms were just waiting to produce goods to swamp the East German market.

The exception were industries bound to the region, e.g. power plants. There, West German capital was quick to act. In August 1990 the general public and especially the local councils were taken by surprise when a contract was signed between the *Treuhand* and three West German electricity companies – *PreussenElektra AG*, Hanover, *Rheinisch-Westfälisches Elektrizitätswerk (RWE)*, Essen; *Bayernwerk AG* – which gave them the majority of the shares in the central electricity network of the former GDR (see below).

Instead of wondering about the lack of capital flowing from West Germany into certain areas of the economy, the last GDR Government and the West German Government would have done better to have paid attention to the areas into which this capital did flow – so quickly and on such a massive scale that a degree of monopolisation was reached far exceeding that in West Germany. A result of this was that large sections of East German industry and agriculture were cut off from markets overnight. So instead of harping on the deficits of GDR industry, critics ought to have resisted monopolisation and retained the competitive elements of the economy.

In line with the rules of free market economics, West German capital was neither encouraged in those areas where it acted hesitantly nor constrained where it wrecked everything. The destruction of industrial potential and the squandering of what had been nationally owned industrial assets characterised the manner in which the *Treuhandanstalt* conducted the privatisation of nationally owned companies in East Germany.

The *Treuhandanstalt*: a State Instrument of Privatisation

The establishing of the *Treuhandanstalt* dates back initially to a resolution passed by the GDR Government under Prime Minister Hans Modrow on 1 March 1990. Its statutes were laid down by decree on 15 March 1990. At the same time provisions were made to transform nationally owned economic units into capital companies.

Both decisions relate to the basic idea and the initial task – to preserve economic assets and protect them against arbitrary take-over and to enable them to adjust to market economy conditions by taking on a new legal status.[13]

However, this initial assignment of the *Treuhandanstalt* was rendered null and void and replaced by the Act on the Privatisation and Reorganisation of Nationally Owned Assets – the *Treuhand* Law – of 17 June 1990, passed by the newly elected *Volkskammer* on 18 March 1990. This Act redefined the task of the *Treuhandanstalt* as follows.

The *Treuhandanstalt* was to promote the 'privatisation and use of nationally owned assets according to the principles of the social market economy' and to assist in the 'structural adjustment of the economy to the requirements of the market by advancing particularly the development and privatisation of enterprises which have a chance of surviving'. According to Article 25 of the Unification Treaty, the *Treuhandanstalt* was

commissioned to continue to restructure and privatise former nationally owned enterprises in line with market economics. The holding company shall be turned into a Federal German Agency with legal competence. The Federal Minister of Finances shall supervise the technical and legal aspects in agreement with the Federal Minister of Economy and the Federal Minister responsible in the particular instance. Shares of the *Treuhand* shall at the same time be indirect shares of the Federal Republic.[14]

Looking back on the first post-'*Anschluß*' year, the last Prime Minister of the GDR Lothar de Maizière said that the conflict between privatisation and restructuring inherent in the *Treuhandanstalt* assignment might have been mastered but for one factor: '*Treuhand*, despite repeated warnings, always gave preference to privatisation'. It was 'sad that in addition some racketeers used *Treuhand* as a kind of self-service shop'.[15] According to repeated statements by its presidents, the *Treuhandanstalt* approached its task from a purely business point of view; namely in wishing to dispose of the former nationally owned property as quickly as possible. Making them competitive, therefore, went by the board. The motto was: 'Privatisation is the best way of rehabilitation.'

At the point of monetary union, the *Treuhandanstalt* owned 8,482 enterprises with more than 4 million employees. By 31 December 1993 some 92 per cent of the firms had been privatised along with 18,813 hectares of real estate, 34,700 hectares of agricultural land and 2,155 hectares of forestry land, which had also been sold off.

The privatising practice of the *Treuhandanstalt* and its results cannot be understood without taking into consideration one additional fundamental aspect: the totally inadequate democratic control of its activities.

A Deficit of Democracy

Officially the *Treuhandanstalt* was a public agency directly responsible to the Federal Government and the Minister of Finances (and not, as would have been far more sensible, to the Minister of Economy), a fact showing clearly that it was the primary task of the *Treuhandanstalt* to get rid of and not rehabilitate the enterprises. As a Federal agency, *Treuhand* was subject to parliamentary control. However, whenever parliamentarians demanded access to the files and documents, it was argued that the *Treuhandanstalt* had to manage like a share-holding company, and that such material had therefore to be regarded as confidential. Even the *Treuhand* controlling committee of the *Bundestag* was not allowed to handle the files for weeks on end until finally certain select members were granted this privilege. And this happened only when the chairman of the committee asked in parliament whether the *Treuhandanstalt* was an 'extra-territorial body' or an 'area outside law', and threatened to go before the Federal Constitutional Court.

The Ministry of Finances did not conduct supervisory checks on the *Treuhandanstalt* or any of its branches. 'In actual fact there is no technical supervision', records a briefing for the *Bundestag* issued by the Federal Audit Office on 17 September 1993.

On the other hand the objective laid down in the *Treuhand* Law to the effect that the former GDR firms were to be merged in five large share-holding companies was deliberately not carried out. Implementing this would not only have made the *Treuhandanstalt* responsible for the financial obligations of its branches, it would also have implied that, as in other share-holding companies, members of the workforce would have had the right to be represented on the management committee with a right to vote. The honorary administrative council of the *Treuhandanstalt* comprised three trade union representatives, but they did not serve on the management committee. The workforce at individual enterprises only learned about the sale of their firms after the contracts were signed. In many cases they had to rely on the media to learn about decisions which so vitally concerned them. The price at which their firms were sold and other important terms of the sale were kept secret anyway.

How Does One Squander an Entire National Economy?

To privatise a whole economy by selling it off enterprise by enterprise must inevitably lead to a squandering of the assets. This is striking proof of the fact that the scale of the whole undertaking was neither recognised nor properly taken into account – the historically unparalleled operation of putting an entire economy on a new property basis by privatising it. As there just could not be enough potential buyers for privatisation on this scale, the headlong disposal of economic assets, *Treuhand*-style, enterprise by enterprise, placed purchasers in a monopolistic position which enabled them to dictate the conditions of sale. They knew that the longer they waited, the more cheaply they could acquire the property.

Who Were the Potential Buyers?

The people of the GDR were not able to accumulate capital or other assets. They had only their savings and benefits from insurances, and the bulk of their savings had in any case been devalued at an exchange rate of 2:1 in the course of monetary union.

Lothar de Maizière was absolutely correct in saying that

> The economic situation is as if one would take away all property from the Bavarians save their cash reserves, and then asked them to buy back the Bavarian assets. The people of Bavaria would not be able to do this. Only those as naïve as Queen Marie Antoinette, could overlook this fact.[16]

The optimistic expectations of many people, including those who had warned against a hasty monetary union, that there would be 'a powerful influx of capital from the Federal Republic and also from other European and non-European countries',[17] did not materialise. The hope that there would be no problem raising the DM1.1 billion required to adjust the GDR economy to the West German model from the private sector was based on the assumption that there was enough floating capital in the Federal Republic in 1990. And indeed, there was more than DM600 billion available; the dilemma was to transform this floating capital into investments – a procedure which poses increasing problems in present-day market economies at the best of times.

Sale for Cash

The *Treuhandanstalt* sold off the companies piecemeal for cash on sale, and that ruled out many sound potential buyers from West Germany.

They could only have afforded to buy at a very low or nominal price. Cash down payment weakened the buyers financially and reduced their investment capital. This in turn stimulated buyers to wait for the firms to get into difficulties and not buy until the price dropped. Again, suggestions were made as to how to solve this problem to the economic benefit of both parties. Had the *Treuhandanstalt* really been interested in achieving good prices for the sale, then it would have adopted these suggestions. Among the proposals submitted was one from Hans-Werner Sinn which called for distributing the companies instead of selling them. He proposed that they should be handed over to West German firms, the *Treuhandanstalt* to start with retaining ownership but waiving its right to influence business policies. Minor firms and retail shops could be passed on to potential East German buyers against registration of a fixed-interest debt to the *Treuhandanstalt*. At a second stage, the shares held by the *Treuhandanstalt* could be distributed among the East German people at the rate of 2:1. This would not have delayed privatisation but would have prevented the squandering of assets, as there would have been no pressure to sell in the face of an insuffucient number of potential buyers. The new owners would not have had to pay for the entire assets immediately but would only have had to remit clear profits from investment. They could have acquired the shares held by *Treuhand* at a later time and at normal conditions.[18] But all such considerations were swept aside by the Federal Government and the *Treuhandanstalt*.

GDR State Property Goes West

It may really be correct to claim that the *Treuhandanstalt*

> developed a lot of commercial initiative, making full use of modern publicity such as public tenders in large journals, sales fairs, distribution of sales catalogues, a direct approach to potential customers. They availed themselves of the services of company agents and investment banks. Smaller and medium-sized companies were offered to the management and/or the staff (management buy-out) or to people from outside (management buy-in). And all these activities were not only restricted to Germany but were also undertaken abroad.[19]

Nevertheless, despite these efforts, the main form of privatisation remained the sale of *Treuhand* property to West German firms in the same branch. Selling in this way ignored the rules of market economics, which would have called for the introduction and sale of capital shares on the capital market and would also have called for the restoration of the enterprises to profitability beforehand. The inevitable outcome was therefore that:

> Calculated on the basis of jobs, less than 6 per cent of the privatised assets were sold to East Germans. Just under 10 per cent were sold to foreign investors. The West Germans got the lion's share of 85 per cent.[20]

The greed and dubious methods employed by some representatives of West German big business in the race for the best bits from among the East German assets, and the assistance they were sometimes afforded in doing this by the *Treuhand* is not the actual problem. What really mattered was the tacit objective of the *Treuhandanstalt*, its concept of achieving a speedy total privatisation as sole priority.

Given this concept, subjective shortcomings in the work of the *Treuhandanstalt* were bound to have devastating effects. Merely delaying decisions on certain privatisations, rejecting reconstruction concepts for certain enterprises, refusing to cancel former debts, which the *Treuhand-anstalt* was entitled to do, meant that East German assets were needlessly squandered. Irrespective of whether this was done deliberately, or for whatever other ulterior motives, or merely as a result of incompetence or indifference, enterprises which would have stood a medium-term chance were in this way ruined, or sold off dirt-cheap to West German firms. If the decision to privatise a firm is long delayed, this stops all reconstruction or reduces activities to minimal maintenance efforts until a prospective buyer's intentions are known; such a firm is doomed because no product or market strategy can be developed and imple-mented; customers forsake the firm, which is considered unreliable. Unless the enterprises still under *Treuhand* administration, whether profitable or not, were guaranteed a sheltered existence for a certain period of time, sales pressures and the fundamental problems of financing the purchase of former nationalised plants would continue to undermine their chances of survival and their workers' chances of staying in employment.

Common Sense Versus the Distorted Logic of Free Market Economics

How was it possible for the sale of an entire economy – the work of nearly two post-war generations in East Germany – to leave nothing but debts? Even if an enterprise is run-down, there are still certain assets left, such as equipment, buildings, real estate, so how can there be nothing left of it after sale, as so often happened in this case?

What seems incomprehensible judged on the criterion of common sense is not necessarily incompatible with the logic of free market economics.

If a firm which has neither debts nor is making any profit is sold in toto, the price will not be based on the value of the fixed and current assets or on the added price of all property involved. Instead, it will be sold for a price based on the capitalised earnings expected at current interest rates plus a certain risk charge. This will then be called the 'profitability value' and will be the foundation of the sales price. This 'profitability value' relates to the amount of capital required to show a profit return at the current rate of interest, equal to the profit to be expected from the enterprise in question in the near future.

Selling enterprises for a nominal one Deutschmark was *Treuhand*'s way out of the inevitable dilemma which arose from a privatisation concept providing for the sale of an entire economy in accordance with the rules of a free market economy. Accordingly the sale of such enterprises at their actual profitability value was logical, and yet at the same time insane from a genuine economic point of view. No sane person wanting to dispose of an enterprise would do such a thing. S/he would not sell the whole firm but go into liquidation and sell off the assets piecemeal.

However, when the *Treuhandanstalt* sold property, social and economic considerations made it imperative that the firms be maintained as places of work. As most of the enterprises were not making a profit, they therefore had to be given away for nothing. Such squandering of property is unavoidable if you don't first reconstruct; it is the price you inevitably have to pay if you insist that 'privatisation is the best form of reconstruction' – the line taken by the *Treuhandanstalt*!

Such crash sales, if conducted in accordance with profitability principles, are actually a gift handed to the buyer. Even if the purchaser went into liquidation immediately after having bought the firm, s/he would still make a profit. And even if s/he complied with the conditions of the *Treuhand* purchasing contracts, which prohibited resales, the purchase would still be a 'potential gift'. If the new owners managed to manoeuvre the company into the black by clever management, by opening up new markets or by modernising their production lines or technology, profits were quickly achieved on the basis of assets bought for a song, in fact for the nominal sum of one Deutschmark. The buyer of course undertook to keep a certain number of jobs and to invest a certain amount in the business, but this undertaking was frequently not carried out and often not insisted on by *Treuhand* officials.

The sample contract for *Treuhand* sales laid down a penalty in the event that fewer than the contractually promised number of jobs was maintained, i.e. DM15,000 to 40,000 per job lost. There was also a penalty if less capital than laid down in the contract was invested, in which case the new owner might have to remit to *Treuhand* up to 20 per cent of the sum not invested. If buyers resold the property bought from *Treuhand* during the first 15 years after purchase, they would have to pay back a portion of the profit thus made. Another clause provided for the re-evaluation of the price of the property bought from *Treuhand* in two to five years after purchase. Should the value of the property have increased by more than a stipulated percentage (e.g. 10 per cent), additional payments might have to be made. Naturally such conditions attracted not only serious buyers but also all kinds of racketeers.

The real 'price' was therefore the buyer's promise not to close down the firm and sell off the company piecemeal, to invest a certain sum in the firm and to preserve a certain number of jobs. But how long and how effectively could such sales conditions be monitored and their implementation demanded? This is in fact a somewhat academic question as the *Treuhandanstalt* announced that on this point, too, it wouldn't be too stringent.

The sales agents in these acts of privatisation were not only West German civil servants, but also managerial staff from the major concerns and employers' organisations of the particular branch of industry to which the firm about to be privatised belonged. There were often complaints about these 'experts' from inside *Treuhand* who handled its privatisation activity. The negotiators of sales of whole branches of GDR industry were thus part of the lobby of West German big business, just as were the chartered accountants employed in such deals or the experts who provided the reports on the enterprises to be sold. This manner of privatisation was characterised by a fusion of interests and persons on both sides of the deals and thus by the likelihood that people would line their pockets; and of course that the nation's assets would be squandered on an even more massive scale.

There were many instances of representatives of West German industrial branches inspecting *Treuhand* firms of the same branch offered for sale. They provided themselves with the relevant business data and then disappeared for good. A little later the management at the East

German firm found that some of their customers had been enticed away by the West German firm in question.

The truth is that the brand of privatisation adopted lent itself to this sort of malpractice. The borderline between making a profit legally or illegally is anyway very narrow. Any officially sanctioned leniency in respect of the regulations of such privatisation would necessarily stimulate illegal profit-making and the squandering of assets – which is what happened. In a letter of December 1992 to the President of the *Treuhand-anstalt*, Birgit Breuel, the Federal Minister of Finance encouraged it to be as flexible as possible in interpreting the regulations in the interests of a speedy privatisation (which, naturally, made it extremely hard to prove that breaches of trust had taken place) and to disregard other aspects as well, including sales incomes.

Privatising Practices

Günter Ogger, editor of the journal *Capital*, writing in 1992, provided a vivid description of West German businessmen in East Germany:

> Hardly had the GDR gone, when whole legions of West Germans eager for booty pounced on their inexperienced East German colleagues, overwhelmed by the political events, in order to snatch from them anything which had been of value in the workers' and farmers' state.
>
> Many of the West German managers sent to the East by their firms acted like colonial masters as they drove up to first-class hotels in Leipzig, Dresden or Berlin in their posh company Daimlers or BMWs. Those who witnessed just how brutally the invading Germans treated their unsuspecting 'brothers and sisters' in the nationally owned companies had reason to be ashamed of being German. Instead of providing the unsuspecting socialists with all possible assistance, the Westerners took every advantage of them, tricking them out of their real estate, factories and stocks.
>
> No trick was too shabby for them as they secured the best chunks of the East German economy. For instance, envoys of renowned West German firms were placed in the management of the *Treuhand* administration in order to tell their bosses where the hidden treasures of GDR industry were to be found, so that they could lay their hands on the juiciest morsels.

Munich-based building contractor Fritz Eichbauer, long-time president of the Central Association of the German Building Trade, was brazen in his attempt to grab one of the largest building companies of the former GDR. First of all he got *Treuhand* to appoint him as chairman of the management board of the former nationally owned *Hochbau AG*, worth DM200–400 million. Then he circumvented the sale of the firm to other German and foreign bidders, before he and his partners submitted a modest offer of DM40 million.

When *Treuhand*, frightened by publications about similar predatory practices, rejected this 'offer', Fritz Eichbauer retired from his mandate, claiming that he had considered it his 'patriotic duty' to help the East.

In a similarly cold-blooded way, Frankfurt businessman Claus Wisser tried to get possession of an East Berlin railway carriage firm, which was worth at least DM100 million, for the symbolic price of one Deutschmark. The Munich-based SIEMENS company was even cleverer; they managed to haul in twenty nationally owned companies with more than 20,000 employees for the discount price of $250 million. The SIEMENS trick: chartered accountants associated with SIEMENS assessed an extremely low value in the opening balance.

Although *Treuhand* removed five dozen West Germans from the boards of East German firms within the first two years after unification, the con tricks in East Germany are still being practised today. Many former GDR firms were pillaged and ruined by their West German opposite numbers, so that they are now more or less unsaleable and have to be refurbished at the expense of the taxpayer.

According to an estimate by the management consultant firm Ward Howell, some 75 per cent of the West German managers working in the East are 'drop-outs' who would never get another chance in the West. For salaries on average 20 per cent higher than those in the West, these bunglers are steering what remained of the nationally owned economy into certain ruin.

There are also smart Westerners such as the former Porsche board member Heinz Branitzki, who helped his cronies into highly paid jobs; and *Treuhand* managers who underwrite bills submitted by lawyer, tax consultant, management consultant or chartered accountant friends, even though their services bear no relation to the exorbitant sums they charge.

Some 10,000 such seedy profiteers and small-time managers are active in the East, according to *Treuhand* estimates. The damage they are causing there is unimaginable. On top of all that, the West German managers, under the guise of having done their patriotic duties, also want to cash in, after robbing East Germany, with regard to pensions. The *Treuhand* administration is planning to hand out enormous retirement sums to their 200 top executives at the termination of the agency's work in 1995. This expense, not provided for in the employment contracts, adds an additional strain on the German taxpayer to the tune of a three-digit million sum.[21]

That was Günter Ogger's picture of things in 1992. Altogether, the varied privatisation practices of the *Treuhandanstalt* provided a bizarre picture.

There was, it is true, the occasional instance of a privatisation which was genuinely followed by the firm's rehabilitation. The new owner produced a successful product and marketing strategy, preserved a large proportion of the jobs, and even created some new ones after a phase of redundancies. But these were exceptions. Of the 3.9 million jobs in the privatised *Treuhand* companies which had been guaranteed by the buyers, only 1.5 million were left by the end of 1993.

There were many instances of adventurers who bought up a number of firms in East Germany, stripped them of their assets and then simply vanished from the face of the earth, so that police investigations had to be initiated.

Certain large concerns and vested interests, for instance major power-supplying firms or even the SIEMENS concern, more or less divided up the GDR economy among themselves. Some very carefully selected the icing on the cake and then abandoned the rest.

Then there was the widespread practice of using East German firms as a potential extension and capacity reserve for the West German parent company. Other firms, individually or in groups, bought up all the enterprises of their branch of industry. The *Kugelfischer AG Schweinfurt* company, for instance, bought up all eight East German rolling mills, and then just closed them down, thus ridding themselves of competition. Being bought up quickly and then closed down was also the fate of the East German sugar companies, which enabled the West German sugar companies to take over the production quota of 847,000 tons laid down by the EC for East Germany.

Speedy Privatisation at Any Cost

Even if there had been parliamentary control of the sales practices, it could only have rectified the worst irregularities, thanks to the lack of transparency in respect of *Treuhandanstalt* sales conditions. The *Treuhand* law did not specify privatisation or sales provisions. Thus the remission of a firm's so-called 'old liabilities' (these dated back to GDR times when enterprises were provided with funds to build social amenities for their workers) was optional.

In many instances, buyers who agreed to invest heavily and preserve jobs were rewarded by a low price, in addition to which the *Treuhand-anstalt* also granted investment subsidies and financial loss compensation, etc. The sales contract with the Norwegian *Kvaerner* concern for the *Warnow* shipbuilding yard was considered perfectly legitimate by the *Treuhandanstalt*. It was priced at DM1 million. The concern undertook to invest DM573 million by 1995, and during the following ten years another DM15 million p. a. The Norwegians also guaranteed 2,150 jobs for a period of three years. In return, the concern received DM549 million in investment subsidies, DM73 million in competition subsidies and another DM614.4 million in loss and risk compensation. The *Warnow* shipbuilding yard was also released from its 'old liabilities' of DM262 million. All in all, the concern received subsidies to the tune of DM1.525 billion from the *Treuhandanstalt*, the Federal State of Mecklenburg-West Pomerania and the fund dealing with 'old' GDR liabilities, totalling DM709,300 per job guaranteed.[22] Such expensive jobs were to be found nowhere else in the shipbuilding industry.

MBO companies (management buy-out, i.e. the firm's management buys the company with the help of bank loans and state subsidies), generally acquired by East Germans, were always at a disadvantage. Some 75 per cent of such firms had no remission of 'old liabilities' and nearly 95 per cent were assessed not at their 'profitability value' but at the value of their assets. No West German firm was expected to buy on such conditions.

In this connection, Hans Richter, head of the legal department of the *Treuhandanstalt* until the end of 1992, said:

As everybody got what they wanted in East Germany, and that at conditions which were extremely favourable, there was no need for delinquency.[23]

The target of achieving speedy privatisation was enhanced by a bonus system for the executive staff of the *Treuhandanstalt* linked to the number of sales effected. The salaries of the top management of the *Treuhand-anstalt* were very high anyway, well above comparative salaries in industry, even though the executives ran no business risks. In 1992, the 46 directors at headquarters received a basic salary of between DM228,000 and 400,000 per year, the 135 heads of department between DM120,000 and 276,000. In addition there was a bonus of DM44,000 to 96,000 for directors and DM29,600 to 77,000 for heads of department. Furthermore the directors were paid lump sums of DM7,000 and heads of department of DM6,000 in separation allowances, and, last but not least, the directors were granted another DM1,482 per month and heads of departments DM1,140 for car-leasing expenses, the latter sum also being available in cash.

Peter Kachel, commenting on this in 1992 in an economic journal, remarked that it was

> the principle of granting *Treuhand* staff bonuses for the particularly speedy execution of their tasks which is questionable. This privatisation-related bonus system only promotes a policy of 'privatisation at any cost' and prevents the development of long-term concepts of corporate modernisation, as it provides an incentive to sell off the 'prime beef' without regard to the 'bones'. The bonus system of the *Treuhandanstalt* creates an incentive structure which rewards the sell-off of companies below their value. The shock on the company market which the *Treuhand* provoked by this practice is seen as the root cause by business people for the steady decline in sales prices and the growing mountain of debt piled up by the *Treuhandanstalt*.[24]

In any case, this type of privatisation turned out to be the most expensive way of transforming the East German economy into a market and private property economy.

The Decline of East German Agriculture

The dramatic drop in agricultural production in East Germany is just as unparalleled as the more or less complete de-industrialisation. Agricultural policy, including *Treuhand* schemes for reprivatisating agriculture, was in no way geared to providing equal opportunities to all types of agricultural ownership, nor did it respect the desire of the bulk of the former cooperators to retain cooperative forms of agricultural management. Had there been a relevant concept for structural adjustment, East German agriculture would have been able to undergo the transition to a market economy under the conditions of EC agricultural policies in a relatively short period of time.[25] With regard to the size of the farms, East German agriculture had a clear and economically significant advantage vis-à-vis West Germany. However, this advantage was likely to be lost because the policy adopted by the Federal Government was aimed at forcing the small family farm concept on to the East Germans, even though EC experience had demonstrated the problems inherent in such forms of agriculture.

The systematic discrimination against the agricultural enterprises which succeeded the cooperatives proved to be one of the main pillars of the Federal Government's agricultural policy. Everything suggested that it was influenced strongly by ideological prejudice rather than by economic considerations. Hence the priority attached to so-called 'victims' of the post-war land reform,[26] who were treated in a privileged manner in respect of land-leasing contracts. Hence, too, the disadvantageous treatment of both the reconstructed cooperatives and members of limited agricultural companies from the Government settlement programme,[27] which handled future sales of land and formerly national property, and was subsequently administered by the *Treuhandanstalt*. Another form of discrimination was the slow and only partial remission of the cooperatives' liabilities dating back to GDR times; even if the former cooperatives were cut down in size these 'debts' were not reduced. The allocation of subsidies was extremely prejudiced and operated to the detriment of the cooperative farms. In 1992, for instance, the new cooperatives, cultivating 70 per cent of the arable land, only got 2.8 per cent of the subsidies paid to family farms.[28]

By comparison, the treatment of so-called land reform 'victims' was a spectacular case illustrating how the ruling and judgement of the Federal Constitutional Court, which bans discrimination against any type of agricultural enterprise, was systematically undermined and, in effect, repealed by administrative means. The result was an economic policy heavily biased against cooperative agricultural enterprises.

Deprived Local Communities

The East German communities might actually have come out of unification quite well, considering the dominance of nationally owned property in the GDR, which could even have given them a degree of affluence. This would have enhanced economic recovery, representing the necessary economic foundation for recovery and equipping local communities with financial resources. But this chance was sabotaged.

The GDR Law on the Assets of Local Communities of 20 July 1990 ruled that former nationally owned property, administered by the local councils or used for the purpose of local self-administration, was to be handed over to the local communities free of charge. This Law was endorsed by the Unification Treaty. But after 1990, these rulings were modified, qualified or cut back. At best, they were implemented only hesitantly. Why was this?

In the GDR, many institutions provided indispensable local community services without actually being subjected to local administration. Precisely this fact was used in an unscrupulous way to circumvent the regulations of both the GDR Law on the Assets of Local Communities and the Unification Treaty.[29] For instance, many sports grounds, kindergartens, health centres, cultural centres and vocational training schools had been run by industrial enterprises or agricultural cooperatives, and not by the local council. They could and should have been handed over to the local councils, if the latter wanted them. But instead they were frequently sold off as part of the assets to be privatised. This also applied to other services such as the electricity and water supplies, sewage disposal, public transport, etc., which again had been provided by state or district enterprises.

Local councillors and deputies quite rightly censured the *Treuhandanstalt* for failing to hand over assets to the local communities, in contrast to their zeal in carrying out their privatisation programme.

It was clearly a grave mistake to commission an agency with the job of allocating assets to local communities, when that commission's primary task was to privatise assets, including property not considered eligible for communal ownership. The *Treuhandanstalt* could opt to hand over the assets free or sell them. It is little wonder that they rejected one-third to one-half of all applications from local councils to be allocated educational, health and cultural property.

By delaying the processing of these applications, the *Treuhandanstalt* and the financial authorities in effect reduced the local communities' economic power, and hindered investments by them. That property handed over to the communities was encumbered with 'old liabilities' was, moreover, clearly in defiance of both the Unification Treaty and the GDR Law on the Assets of Local Communities, which had envisaged the allocation of nationally owned property free of charge. Because of these liabilities many local councils dared not file applications for an allocation of such property. The result was their privatisation or closure.

The so-called 'Electricity Contract', which the *Treuhandanstalt* concluded with three large West German firms – *PreussenElektra AG, Rheinisch-Westfälisches Elektrizitätswerk* and *Bayernwerke AG* – is a special chapter in the discrimination against local councils with regard to GDR assets. West German concerns were given the majority shares in the large soft coal power plants and the high-tension transmission system, which meant that East German communities had no chance of operating independent power-producing plants, again in stark contradiction to the GDR Law on the Assets of Local Communities. This had provided for the allocation of at least the 164 local power plants to the local authorities which before 1945 had held a prominent position in the energy industry in East Germany.

On this point the Unification Treaty (Part II, Chapter IV, Section III, Number 2 b), signed one month after (!) the 'Electricity Contract', amended the GDR Law on the Assets of Local Communities (4, Section 2) as follows:

Insofar as the shares of the urban and rural communities exceed 49 per cent of the capital of a joint-stock company for the supply of network power, this share shall be reduced to that percentage.

This ruling contrasts with the situation in West Germany, where nearly all major towns, some 10 per cent of all local administrations operate their own local power works. There the trend towards setting up or buying back local power plants has increased considerably in recent years. There are important reasons for this development, namely that local power plants are an important source of income for the local authorities, and also produce cheaper and ecologically sounder electricity, far more in keeping with the modern trends in this field. In contrast, the large concerns rely mostly on centralised electricity production in large power plants, which calls for cross-country transmission lines. Though, of course, indispensable to a certain degree, these spoil the countryside. The local power works provide a more decentralised energy production, and have the decisive economic and ecological advantage of being able to combine the generation of heat and power in a way not possible at centralised large plants.

Following a complaint about unconstitutional procedures filed by 164 East German communities, a compromise suggested by the Federal Constitutional Court came into force which allowed communities to produce their own electricity if they could obtain the necessary permission. In that case, relevant property would be allocated to them, failing which they would receive 49 per cent shares in the regional power supply company free of charge. In this instance, too, the transfer of the assets to the communities was much delayed and the 'old liabilities' had to be acknowledged.

'Old Liabilities'

The Federal Government and the *Treuhandanstalt* claimed that the GDR had not contributed any assets at all to unification. The Federal Government had, however, failed to take stock of nationally owned property and the economic potential as prescribed by the Unification Treaty, arguing that GDR liabilities were so blatant that there was no point in making such an inventory. The *Treuhandanstalt* also disregarded the *Treuhand* Law, which ruled that an opening balance be made of the property value (at current market values). The opening balance issued in October 1992 evaluated the nationally owned assets on the basis of predictable privatisation proceeds. This of course meant that the implementation of the *Treuhand* privatisation policy was already taken for granted. The entire industrial, banking, insurance and trade property was estimated to be worth DM78.9 billion and the value of agricultural assets DM16 billion.

This 'balance sheet' showed a deficit of DM229 billion. The foreseeable results of privatisation were integrated into the opening balance in 'anticipation'. But this opening balance was used as the basis for the Federal Government in assessing GDR liabilities. A different approach to balancing assets and liabilities at the time would have produced totally different results:

• The national debt per GDR citizen at the point of monetary union (liabilities of the state to banks, foreign debts, housing loans and remaining balance items from the monetary exchange) amounted to about DM6,800. To compare, the public debt of the Federal Government amounted to DM10,800 per West German citizen (not counting the individual German Federal States).

• The East Germans justifiably expected a revenue of several billion Deutschmarks from the privatisation of GDR assets. At the end of 1991, the late President of the *Treuhandanstalt*, Detlev Rohwedder, evaluated these assets at DM600 billion. The total value of national assets (including GDR assets abroad, e.g. the real estate belonging to former GDR embassies) was at least 50 per cent higher.

• The East Germans also expected that the money paid by the GDR in war reparations on behalf of the whole of Germany would be included in the balance of their liabilities.

On 28 November 1989, Professor Arno Peters of Bremen presented a 'Reparations Balancing Plan' at the Federal Press Conference in Bonn, showing that the GDR had paid 98 per cent of German war reparations to the victorious powers of the Second World War, amounting to a sum of DM16,124 (including interest) per inhabitant, whereas the West Germans merely paid reparations of DM128 per head. Professor Peters said that it was his aim 'to make clear that when we make resources available for the GDR today, this cannot be considered "Aid" and it is by no means "altruistic".' The capital we saved as a result of the 'people of the GDR undertaking the reparation payments, is held by us in trust. These financial means entrusted to us have to be returned of course.' As early as the end of the 1950s, Professor Fritz Baade, then Director of the Institute of World Economics in Kiel, had assessed the financial obligation of West towards East Germany at DM100 billion.

As East Germany's economic position at the time of unification was the weaker, considerable transfers from West to East Germany were required to allow East Germany to thrive and balance living conditions in East and West. To take account of reparation payments made by the GDR and waive its liabilities might have been a just way out of the dilemma, and one which would very probably have been accepted by the East Germans.

But this was not the approach adopted. Every single one of the GDR liabilities was pedantically listed, and all the blame for the present disaster attributed to that country.

- The many serious arguments put forward by economic institutions and researchers, that these 'old liabilities' of GDR enterprises had no economic significance and made even less sense in market economic terms, were ignored. No civil court would endorse the bank loans (allocated by the GDR planning authorities according to the mechanisms of a planned economy, regardless of economic success or failure of the respective company) as debts.
- No internal clearing or balancing of the 'internal liabilities of a planned economy' (for instance, those of nationalised companies towards the state bank) was ever made. The fact was just ignored that when a nationalised economy collapses, it can only leave such debts as result from foreign loans or liabilities relating to people's savings in the nationalised banking institutions.

- The 'GDR debt' was not taken over by the Federal Republic, as would have been appropriate. The individual companies and housing societies were all burdened with these 'old liabilities' of the GDR (the latter contradicting the 1977 GDR Housing Construction Law, according to which the state was responsible for payment of loans and interest). Housing societies found it hard to recover from this blow as it meant that tenants would have to pay back these debts to the last pfennig – an impossible task if the current regulations remained in force.

- The war reparations paid by the people of East Germany were not taken into consideration in evaluating the debt inherited from the GDR; yet many minor items such as GDR liabilities from trade with the Federal Republic which amounted to DM5.8 billion, were meticulously listed.

A grotesque aspect of this matter of the GDR 'liabilities' was that the Federal budget would finally end up with a much higher debt than the liabilities West Germany should have taken over from the GDR on the day of monetary union, 1 July 1990: as the new liabilities which the *Treuhand* property was encumbered with could not be passed on to the buyers in *addition* to the profit-related value, the *Treuhandanstalt* was finally going to end up with a 'mountain of debts' which it would pass on to the Federal budget.

When the *Treuhandanstalt* was officially dissolved on 31 December 1994 by the Federal Government, not only did the deficit of DM270 billion, resulting from the disastrous policy of privatisation, have to be transferred to a so-called 'GDR Liabilities Repayment Fund', but also the liabilities under the Credit Transaction Fund, which had negotiated GDR liabilities in respect of payments to banks to balance the currency exchange involved in the monetary union and GDR foreign debts. All these 'debts' added up to at least DM400 billion. This was quite a considerable portion of the total Federal debt, which (naturally) would be blamed on the GDR for years to come.

The End of the *Treuhandanstalt*?

The Federal Government submitted a bill on the remaining tasks of the *Treuhandanstalt*, which was debated by the German *Bundestag* in a first reading on 4 March 1994. The Government was confident that the privatisation task of the *Treuhandanstalt* would be more or less completed by the end of 1994, and that its parliamentary mandate would then run out. The tasks remaining would have to be taken over by private institutions or other Federal agencies. There was reason to assume that this was to be a way of removing the target of criticism and reproach from the public eye, and of distracting attention from the destruction and wastage of East German public property for which the *Treuhandanstalt* was partly to blame.

Faulty Economic Cycles

After the '*Anschluß*' of the GDR, economic cycles with long-term effects developed between East and West Germany:

- Three-fifths of the monetary transfer to East Germany were used for paying social benefits (i.e. social security, pensions, students' allowances, etc.). However, as has been pointed out already, such figures distorted the true relationship of giving and taking. Saxony's Finance Minister pointed out that the 'unification-related expense' of the state budget estimated at DM91.9 billion was balanced by tax revenues to the Federal budget of DM42 billion in East Germany. 'Unification-related expense' totalled only DM79.1 billion, which, given the Federal German budget of DM430 billion, certainly did not overburden the Federal budget.[30]
- The demand for consumer and investment goods concentrated primarily on products from West Germany. Thus the money transfer actually flowed back again to the West, stimulating the economy there and leading to higher tax revenues than the Finance Minister ever expected. This trend was even increased by the fact that Eastern enterprises taken over by West German firms whose headquarters were in the West actually paid their taxes there. These profits and taxes from East Germany in turn fed the transfer of money back to East Germany.
- Not only industrial property but also a substantial amount of real estate was being transferred from East to West. The figures presented by Frau Breuel, President of the *Treuhandanstalt,* on the East German share in the acquisition of East German property in the course of privatisation obscured the realities – 80 per cent of the shops went to East Germans and among the 7,000 privatised enterprises 1,256 were management buy-outs. But no mention was made of the fact that

the major concerns, prestigious shops and housing property were not
among those passed into East German hands.
• The cycles between East and West and the flow of money and
capital, led to a considerable redistribution of wealth. That the West
Germans had to 'pay for unification' was as imprecise as the reproach-
ful statement often made by East Germans to the effect that West
Germans were 'expropriating' them. The real social developments
taking place were not accurately described either way. While the West
German taxpayer, especially in the low-income groups, really did
have to pay the lion's share of what was transferred to the East, the
big West German concerns made enormous profits from the '*Anschluß*'
of the GDR.

From the point of view of creating wealth, the East–West cycle was
characterised by private property-owners amassing a fortune while the
national debt escalated. For the private property-owners the East was
something of a gold-diggers' paradise, where they did not even need
good luck to get rich. East Germany experienced a hitherto unknown
materialisation of the phrase 'unto every one that hath shall be given',[31]
the giver in this instance being the Federal German state, and the gifts
valuable property to be had for a song. True to the nature of a market
economy based on private property, state investment and subsidies
were nothing but gifts of money by the state to the private owners.

The items of economic support granted to big business in the Eastern
part of Germany read like a catalogue of a gift shop for businessmen.
It comprised:

• investment subsidies of 12 per cent of the purchasing or producing
costs;
• special depreciation of 50 per cent of the purchasing or producing
costs;
• the creation of tax-free reserves when transferring certain industrial
commodities to a joint-stock company in East Germany alternating
with tax deductions for losses incurred by West German firms, if these
arose from shares in East German firms;
• investment funds from the joint programme to 'Improve the Regional
Economic Structure' under the European Regional Fund;
• providing loans for people setting up new firms.

This support for the up-and-coming investors was summed up in the
'Prosperity for the East' programme of the Federal Republic. To expect

that such subsidies would lead to genuine economic prosperity and reduce unemployment was as naive as the hope that those who had benefited from unification would, under market conditions, be made to finance the unification. This was clearly not the case – the Government was not concerned with promoting the economic development in the East so much as with serving vested interests in the East.

• The particular nature of the economic and social cycles between East and West Germany provoked a migration of people from East to West which may have lasting effects. Especially the young and qualified workers and a large number of the research and engineering personnel migrated from the East to the West. Here again, it was the cream that left. This exodus contributed to the dramatic drop in the East German birth rate:[32] the figure of births per 1,000 inhabitants sank from 13.6 per year in the GDR in 1987 to 6.6 in 1991; in West Germany the birth rate rose during the same period from 10.5 to 11.3. There is the genuine danger of a disproportionately large number of elderly people; of derelict areas forming, especially in the border areas to West Germany. This migration of people and property and of firms and property from East to West is likely to influence the development and conditions in Germany more than the transfer of money from West to East.

What Should Be Done?

Many suggestions have been put forward on how to kick-start the East German economy. Obviously priority should be attached to an active industrial and job-creation policy in the Federal States and regionally, to investment incentives and to preferential treatment of local firms. This would revitalise and strengthen the East German economy and help it to become more independent. The firms still in *Treuhand* hands would need a certain period of time to stabilise, along with decreasing temporary supporting measures. Experience shows that without an industrial core there can be no prosperity for medium-sized businesses and the services sector. It would require tremendous efforts to prevent East German property, not yet privatised, from being squandered. However, it is vital that it should not be privatised in the way hitherto practised. On 31 December 1993 this property comprised 951 firms employing 187,000 people. In addition there were some 4 million hectares of land (1.9 million hectares of farm land and 2.1 million hectares of forest) which represented a value of DM250-300 billion.

Needless to say, *Treuhand* contracts would require rigid monitoring to keep a check on the promised investments and job guarantees.

Conclusions

There was never any public political debate to establish which GDR socio-economic structures would be viable under market economy conditions and would, therefore, have contributed social and economic assets to a unified Germany.

The decisions to incorporate the GDR into the Federal Republic and to transform the planned to a market economy were inseparably linked with privatising major parts of the nationally owned economy in East Germany. There was no experience to fall back upon to gauge the effect of such an historically unparalleled transition from a planned economy, based on nationally owned property, to a market economy, based primarily on private property.

It is true of course that nothing could have remained as it was. But no serious consideration was given to the question of how to conduct this socio-economic upheaval in a manner that would preserve the economic assets and enable enterprises to survive in a market economy and to restructure individual elements of the social and economic structure of the GDR to match market conditions. So doing would also have undoubtedly provided an impetus for a 'modernisation' of the Federal Republic.

It would have been productive and well worth the trouble to have activated the political, scientific and cultural potential in the whole of Germany in a comprehensive discussion on how to conduct unification so that it would be of maximum benefit to the German people in East and West. There was in fact a general readiness for such an exchange of ideas; the political and intellectual energies released by the changes, especially in the Eastern part of Germany, might well have been utilised or even expanded in such a process. Academic institutions dealing with economic and social problems supplied a wealth of analyses and ideas on how best to adjust and restructure the two Germanies. These included substantial contributions made by East German social and economic researchers.

The Federal Government did not avail itself of these opportunities:

- The Government ignored the discussion that had been carried on in West Germany for many years about whether to regulate or de-regulate the economy, on more state intervention or more market forces. In East Germany it put into practice a radical market policy, following the 'pure' doctrine of a free market economy.
- The Government completely ignored Germany's historical experience of state support for regional economic development, of state protection for the domestic economy against foreign competition, which, especially in the 1950s, was still applied in certain areas. Without protection, and overnight, the East German economy was exposed to the rigours of world market competition.
- The Government ignored all advice, analyses and reports from experts which did not correspond with its political course. In so doing, it destroyed almost totally the socio-scientific potential of East Germany when it closed down the established institutions and dismissed their staff.

There was not the slightest attempt of an exchange of political opinions, or public discussion on the social and economic restructuring of East Germany. Those who tried were thwarted, which has since proved to be a serious political drawback in the process of unification. It has damaged the united Federal Republic of Germany seriously for a long time to come.

The basic decision in favour of a market economy and of privatising the bulk of the nationally owned industry and agriculture need not necessarily have been carried out so rigorously. A plurality of ownership forms, including public (federal, state and local property) and cooperative property, would have made the transition of the East German economy to a market economy much easier and would have prevented much of the economic loss.

A market economy can operate quite successfully, given a variety of ownership forms. It is an unwarranted prejudice to assume that nationally owned property is always inferior to privately owned property and always managed less efficiently. The differences between nationally owned property and modern forms of private property are less than is generally assumed. Private property is rarely owned by one entrepreneur, but is normally corporate property. On the other hand, state property can adopt the legal form of joint-stock company. Thus the differences in style of management and democratic participation in management are not significant. A variety of ownership forms, whether private, the property of the German Federation or the Federal States, of local communities or cooperatively owned, would have promoted rather than hampered the competition acclaimed as the main principle of a market economy. Had such a mixed economy been established, this would have cost less than the rigid privatisation approach adopted by the *Treuhandanstalt* .

Nationally owned and cooperatively owned property has the advantage that it is more open to democratic control and participation; in addition, it has economic and social advantages relating particularly to jobs. Private investors will only invest if they are sure of getting a return in line with the current interest rates plus a risk charge. If this cannot be expected, they will turn to financial investments, which is one of the reasons for the increasing transfer of capital from industry to financial assets (e.g. national bonds). Nationally owned and cooperative enterprises, on the other hand, can operate at a minimum yield rate. They provide tax revenue for the state and save unemployment benefits. Especially in East Germany the retention of some property would have curbed the escalation of unemployment. But no such path was adopted – it would have been anathema to the victorious neo-liberals. Thus expedients which would have tempered the wind to the shorn lamb were not resorted to.

Notes

1. With monetary union on 1 July 1990, the GDR Mark was replaced by the Deutschmark of the Federal Republic at a ratio of 1:1 for wages as well as savings of the population up to a sum of 4,000 Marks per person. Assets of companies and institutions as well as loans and savings of more than 4,000 Marks were exchanged at a ratio of 2:1.
2. 'There are three decisive causes of the East German transition crisis:

   • the little productive and declining GDR economy, with its portion of outdated and run-down capital assets, was uncompetitive;
   • monetary union of 1 July 1990 with the shock-like upgrading effect of more than 300 per cent;
   • an economic policy which for a long time misjudged the effects of monetary union and underestimated the problems of transition.'

Jan Priebe and Rudolf Hickel, *Der Preis der Einheit* [The price of unification] (1991: Fischer Taschenbuchverlag, Frankfurt/M), p. 13.

3. *IFO-Schnelldienst*, Berlin, No. 28, 1990.

4. Peter Fleissner and Udo Ludwig, *Ostdeutsche Wirtschaft im Umbruch: Computersimulation mit einem systemdynamischen Modell* [East German economy under transformation: Computer simulation with a system-dynamic model] (1992: Vieweg Verlag, Brunswick, Wiesbaden), p. 98.

5. Alfred Graf Matuschka in *Berliner Zeitung*, 8 March 1990.

6. Ingrid Matthäus-Maier, 'Für eine Wirtschaftsunion schon in diesem Jahr' [For a monetary union already this year], *Wirtschaftsdienst*, February 1990, p. 63.

7. Lutz Hoffmann, 'Wider die ökonomische Vernunft' [Against all economic reason], *Frankfurter Allgemeine*, 10 February 1990.

8. Herbert Schui, *Die ökonomische Vereinigung Deutschlands* [The economic unification of Germany] (1991: Distel Verlag, Heidelberg).

9. See pp. 82–83 above.

10. 'Das westdeutsche Wirtschaftswunder läßt sich im Osten nicht wiederholen' [The economic miracle of West Germany cannot be repeated in the East], *Handelsblatt*, 2 June 1992.

11. Lutz Hoffmann, *Warten auf den Aufschwung* [Waiting for prosperity] (1993: tv Verlag, Regensburg), p. 25.

12. Ibid., p. 47.

13. Hans Modrow, 'Die Treuhand: Idee und Wirklichkeit' [The *Treuhand*: Idea and reality], in Horst van der Meer and Lothar Kruss (eds), *Vom Industriestaat zum Entwicklungsland?* (1991: Dieter Joester Vertriebsgemeinschaft GmbH, Frankfurt/M), p. 197.

14. *Der Einigungsvertrag* [Unification Treaty] (1990: Wiesbaden), p. 22.

15. Lothar de Maizière, interview in *Berliner Zeitung*, 2 October 1991.

16. Ibid.

17. Hoffmann, 'Wider die ökonomische Vernunft', p. 15.

18. Sinn, 'Verteilen', p. 78.

19. Ulrich Drobing, 'Privatisierung von Staatsunternehmen in Deutschland' [Privatisation of nationally owned enterprises in Germany], *Wirtschaftsrecht*, December 1992, p. 493.

20. Hans–Werner Sinn in *Wirtschaftswoche*, No. 1/2, 7 January 1994.

21. Günter Ogger, *Nieten in Nadelstreifen* [Twits in pinstripes] (1992: Droemer Knaur Verlag, Munich), pp. 136–8.

22. *Berliner Zeitung*, 23 September 1993.

23. *Die Zeit*, 2 July 1993.

24. Peter Kachel in *Wirtschaftsbulletin Ostdeutschland* (Hans-Böckler-Stiftung, No. 4, 1992, Berlin), p. 29.
25. See Chapter 4 below.
26. In 1945/6 a land reform was carried out in the former Soviet occupation zone of Germany which expropriated land-owners with more than 100 hectares (some 2.2 million hectares, a third of the farm land). This land was handed to 559,000 agricultural labourers, refugees from Polish occupied territories and landless labourers. It remained the private property of the farmers when they joined agricultural cooperative farms. Cooperative farming profits were distributed according to the member's land property. The Unification Treaty's stipulation that expropriations from 1945 to 1949 cannot be reversed was upheld by a ruling of the Federal Constitutional Court dated 23 April 1991.
27. See Chapter 1 above, pp. 15–18.
28. See Chapter 4 below.
29. Ibid.
30. *Neues Deutschland*, 11/12 June 1992.
31. Matthew 25:29.
32. See also Chapter 5 below.

4 Changing the East German Countryside

Christel Panzig

While mass demonstrations in Berlin, Leipzig, Dresden and other East German cities, chanting 'We are the people', swept away the obstinate and politically blind dictatorial SED government in October/November 1989, all was quiet in the countryside. The rural communities certainly did not speed up the course of history with comparable emotional spontaneity.

The new slogans at the demonstrations after the fall of the Wall on 9 November 1989 of 'We are one people' did not inspire the villagers to take to the streets either. This may suggest that farmers in the GDR, who were cultivating several million acres of land they had been allotted by the land 1945 reform,[1] had a keener interest in retaining the GDR than people in urban communities. But when, in March 1990, just a few weeks away from the GDR parliamentary elections, the villages were decorated with Federal German flags and CDU election posters, especially in the southern regions of the GDR, this appeared to belie this assumption.

The headlines said afterwards that the elections had been decided in the countryside. The Christian Democratic Union had won with the unexpectedly high polling results of 40.59 per cent, in a coalition with the German Social Union[2] (DSU), who polled 6.2 per cent, and Democratic Awakening[3] (*Demokratischer Aufbruch*; DA), with 0.93 per cent. However, a more detailed analysis of the election polls showed that for the northern regions of the GDR, where most of the land reform property was to be found, things were different. There a surprisingly large number of up to 20 per cent (national average 2.17 per cent) voted for the Democratic Farmers' Party (DBD), who were against a quick '*Anschluß*' to West Germany and had always supported the agricultural policies of the SED, the GDR ruling party. It was very much to the disappointment of many members that the DBD leadership decided, after the 1990 elections, to merge with the Christian Democrats.

In Mecklenburg-West Pomerania, the Conservative Alliance for Germany, in coalition with the Liberals, only won about 40 per cent

119

of the polls. Against that, it won the absolute majority in the six southern districts of the GDR, and in the district of Karl-Marx-Stadt (now again Chemnitz) even two-thirds of all votes. In the villages of Saxony and Thuringia, voters contributed considerably to the election victory of the East German Christian Democrats on 18 March 1990, who were in favour of a quick '*Anschluß*' of the GDR to the Federal Republic and had fought their election campaign under the slogan 'Freedom and prosperity instead of socialism' (*Freiheit und Wohlstand statt Sozialismus*).[4]

Did the agricultural policy of the CDU/CSU live up to the expectations of their voters among the East German farmers?

What did they and the other members of the rural communities gain from the merger of the two German states?

What is the situation today in the countryside of East Germany?

The Situation Before the Fall of the GDR

In order to assess the changes, it is necessary to look back to the year 1989: at that time, nearly 930,000 people (10.8 per cent of the total workforce, or every ninth gainfully employed person) worked in GDR agriculture and forestry.[5]

The careers and biographies of former cooperative farmers and agricultural workers on state farms in East Germany differed greatly from those of West German farmers, who still lived on family farms of an average 30 hectares of agricultural land and a corresponding number of livestock. Out of the 630,000 agricultural enterprises which existed in West Germany at that time, some 80 per cent had no more than 29 hectares to farm.[6]

Contrary to the situation in West Germany, in the East German countryside 1,162 crop-farming cooperatives and 78 state farms had an average of 3,000 hectares of agricultural land at their disposal. The crop-farming cooperatives and state farms formed so-called 'associations', supervised by association boards, of sometimes 40 km in extent, with the remaining 2,682 cooperatives and 312 state farms specialising in livestock-breeding.[7]

Despite the fact that quite a number of cooperative farmers earned extra money by breeding and selling livestock privately, farming life in the East German countryside was characterised by large agricultural enterprises with an average of 400 to 500 employees and several thousand hectares of farm land or correspondingly large numbers of livestock.

Whilst the rural areas in West Germany had developed various trades, small businesses and medium-sized industrial firms, the East German countryside was, by contrast, almost completely dominated by the agricultural enterprises. Their economic structure bore little comparison with that of the West German farms. In the GDR, various producers and services connected with agricultural primary production were integrated into the cooperative agricultural structures. Large technology sections even developed and produced the means to automate production, thus supplementing the increasingly poor performance of industry.

In the villages of the GDR, agricultural enterprises also fulfilled many functions going beyond their actual production activity, which in West Germany are the responsibility of the local authorities. The agricultural cooperatives and state farms:

- were the social and cultural centre of the villages;
- trained young people, among them many women, at their own training schools;
- offered apprentices from outside the locality inexpensive accommodation, board and meals in their own apprentice hostels;
- offered most of the vacancies for graduates from agricultural university and college courses;
- conducted further training courses, giving women with children preferential treatment;
- financed and looked after social institutions such as crèches and kindergartens and communal kitchens, which took the burden of cooking from the women and also supplied meals to old age pensioners, schoolchildren and children at pre-school institutions;
- owned and ran children's holiday camps, holiday homes, and other holiday schemes for their employees;
- often organised leisure-time activities and provided facilities such as youth clubs, riding and other sports clubs, folklore and music groups, ceramics and textile art groups, etc.;
- built and maintained cultural centres, pubs and restaurants, shops, medical and physio-therapeutical institutions, roads, sewerage systems, and also flats for their employees, which attracted labour from the towns and cities;
- financed and implemented many local projects, which the local communities would not have been able to see through because of the GDR policy of stripping the local authorities of practically all their funds.

These conditions contributed to most employees often staying for several decades in 'their' agricultural enterprise, not uncommonly beyond retiring age. The closeness to the place of work and the rising income, especially in prosperous cooperative and state farms, as well as the social amenities, persuaded many a villager who had drifted into industry or other gainful employment to return to the countryside.

In the course of generations, and with the many changes and frequent restructuring which took place in East German agriculture from the foundation of the cooperatives in 1952 to 1989, membership of cooperative farms also changed. More than two-thirds of the cooperators had contributed neither land nor inventory to the cooperative farms and only became members after the last wave of collectivisation was over.

In the course of time the level of qualification, too, changed considerably among those permanently employed in agriculture and forestry. In 1961 less than 17 per cent had any kind of qualification (0.36 per cent university graduates, 1.54 per cent college graduates, 2.18 per cent with a craftsperson's certificate, 12.75 per cent with a skilled worker's certificate),[8] whereas by 1989 nearly the entire workforce had obtained some kind of qualification.[9]

The fact that women working in GDR agriculture were better qualified than their opposite numbers in industry is striking and unusual, even in Europe. Of the 350,000 women farmers and other women working in GDR agriculture and forestry, nearly 92 per cent had some qualification (30,000 held university or college degrees) by the end of 1989. In contrast, only 84 per cent of the women working in industry had a qualification of some nature.[10]

As for their production yields, GDR farmers were among the foremost of the COMECON countries and also ranked highly on a European scale. However, even though some cooperative and state farms achieved very high yields of various crops, the average yield per hectare was lower than in West Germany or Great Britain. One reason was the high degree of self-sufficiency and the drive for a surplus of agricultural produce for export, especially to West Germany and other hard-currency countries. In the GDR, therefore, land of low soil value also had to be cultivated. GDR industry was, moreover, less and less able to meet the demand for mineral fertilisers, agricultural machines and equipment or sufficient spare parts of good quality. In spite of serious efforts, the GDR never reached the output of mineral nitrogenous, phosphate and potash fertilisers per hectare of the Federal Republic or other EC countries such as Denmark and the Netherlands.

These were reasons why the optimal times in the year to put mineral nitrogenous fertilisers into the soil were often missed. Thus losses in yield were unavoidable. The GDR exported tractors to the Soviet Union and to developing countries in exchange for the urgently needed petrol and other raw material while there were not enough tractors available for agriculture in the GDR.

In the mid-1980s the life-span of agricultural machines was raised from 10 to 15 years, which meant that they could not be written off completely and replaced by new ones before they were 15 years old.

An increasing stock management of spare parts and a bloated repair sector developed in order to prevent machines from breaking down at tilling or harvesting time. This even led to such economic insanity as the dismantling of a brand new combine harvester to repair three broken-down ones.

The lack of machines and materials also meant that maintenance of the buildings belonging to agricultural enterprises was seriously neglected – cow-sheds, pig-sties and other stables – and industrial facilities for the livestock as well as production and storage buildings fell into disrepair. The steadily decreasing performance of industry, which became increasingly evident, forced farmers to use extra labour and input without actually achieving higher profits.

The growing discontent among the farmers at the inadequate supply of materials and technology, and the deterioration of their working conditions as a result of this unsuccessful economic policy, increased as a result of their frustration at the political indoctrination attempted by the stagnating SED regime, which had proved as incapable of reform as it was of democracy. That these shortcomings could not go on for very much longer was the considered opinion shared by the rural population as much as by most other GDR citizens. But the conceptions of what changes were needed differed greatly.

After 'Enforced Collectivisation' Now 'Enforced Privatisation'?

While in the 1990 parliamentary elections a little less than half of the GDR population voted for the Social Democrats (SPD), the Party of Democratic Socialism (PDS) and other political groupings which were against a quick unification of East and West Germany, the others, the majority, including many farmers, voted for a quick merger.

Many farmers opted for 'Freedom and prosperity instead of socialism' and were to become the first in the East to understand the meaning of the word 'freedom' under free market conditions.

Even before the merger of the GDR and the Federal Republic (3 October 1990) dairy and other agricultural products from West Germany were flooding the East German market as a consequence of the economic and monetary union of 1 July 1990. On the other hand, Ignatz Kiechle, then Federal German Minister of Agriculture, never dreamed of lifting the restrictions on East German products imported into West Germany.

At the same time, nearly all large state-owned GDR shopping centres were bought up by a few large West German chains, and stopped selling East German products overnight, as these were, naturally, not on their lists of commodities. Dairies, slaughter-houses, bakery firms and other food-processing enterprises in the GDR, which in most instances had considerable modernisation deficits anyway, were left stranded with their products and were no longer able to buy up the milk, meat and grain produced by the agricultural cooperatives. But what were the cooperatives and state farms to do with their livestock of up to 20,000 fattened pigs or several thousand beef cows?

Every additional day created new costs for feeding the livestock and paying wages and thus increased losses. The de Maizière government did precious little to help sort out this chaos. The West German and Dutch livestock dealers, however, were quite ready to step in. Making unscrupulous use of the dilemma of the farmers, they bought up whole herds of cattle at DM120 a head. In this way the East German agricultural enterprises suffered losses of millions of Deutschmarks. Professor Klaus Böhme, editor-in-chief of *Neue Landwirtschaft* (New Agriculture) wrote:

> Those who had not fallen into debt before ran into difficulties now. Our calculations show that in July 1990 alone East German agriculture lost an additional DM1.7 billion in addition to losses expected for that month. In the course of 1990 losses amounted to more than DM3 billion due to this additional set-back.'[11]

The mighty farmers' demonstration of 15 August 1990, organised by the GDR Association of Farmers and Cooperatives, forced the GDR Government, by now economically directly dependent on Bonn, to pay adjustment compensation and introduce surcharges on imports to East Germany. These measures were needed to help cooperative farmers to restructure their enterprises from a planned economy isolated from the Western world, to a free market economy. The Law on the Structural Adjustment of Agriculture in the German Democratic Republic to the Social and Economic Market Economy (LAG), dated 20 July 1990,[12] was passed, but none of these steps prevented the collapse of many enterprises, at best they just delayed it.

The unprotected exposure of East German agriculture to the conditions of the EC agricultural market, especially the sudden cuts by half in the prices for cereals and cattle feed and by two-thirds for animal products, led to a sharp decline in animal stocks between the end of 1989 and the end of 1992: of cattle by 43 per cent, pigs by 61 per cent and sheep by 69 per cent. In the financial year of 1990/1, some 13 per cent of the arable land was left fallow.

The positive change hoped for by the East German farmers after the '*Anschluß*' of the GDR to the Federal Republic on 3 October 1990 never materialised. The promises made in the CDU election programme, its slogan of 'Together we'll manage it!', pledging 'effective help for the farmers of the new Federal States[13] allowing family farms and cooperatives to hold their own on the market',[14] proved empty.

The East German farmers' expectations of being rid of the political and state interference in their enterprises which they had suffered from in the SED state were soon dashed, as were their hopes to be able, under the improved economic conditions, to buy and use modern agricultural machinery and other means of production now available in adequate quantity and quality.

The new bureaucracy soon taught them the facts. The agricultural policy of the German Government made them realise very quickly that an agricultural policy can be enforced by a refined system of subsidies and tax regulations even more effectively than by political directives.

The farmers in East Germany were confronted with the plans of the Federal German Minister of Agriculture, Ignatz Kiechle, to restore 'family-style agriculture' in the East and repeal 'enforced collectivisation'. Although the structural development of West German agriculture had shown quite clearly during the preceding years that the traditional family farm, kept alive only with the help of a lot of taxpayers' money, stood no real chance in the future, this did not stop the drive towards revitalising it in East Germany.

Martin Irion, long-standing RIAS[15] editor on agricultural affairs, commented that in the field of agriculture 'socialism had achieved something to be proud of'. The problems faced by the agricultural enterprises in East Germany after the '*Anschluß*' to West Germany were not the result of an inability to compete with the output of the family farms but were due to other reasons:

> There is no difference of opinion with regard to the economic potential of Eastern agriculture, there are only those interested in crippling a potent competitor.[16]

To eliminate these unwanted competitors, who also cultivated the much coveted land reform estates, the former large socialist enterprises had to be broken up. It was therefore the aim of Bonn's agricultural policy-makers to eliminate the cooperatives, products of SED 'enforced collectivisation', as quickly as possible and replace them by family farms![17]

The amendment to the Agricultural Adjustment Law of 3 July 1991[18] was the first step in this direction. The original version, embodied in the Unification Treaty, provided for a transformation of the coopera-tives into cooperative enterprises in accordance with West German legal provisions, the settling of property rights by the members of the coop-eratives themselves and the continued use of cooperative property for relevant purposes. In defiance of these basic principles, the modified version was now geared towards redistributing the property and dissolving the cooperatives. Unless they were restructured in line with the com-plicated Federal German cooperative laws by 31 December 1991, their liquidation would, according to the amended law, be enforced.

Thus the cooperatives were faced with the overwhelming task of re-evaluating their basic assets with the help of lawyers, at great expense, and of settling the very complicated property issues in just a few months. They had to find everyone to whom every single share of the land farmed collectively for decades had belonged. In many instances these shares consisted of land of less than 10 hectares. Owners might have long retired, or died, or moved from the region. Leasing contracts had to be agreed either with the owners or with their heirs. Former cooperators who either could not or did not wish to continue to work for the cooper-ative had to be paid what was due to them according to what they had earned and how long they had been members, either in money or in machinery and livestock, and were also entitled to the land and inventory they had once given to the cooperative.

The cooperatives had to work out plausible schemes acceptable to the banks of how they were going to restructure the enterprises, as this was the prerequisite for applying for the desperately needed interim loans.[19]

Cutting the large farms down to manageable sizes, ranging from several hundred to over 1,000 hectares, ending the separation of plant and animal production, reducing surplus staff, bringing agricultural machinery up to modern standards and improving marketing would have ensured prosperity, given time. The costs of restructuring GDR agriculture according to West German requirements would have been much less than in industry.

Many dubious advisers from West Germany used the predicament of the cooperatives to drive them into total economic ruin or to make them dissolve themselves, by which these advisers, acting as receivers in bankruptcy proceedings, gained additional profits. Some cooperators decided to dissolve the cooperatives because they thought they could make big money by leasing or selling their individual plots of 8 or 10 hectares of land to potential clients in West Germany.

Notwithstanding this development, the expectations of the agricultural policy-makers in Bonn were disappointed. The bulk of the farmers wanted to continue working collectively.

Why didn't the farmers in East rush to throw off the 'yoke of 40 years of enforced collectivisation'? One reason was that two-thirds of all cooperative farmers only joined after 1960 and had not experienced any coercion, and most of those who had been coerced into the cooperatives, or their successors, still held on to collective production methods after 1990, showing little enthusiasm for Kiechle's concept of family farms, which would entail having to become so-called 'moonlight farmers' working from morning to night.

Their approach was incomprehensible to those in authority at the Federal Ministry of Food, Agriculture and Forestry. Their ideas were based on agricultural experience in West Germany. They transferred these to East Germany, as other politicians in Bonn did, without any consideration for the feelings, lives and ideas of the people actually living there. The 'obstinacy' of the East German farmers who stuck to collective large-scale production was, in their eyes, evidence that the latter had degenerated into mere agricultural labourers, even though they were running agricultural enterprises of 10,000 hectares in size and larger. They had clearly lost the virtues of a farmer, it was argued, and weren't able to run a family farm of the usual West German size of 29 hectares.

Why did only very few farmers want to go back to being independent farmers on their own free land? Representative polls conducted in 1990–91 revealed why the majority were unwilling to revive this concept. There was often neither enough land nor the other material conditions, for instance cow-sheds, pig-sties, barns, machinery or money. The bulk of such savings as they had from socialist days had been halved at monetary union. The DM23,500 in subsidies[20] from the

Federal Ministry of Food, Agriculture and Forestry allotted to every farmer up to the age of 55 who was willing to establish a family farm was a pittance, inadequate to cover investment needs.

More importantly, most of those who decided against a family farm did not want to throw overboard the material and technical advantages of large-scale production, especially as the trend in France, the Netherlands and Britain and even in West Germany itself had been moving towards concentration and specialisation for several years, with more small farms having to give up every day. The farmers knew about this development and saw the family farm concept as a ruse on the part of the big West German agricultural estates to eliminate competition in the East.

A number of men might have taken their chance of a 'family farm' had they been younger. Most women, however, rejected it, especially those of the war or immediate post-war generation. They still remembered vividly their lives on their own farms, the backbreaking work, the scrimping and saving with no chance of a holiday. Apart from restrictions imposed by the authorities, the satisfaction of cultivating one's own land was always lessened by the risks involved in open-air production.

Women, who had more often than the men been coerced into joining the cooperatives, had helped to turn these enterprises into stable production units, sometimes under the most adverse conditions. If there was need, they even learned to drive tractors, combine harvesters, fork-lift trucks, etc. They had also undergone further training for a qualification in addition to rearing children and working in the fields. By 1989 most women in rural areas had qualified for a full (77.3 per cent) or at least a semi-skilled (2.3 per cent) worker's certificate; 3.1 per cent had a craftsperson's certificate and 9.3 per cent a college or university degree.

Looking back, women said that the radically improved working conditions in the GDR had changed their lives. They had had the chance to gain a certain degree of independence from the rural family, to earn 'their own money' and become eligible for a pension of their own. This, too, undoubtedly led to a strong identification of the women with their cooperative farm.

A survey conducted at various cooperatives in different regions proves this.[21] Asked for their reasons for opting against a family farm, the men's first argument was the trend towards large agricultural enterprises in the EC. This reason was only named third by the women who were interviewed. Their first choice was the social network offered by the cooperatives, followed by the advantages they experienced in working together.

Younger women, who only knew the family farm from the tales of the older generation, shied away from the amount of time and effort to be invested out of all proportion to the benefit gained. GDR agriculture had allowed them time for hobbies and to develop their leisure time needs in similar ways to urban women – to spend time with their families and go for holidays together with their husbands and children. They were therefore in favour of the large-scale agricultural enterprises which they were familiar with through their work on cooperative or state farms. They had grown used to fairly regular working hours. They also considered production risks a further handicap of individual farming, namely, the risk of poor harvests, price cuts for agricultural commodities, not being listed by chains, EC restrictions, etc., and therefore not being able to repay loans, mortgages and interest.

Also, working in a group, in 'their' teams, 'their' cooperative played an important part in the lives of nearly all these women. Similar to unemployed East German women in other trades, most of them felt it a loss not to be integrated in a work process any more and having to forgo the regular social communication. Through their work many of them had acquired self-confidence and recognition in the village community.

They were independent and well able to look after themselves. They saw their jobs as the basis of this economic independence and considered the communication with colleagues on topics such as the family, the village, the job and politics to be an important constituent of their everyday lives. These losses were a great problem for many women and men who had become unemployed, especially in the countryside.

For those who were coerced into some form of early retirement, the termination of their employment was not only an economic loss but above all posed a psychological and social problem to them. Without exception, women and men found unemployment to be painful and a genuine deterioration of the quality of their lives. Even women who attended a seminar on family farms in October 1990 regretted having had to give up the cooperative. Asked why they and their men had chosen to establish a family farm, they answered 'What else is there left for us to do? Our cooperative doesn't exist anymore. There is no hope of getting another job, unemployment is too high. We have no choice!' While this may not have been typical of all the women who had opted for the family farm, it still challenged the statements by West German politicians about the 'free choice farmers have to opt for the family farms' in East Germany.

The free decision taken in favour of the cooperative and other forms of collective farming met with little enthusiasm on the part of the Federal Government in Bonn; the official subsidy and support policy, which put any form of collective enterprise at a disadvantage, made this quite evident.

The Empty Promise of Prosperity in the East[22]

The economic transformation of East Germany also brought about deep structural and social changes for the regions where agricultural areas dominated. They had grave consequences for the people working in this sector of the economy. Long-standing agricultural structures, though at one time established under pressure, had meanwhile developed new social relations within the villages. They were destroyed again under pressure 'from above'.

Full of bitterness, many of the former cooperative farmers had to suffer an 'enforced privatisation' following the previous 'enforced collectivisation'. Sticking rigidly to their agricultural policy, the Christian Democratic Party leadership would not listen to appeals from their own ranks in East Germany 'to also respect the will of the overwhelming majority of farmers to continue working collectively and not only the drive towards setting up family farms'.[23]

Without the transition periods usual in the European Community, the cooperative farms were forced into a crash adjustment to Federal German agricultural legislation and structures. The fears expressed by the CDU in the Brandenburg parliament in April 1991 applied to many rural regions:

At the moment massive bankruptcy and liquidation threaten agricultural enterprises ... Due to the chaotic dissolution of the cooperatives, farming property will be destroyed and squandered, jobs eliminated and production given up. The agricultural market will vanish.[24]

In transforming agricultural enterprises into commercial ventures according to West German law, the Agricultural Adjustment Law and the one-sided agricultural policy of the Federal Government, discouraging all forms of collective farming, drove 1,200 agricultural and gardening cooperatives into bankruptcy or disintegration by the autumn of 1992, and thus led to a massive axing of jobs and training facilities as well as to the abandoning of 623,555 hectares of agricultural land by 1993.[25]

The majority of GDR cooperative farms, however, succeeded in transforming their enterprises into West German-style joint-stock companies etc. More than 20,000 private farms and nearly 2,000 general partnerships of various forms were established by May 1993. Although favoured by the authorities, these latter forms of agricultural enterprise cultivate no more than a third of the much reduced arable land, whereas collective farms operate the remaining two-thirds (1,388 cooperatives farm 38.8 per cent and the 1,302 limited and 64 joint-stock companies and other commercial enterprises 25.1 per cent).[26] This development, unwanted by politicians and in defiance of their agricultural objectives, had to be acknowledged even by the Federal Ministry for Food, Agriculture and Forestry, which declared East Germany was building up 'an efficient, market-oriented and environmentally sound agriculture'.[27]

Even though these new cooperatives achieved some security economically, their existence was jeopardised by political handicaps. The former socialist cooperatives often farmed nationally owned land taken over by *Treuhand* on behalf of the Federal Government. The new enterprises had to negotiate leases with the Federal agency responsible for selling off GDR national property. The cooperatives needed long-term leases for their vital bank loans, but efforts to obtain such leases were resisted. The guidelines governing the allocation of such land, elaborated jointly by the *Treuhandanstalt*, the Ministries of Agriculture and Finance and the West German Farmers' Association, provided that newly established family farms and 'victims of the land reform'[28] were to be given priority, while the successors to the GDR cooperative farms were treated unfairly.

Under a programme allocating former GDR nationally owned land to new settlers, due to start in 1995–96, cooperatives were discriminated against.[29] That is to say, the people who worked the soil for decades were only to be given a very restricted option to buy it.

The aim of this policy was crystal-clear. The Federal German Government wanted to favour the big land-owners. Expropriated in 1945, they or their heirs were given compensation in West Germany in the 1950s. The Federal German state took over the land reform estates as legal successor to the GDR. They planned to transfer this land to its former owners again, in contravention of the stipulations in the Unification Treaty and the pronouncement of the Federal Constitutional Law Court. As this jeopardised the very existence of many East German farmers and was consequently resisted bitterly by their representatives and provoked conflicts in the rural area of East Germany, a compromise was found[30] which gave cooperatives the option to buy land, but, however, only an eighth of the area they cultivate.

Evidently those in power considered neither the social dimension nor the importance of the cooperative farms and their successor institutions for regional economic development, or the consequences arising from their discrimination for the rural areas and the people living there.

The Labour Market in the Countryside

The German Government's agricultural policy produced a situation in which the problems not of work but rather of unemployment determined the everyday lives of the rural population in East Germany.

In its Unemployment Report of December 1993, the Federal Labour Office stated that there had been a drastic cut in agricultural jobs in the East. From November 1989 to November 1992 more than two-thirds (70 per cent) of those employed in agriculture lost their jobs.[31] That is to say, within three years, 629,000 of the former 915,000 people employed in GDR agriculture and forestry lost their jobs. Of these 200,000 were pensioned off or sent into early retirement, i.e. were ousted from work at the age of 55 with an early retirement pension of 63 per cent of their previous wages (GDR wages were an average of 1,242 Marks in 1989 as compared with the much higher ones in the West).

Whereas 240,000 mostly younger and well-trained people abandoned their agricultural and forestry jobs for other fields, 135,000 were faced with unemployment. Most of them were women but older male workers were also affected. Of these, 105,000 found places in job-creation schemes, limited to one year, or retraining programmes which they hoped would provide the basis for a new beginning – hopes which were later generally dashed.

By June 1993 only some 170,000 people were still gainfully employed in East German agriculture, of which 10,000 were on short time.[32] At the end of 1992, their net monthly incomes, averaging DM1,390, were about DM350 lower than the average net income even in East Germany.[33] By the end of 1993, people employed in agriculture and forestry, with an average gross income of DM2,355 then, were still last on the table of East German incomes, and earned little more than half (51.48 per cent) of the average monthly income in West Germany.[34]

The process of 'redundancy', which had taken place in West Germany over a period of four decades, was effected so ruthlessly in the East that the average number of workers per 100 hectares of farm land sank to 3.4, i.e. considerably below the West German agricultural level of 5.7 workers per 100 hectares.[35]

The structural changes in East German agriculture brought about devastating consequences for the economic sectors related to agriculture and for the rural communities.

In the Federal State of Mecklenburg-West Pomerania, where before 1989 every sixth person was gainfully employed in agriculture and forestry, but also in many parts of Brandenburg as well as in the rural regions of Saxony-Anhalt, Thuringia and Saxony, mass unemployment and lack of prospects became the order of the day. There were many villages where practically nobody had a job.

East German Farmers' Response to the Situation

The future of many former cooperative farmers was thus very uncertain. One year after unification, at the end of 1991, some 48 per cent of the people in Mecklenburg-West Pomerania assessed their general economic situation as poor (40 per cent) or disastrous (8 per cent); in Thuringia the figure stood at 43 per cent, in Brandenburg at 39 per cent and in Saxony-Anhalt and Saxony at 38 per cent.[36]

Meanwhile not only the general economic situation but also the response to it by large sections of the East German population deteriorated drastically. Women especially felt at a great disadvantage, marginalised after three years of experience with the free market economy and their new 'fatherland'. Brandenburg's Minister for Employment and Social Affairs, Regine Hildebrandt, confirmed on 8 March 1993[37] that some 80 per cent of the women in the Federal State of Brandenburg felt that they were now worse off than before the fall of the GDR.

In 1988 agriculturist earnings only averaged 1,242 Marks (with 60 per cent of the women earning less than 900).[38] These rates, however, did not include the GDR state subsidies or the bonuses at Christmas and on other occasions (worth 50 to 200 Marks a month) and they did not include the supplements for shift- and night-work or overtime. Pensions, unemployment benefits and early retirement money were worked out on the basis of the former net wage. In 1993 the average pension in the Federal State of Brandenburg was therefore only DM761 for women and DM1,000 for men, with pensioners in agriculture who retired before 1989 still worse off.[39]

Even the 90 per cent increase which brought women's pensions up to DM826 within two years,[40] a step the Federal Government prided itself on, cannot obscure the fact that the living standard of East German newly unemployed workers and those in early retirement as well as pensioners had deteriorated and would remain well below that of the West Germans.

Rents went up by 500 to 800 per cent, electricity by 200 per cent, public transport by up to 1,800 per cent; the cost of living in many areas was already above West German levels while many former benefits for pensioners in the East were lost (e.g. there had formerly been no extra charges for medicine, no fees for television and radio licences, 60 per cent reduction in public transport fares, free or extremely cheap cultural and other leisure pursuits).

Older and single women and men still in gainful employment and mothers with young children living on their own in rural areas had practically no chance on the labour market and were, therefore, doomed to a life on social security. Unemployed single parents' livelihoods were jeopardised if they were given possession of their marital homes after a divorce and had to pay interest on their mortgages which rose from 1 per cent in GDR times to 13 per cent after unification.

Private husbandry, which had provided an additional income in GDR days, was not profitable any more in view of the low prices paid for agricultural products. Even to grow one's own vegetables and to consume home-reared livestock was becoming more and more expensive due to the excessive costs for seed, fodder, water and electricity. Some families who owned farmland, including many early retired and old age pensioners, opted for the cultivation of fruit and vegetables as a sideline, as this provided them with reductions in certain taxes. A large number of those who still worked in East German agriculture did it for the extra income. Only very few people could survive in full time jobs in East German agriculture.

The cuts in child-care facilities and the rapidly rising cost of accommodation in old people's homes forced women to take over these obligations themselves, because they could not afford to avail themselves of the relevant social services. If the exodus of young people from the East German villages, especially in the Federal State of Mecklenburg-West Pomerania, continued, these places would be reduced more and more to homesteads for the elderly without support.

With the slashing of state subsidies, the chances for people who lived in rural areas to requalify and retrain as the unemployed and school-leavers could do in the urban areas were minimal. They were often hampered by a poor infrastructure, restrictions in public transport and increasing prices for other services. The same problems assailed them in respect of leisure time activities. Apart from numerous videotape libraries, cultural, sports and folklore activities were drastically curtailed or abolished altogether after the fall of the GDR, because the dissolution of agricultural cooperatives immediately put an end to the cultural and social institutions they had run. This not only did away with even more jobs for women, but robbed the people of their cultural centres, galleries, crafts groups, youth and senior citizen clubs, etc., for which there was little replacement, thus further impoverishing the quality of life. There was not much hope that the destitute local councils would re-establish such institutions in the foreseeable future. Culture in the East German villages would have to find new patrons or be commercialised. Even shopping became difficult for those in the low-income bracket when the many small village co-op shops were closed and public transport was cut.

Although East German agriculture is well on its way to winning back the East German market, and despite the fact that cooperative farming still prevails, the economic situation has not noticeably improved. Once thriving and providing all those who lived in the countryside with a livelihood, East German agriculture, through it has become an efficient and prosperous industry, is now profitable to far fewer people than before.

Notes

1. The land reform in the Soviet occupation zone, which had been initiated by the Communists (KPD) under the slogan 'Junkerland in Bauernhand' ['Give the land of the *Junkers* to the small farmers'] and supported by the Social Democrats (SPD), was aimed at expropriating war criminals and major land-owners with more than 100 hectares. It also found a backing among the Christian Democrats (CDU) and the Liberal Democrats (LDPD). A total of 2.1 million hectares were distributed in lots of 5 to 10 hectares among the landless and the refugees. The land reform legislation was passed by the administration of the Province of Saxony on 3 September, by the State of Mecklenburg on 5 September, the Province of Brandenburg on 6 September, and the States of Saxony and Thuringia on 10 September 1945.

2. The German Social Union (DSU) was formed in East Germany after the fall of the Wall as a sister party to the conservative Bavarian Christian Social Union (CSU). (See Chapter 2, pp. 47–8 above).

3. Democratic Awakening [*Demokratischer Aufbruch*; DA] had emerged as an insignificant conservative off-shoot of the civil rights movement of 1989 and soon folded. (See Chapter 2, p. 42 above.)

4. Election figures from *Berliner Zeitung*, 20 March 1990.

5. Figures taken from the Statistisches Amt der DDR, *Statistisches Jahrbuch der Deutschen Demokratischen Republik 1989* [Statistical Yearbook of the GDR for 1989] (1989: Staatsverlag der DDR, Berlin), p.18.

6. Figure based on *DBV 91 report*, (1991: Deutscher Bauernverband, Bonn), pp. 32–3.

7. They totalled 3,844 agricultural cooperatives (LPG) and 464 state farms (VEG). All figures based on *Statistisches Jahrbuch der Land-, Forst- und Nahrungsgüterwirtschaft 1990* [Statistical Yearbook of Agricultural, Forestry and Food Processing for 1990] (1990: Statistisches Amt der DDR, Berlin), pp. 10–11.

8. Figures based on *Statistisches Jahrbuch der Deutschen Demokratischen Republik* (1963: Statistisches Amt der DDR, Berlin), p. 235.

9. *Statistisches Jahrbuch der Land-, Forst und Nahrungsgüterwirtschaft 1990*, p. 57.

10. Figures based on *Statistisches Jahrbuch der Deutschen Demokratischen Republik 1971*, (1971: Statistisches Amt der DDR, Berlin), p. 196; *Statistisches Jahrbuch der Deutschen Demokratischen Republik 1989*, (1989: Statistisches Amt der DDR, Berlin), p. 186; *Statistisches Jahrbuch der Land-, Forst- und Nahrungsgüterwirtschaft 1990*, pp. 56–7.

11. Klaus Böhme, 'Die Diskussion um die Zukunft der landwirtschaftlichen Betriebe im Osten Deutschlands – Bäuerliche Familienbetriebe, Produktive Genossenschaften, Agrarunternehmen?' [The discussion about the future of the agricultural enterprises in East Germany – Family farming, productive cooperatives, agricultural companies?], in Thomas Brückner, Antje Peters, Jörg Rhode and Ingrid Saalfeld (eds), *LPG – Was nun? Agrarkonzentration im Osten Deutschlands – Die Neugestaltung des ländlichen Raums* (1992: Reisende Hochschule, Hanover), p. 55.

12. Landwirtschaftsanpassungsgesetz [Agricultural Adjustment Law], in *Deutsche Bauernzeitung* No. 29, 1990.

13. New Federal States – term used for the former GDR as opposed to the old Federal States, the Federal Republic of Germany before unification.

14. *Gemeinsam schaffen wir's. Ja zu Deutschland – Ja zur Zukunft. CDU. Freiheit. Wohlstand. Sicherheit* [Together we'll manage it. Yes to Germany – yes to the future. CDU. Freedom. Prosperity. Security] (1990: CDU-Bundesgeschäftsstelle, Hauptabteilung Öffentlichkeitsarbeit, Bonn).

15. RIAS – *Radio im Amerikanischen Sektor* (Radio in the American Sector) – was set up by the Americans in Berlin after the war to bring Western ideology across the trenches of the Cold War.

16. Martin Irion, 'Der RIAS lügt nicht: Ansichten eines Experten – West zur Landwirtschaft – Ost' [RIAS doesn't lie: Views of an expert from the West on the agriculture of the East], in *Journal für Recht und Würde*, No. 3, March 1993, p. 20.

17. See Chapter 3, pp. 104–5 above.

18. (1990 edition: Bundesanzeigeblatt, Bonn), pp. 1418–29.

19. See Chapter 3, pp. 104–5 above.

20. 'Fördergesetz' (Law on Subsidizing Agriculture), *Deutsche Bauernzeitung*, 27, 1990, pp. 63f.

21. Christel Panzig and Klaus-Alexander Panzig, 'Die Stellung der Bauern zur Transformation der ehemaligen LPG zu privatwirtschaftlich, marktorientierten Betriebsformen in den fünf neuen Bundesländern unter besonderer Berücksichtigung der Länder Brandenburg und Sachsen-Anhalt' [The position of the farmers regarding the transformation of former cooperatives to private and market-oriented companies in East Germany, with a special emphasis on the Federal States of Brandenburg and Saxony-Anhalt], unpublished ms, Berlin 1991.

22. 'Prosperity for the East' – the name of the Bonn Government's programme to transform East Germany into a market economy.

23. The CDU party of the Brandenburg parliament, *Standpunkt zur Entwicklung der Landwirtschaft* [Position on the development of agriculture], March/April 1991, p. 1.

24. Ibid., p. 2.

25. *Argumente: Situationsbericht 1993* [Arguments: Report on the situation in 1993] (1994: Deutscher Bauernverband, Bonn), p. 96.

26. *Agrarwirtschaft in den neuen Ländern: Aktuelle Situation und Maßnahmen* [Agriculture in East Germany: Current situation and measures] (1994: Bundesministerium für Ernährung, Landwirtschaft und Forsten, Bonn), pp. 2ff.

27. Ibid., p.1.

28. See note 1.

29. See Chapter 1, pp.15–18.

30. See ibid., p. 16ff.
31. *IAB Kurzbericht* [Institute for Job Market and Vocational Research of the Federal Agency of Employment: Short Report] (December 1993: Institut für Arbeitsmarkt und Berufsforschung der Bundesanstalt für Arbeit, Nuremberg), No. 20/28, p. 1.
32. *Argumente*, p. 103.
33. *IAB Kurzbericht*, p. 5.
34. *Neues Deutschland*, 8 April 1994.
35. See 'Strukturelle und rechtliche Rahmenbedingungen der deutschen Landwirtschaft' [Structural and Legal Framework of German Agriculture] (1993: Bundesministerium für Ernährung, Landwirtschaft und Forsten, Bonn).
36. See Bundesanstalt für Arbeit (ed.) *Arbeitsmarkt Monitor für die neuen Bundesländer. Schnellbericht: Daten für November 1991* [Labour Market Monitor for East Germany. Express Report: Figures for November 1991] (1991: Infratest Sozialforschung, Munich), p. 60.
37. In the GDR 8 March was celebrated as International Women's Day.
38. Figures from Gunnar Winkler (ed.), *Frauenreport '90* [Women's report '90] (1990: Die Wirtschaft, Berlin), p. 89.
39. Deutscher Bundestag, 12th legislative period, Protocol of the 149th Session (Thursday, 25 March 1993, Bonn), p. 12836.
40. Deutscher Bundestag, 12th legislative period, answer by the Federal Government to the interpellation by MP Petra Bläss and the PDS/Left-wing List (3 December 1992: Deutscher Bundestag, Drucksache 127/3910, Bonn), p.11. Pensions have since been raised but remain below West German levels.

5   Rolling Back the Gender Status of East German Women

Anneliese Braun, Gerda Jasper and Ursula Schröter

Equal opportunities for men and women depend on whether or not and to what extent both are able to secure their existence and consequently their economic independence through gainful employment. Post-unification East Germany shows that a significant roll-back in gender relations arises when women are pushed out of employment on a massive scale, especially out of qualified jobs, with leading positions reconquered by men. Equally, GDR history shows that the reversal of this thesis is wrong: (nearly) full employment of women is no guarantee of equal opportunities.

But let us first ask: What was the position of women in the GDR? What decisive changes in this position did the East German state bring about in the course of its history? What were the consequences of the deficits in women's equality in the GDR?

Foundations of the GDR's Equal Opportunities Policy

At the end of 1989, 91 per cent of women between the ages of 16 and 60 were gainfully employed or underwent training in the GDR.[1] This high rate of employment among women, also in comparison with other 'socialist' countries, had several causes. On the one hand, it was due to the theoretical, more precisely economistic, assumption in the Marxist branch of the labour movement that the emancipation of women required their full integration into a working life outside the home. The patriarchal political system of the GDR was based, among other things, on the theory that by solving the social question and socialising the means of production the 'woman question' would automatically be put right. Apart from the fact that a true socialisation of the means of production never took place, the view of the 'class question' as the main contradiction and the gender and woman question as one derived

139

from it was not only one-dimensional but simply incorrect. 'Gender', just like property, race, generation, etc., is an independent structural category of society, though very closely linked to the others. However, this does not mean that the expropriation of capital automatically leads to the abolition of the patriarchy.

Nevertheless, the above monocausal view in respect of equal opportunities of men and women produced a socially effective emancipatory impulse during the first two decades of the GDR. Equality of the sexes was made a constitutional principle and at the same time an acknowledged guideline for the state. In the 1950s and 1960s, women left the narrow confines of their existence in the home, got qualified and took over public responsibilities, thereby also changing their position within the family.

The social image of the full-time employed woman and mother was also due to straightforward economic reasons. The (re)construction of the country and the constant economic shortcomings led to a great demand for labour, which could never have been met satisfactorily without taking advantage of the female population.

The more or less complete incorporation of women in gainful employment, however, did not fundamentally change the traditional allocation of gender roles. Women remained primarily responsible for the unpaid reproductive work, i.e. child-rearing and household chores. Two-thirds of this work (according to statistics for 1985) was done by women and a third by men[2](which was, however, still an improvement on the time before 1945 or on West Germany).

Despite the advancement[3] of equal opportunities which women in the GDR underwent, the patriarchal system was never seriously challenged.

Stages of the GDR's Equal Opportunities Policy

The first stage, which some authors call the policy of 'jobs for women'[4] (a very reductionist and one-sided term), was geared to getting women into gainful employment and lasted until about the mid-1960s. The social image of the full-time working woman was developed at that time. To implement this policy, certain family duties and household chores were delegated outside the family. Child-care facilities were set up such as kindergartens, crèches and after-school centres. Other services, e.g. school meals and works canteens, were introduced to relieve women of some of their domestic duties. Qualification opportunities were opened up for women both in primary and in supplementary job training. Special importance was attached to the training and employment of women in typical men's jobs (e.g. engineering).

Women from the lower social strata were able to undergo job training for the first time. There was a change in the social position of women; they were given individual development opportunities and availed themselves of these. For example, special programmes were set up at the workplace to help them in their qualification and promote them to executive positions.

Equal opportunities for women, however, spelled their integration into the world of gainful employment still dominated by men, or, in other words, their adjustment to male employment patterns. Women of the post-war generation were the trail-blazers, not only going out to work but also remaining mainly responsible for child-rearing and household chores, at the time without the network of child-care facilities or the social services and support later generations of women enjoyed, which alleviated the combination of a job and a family. Despite everything women gained by this development, it also meant a high degree of physical and psychic strain. The women of the post-war generation especially had to fight hard for every step taken towards emancipation both at work and in their private lives.

With the introduction of the first Family Code of the GDR in 1966, the equal opportunities policy was modified and with this also the image of woman in society. Child-rearing in the family was officially acknowledged as work and thus gained an independent status alongside gainful employment.[5] The background to this development was that women were trying to relieve themselves of the double burden of gainful employment and family duties either by having no or fewer children and by attaching priority to their own careers at work or by taking a low-key approach to their careers and concentrating more on the family.

During this second stage, which followed the introduction of the Family Code, special university or college courses were established which enabled mothers of young children to take up studies suited to their specific personal situation. To ensure population growth in the face of an unsatisfactorily low birth rate, family policy began to emphasise women's reproductive duties.

Thus the policy of equal opportunities, in the third stage during the 1970s and 1980s, focused on legislation designed to harmonise motherhood and gainful employment. Regulations included: shorter working hours for women with two or more dependent children; sick leave with pay in the event of children's illness, which was far more generous than in West Germany, one paid day a month, the so-called 'household day'; the introduction of the 'Baby Year' (a year's paid leave for each of the first two children and 18 months for the third and any further children); financial support for parents with three and more children; interest-free loans for young married couples, etc. These measures must be considered positively even though, inasmuch as they were available almost exclusively to women, they had at least two serious deficits which already proved harmful to women in the GDR but have become much more so since unification.

First, household chores and reproductive work were associated with women. The traditional division of labour within the family thereby remained biased against women. The policy of equal opportunities became mere family policy. The image of women in society changed from the 'full-time working woman' to the 'lovingly caring mother' (of at least two children), who also went to work.

Second, already in the GDR, young women were considered a 'risk factor' in enterprises and institutions on account of their frequent absences due to childbirth or children's illnesses. Thus career opportunities, especially for younger, even highly qualified women, were curbed. In the 1980s young women again tended to take up typical women's jobs, where working hours and conditions allowed them to combine the job and family duties.

Nevertheless, the cuts and even the complete abolition of the social measures after unification, which had enabled women to combine a job and family duties, hit them especially hard.

This was all the more serious as, after the fall of the GDR, most East German women had to continue lifestyles which they had chosen under different social conditions (e.g. single with children). In the GDR women were seldom faced with the alternative of either a child or a career.[6] At the end of the 1980s, 95 per cent of children were born to gainfully employed mothers, 4 per cent to young women still undergoing training and only 1 per cent to housewives. Women had been able to combine career and children, though it was at the price of much strain and hardly any leisure for themselves.

From 1972 onwards pregnant women were able to decide for themselves whether they wanted to bear a child or not; abortion was legalised and free of charge. Thus the majority of children born were wanted and welcome. The recent Federal German legislation in this area is a clear step backwards, to which East German women did not offer enough resistance, very probably because they had never needed to fight for legal and free abortion or for any of the other social benefits they enjoyed, but had been given these as a free gift by the paternalistic leadership in the GDR.

Gender-related Differences in Training and the Labour Market of the GDR

The inequality in respect of family duties and household work burdening women in the GDR had far-reaching consequences for their position at work and in society in general. The unjust division of labour at home, in the so-called 'private sphere', also produced a gender-specific segmentation of the labour market and reproduced different types of socialisation of girls and boys in the GDR.

Even though women made up just under 50 per cent of all gainfully employed people in the GDR, their proportionate share in the different branches or employment differed greatly. In 1981 some 41 per cent of all industrial workers in the GDR were women and they accounted for a quarter of all employees in typical men's jobs – in the iron and steel industry for instance. In the 1950s and 1960s women took over jobs which up until then had been purely male domains, e.g. they became crane operators, mechanics, electricians and quite often also engineers. This fact should be duly appreciated even though women's workplaces were not equal to men's with regard to income, working conditions, qualifications required and career prospects.

Hildegard Maria Nickel rightly stated shortly before the end of the GDR that 'in industry women have the less attractive jobs and even if they do work on modern production lines these often don't allow much communication. Furthermore, women are exposed to less satisfactory work hygiene. Their jobs require lower qualifications.'[7] Consequently, 60 per cent of unskilled or semi-skilled jobs were held by women. This had and continued to have detrimental effects on women, especially as, under the later restructuring and rationalisation in industry, these were the first jobs to go.[8] This also applied to the status of working women in agriculture.[9] Most of the women in the GDR worked in typical women's jobs such as in retail trade and in other services, where they made up nearly three-quarters of all employees.[10] In health care and education the share of women was even higher, at 83 and 77 per cent respectively.[11]

The gender-related differences regarding opportunities in the labour market and the differing socialisation of girls and boys had a great influence on their choice of a career as well as on career guidance work, despite all the progress made in opening up men's jobs for women in the GDR.

As a result, there was a clear gender differentiation in the various training courses at all levels of education. In the period between 1982 and 1987, some 60 per cent of the female school-leavers took up training in 30 different trades (which represented 10 per cent of the total range of trades and vocations offered). They filled some 85 per cent of the vacancies in these 30 categories of jobs (e.g. shop-assistant, secretary, jobs in the catering trade). In the processing industry, girl apprentices were concentrated in jobs in the textile and clothing industries, which had bleak prospects after unification. In the more attractive technical jobs, the proportion of girls was higher than in West Germany but still considerably lower than that of boys. Between 1980 and 1989, the proportion of girls working as electronics specialists dropped from 50 to 20 per cent; for machinists controlling and measuring jobs from 23 to 12 per cent; for machine tool operators from 28 to 15 per cent; in telecommunications from 25 to 18 per cent; and for mechanics from 45 to 31 per cent.[12]

There was also a strong polarisation of the genders in university courses in the GDR. Before the *Wende*, the overall percentage of woman students was 48 per cent; in natural sciences and mathematics it was 46 per cent; in economics 67 per cent; and in the technical branches 25 per cent.[13] The relatively low proportion of women in the technical field was rarely a topic of public discussion, whereas their disproportionately large numbers at medical schools and teacher training courses was considered a problem. Whenever there were not enough applicants for the technical university courses women were encouraged to apply to fill the vacancies. Even so, women were much better represented on these courses in the GDR than in West or post-unification East Germany. This was probably due to girl school-leavers having resigned themselves to being marginalised on the labour market in those professions.

The present training situation consolidates the gender-related GDR structures, adjusting them to the West German pattern to the extent that they might even overtake the level of discrimination against young women traditional in the West.

The gender segmentation of the labour market in the GDR resulted from and reproduced considerable differences in income between typical men's and typical women's jobs. In 1988 the net income of fully employed women was only 76 per cent of men's.[14]

This difference in income does not only reveal that women's jobs were less well paid than men's. Women were also at a disadvantage and discriminated against in employment in other ways.

First, bringing up children made a considerable number of women change their jobs. They stopped working shifts, thereby losing the supplementary pay for shift-work, or looked for jobs with more convenient working hours or closer to home in order to be able to harmonise family and job better. In many cases they gave up the job they were trained for and took up unskilled work or work requiring only some initial job training. Women, more often than men, accepted work below their original qualification and thus loss of qualification status and lower wages. In other instances, however, women took up training for a different kind of job.

Second, women's chances of promotion were poorer than men's because women with young children were unable to work overtime or take up a job irrespective of transport facilities available. Gender inequality varied too according to the different levels in professional or workplace hierarchies. In 1989/90 a third of all executives in enterprises and in the administration, as well as of mayors of towns and villages, were women and they made up 50 per cent of all judges and medical practitioners.[15] This was well above the West German average at that time. However, women mainly held the lower executive jobs at workplaces. Only 2 per cent of managing directors were women and only 12 per cent of deputy managing directors. In the academic field the situation was similar. In 1988 women represented 40 per cent of those who took a doctorate, but only 14 per cent of those who took their second doctorate (which made graduates eligible for a professorship) and only 5 per cent of newly appointed professors.[16] This was all the more serious because even if the women were equally qualified, men would be appointed.

In October 1989 some 6.7 per cent of women working in industry had a university degree, 18.5 per cent had attended a training college, 1.2 per cent had a craftsperson's certificate, 58.5 per cent were skilled workers, 2.9 per cent were semi-skilled and 12.3 per cent were without any training.[17] An investigation of non-academic qualifications and the employment of women in the GDR, commissioned by the Federal Minister of Education and Science, also confirmed that professional qualification was a typical component in the working lives of women. A representative survey of the mid-1990s revealed that 70 per cent of the women interviewed had some qualification for the job they were actually doing. More than half the women said that they had to undergo additional training at their current place of work.[18]

The following trends in the gainful employment of women and their qualifications, and the women's reaction to these changes, developed after the fall of the GDR.

Radical Changes in Gainful Employment

Though East German men also had to cope with changes in the social system, women were faced with three additional problems.

First, in contrast to GDR days, women no longer enjoyed full legal independence, e.g. unmarried mothers were subjected to an official guardianship on behalf of their children. Another step backward was that women wanting an abortion were coerced by the state into accepting official medical and social advice. This was humiliating for women who, for the past two decades, had been able to decide for themselves whether to continue their pregnancies or not. There were other retrogressive aspects in family, labour and social legislation, more subtle but no less effective. The Federal German social constitution reduced the pronounced economic independence of women in the GDR to the 'marginal Federal German level'.[19] This especially concerned social benefits with regard to childbirth and the care of children. Thus, paid leave for the care of sick children was reduced to no more than 10 days for each parent or 20 days for single parents. The system of joint annual tax statements for both spouses favoured the non-gainfully employed wife vis-à-vis the gainfully employed. The state thereby subsidised unwaged married women. The 1992 Law on Pensions Adjustment (for East Germany) did not promote women's economic independence. Even in old age, their claims for maintenance and dependants' pensions were derived, at least partially, from their partners. Only married women, regardless of whether they had any children, could claim; single or divorced women were not eligible.[20] The family support principle was introduced, which meant that first of all the family (partner, parents, children) had to assist an unemployed or needy person before he or she could claim social benefit; this put women at a disadvantage more often than men.

Second, women were unemployed more often than men and thus lost their previous (relative) financial independence. Even though in the GDR this independence was on a modest scale, it gave women freedom of action which they greatly missed after unification. Unemployment was the chief agency by which East German women were massively robbed of a continuous working career and driven into economic dependence on their husbands or a state welfare institution. This segregation of women was expected to gain momentum as their claims to unemployment benefit ran out, as the Federal Employment Agency axed the job-creation schemes and as more qualified and flexible women took the jobs of the less qualified.

Third, women were more affected by growing, escalating discrimination than men. Unemployed women, for instance, were labelled as 'hard to place' by the labour exchanges. Their prospects on the labour market were reduced still further if they were single parents with young children, or 'too old' (40/45 years upwards), or if they were foreigners, or had health problems.

When firms wanted to fill vacancies, they preferred men. Only the Federal State of Brandenburg offered enterprises tax reductions and other incentives if they employed women.

General discrimination on the basis of gender, age or ethnic origin was stepped up even to the extent of making the applicant's qualification and professional competence irrelevant.

Trends in the Labour Market

A process of displacement and polarisation was under way in East Germany. Men were displacing women, academics were displacing skilled workers, women without children were displacing those with children, the young were displacing the old, etc. At the end of 1989 some 4.7 million women and 5 million men were gainfully employed in the GDR. Three years later, at the end of 1992, only 2.8 million women were still in regular employment in the 'first' labour market (the 'second' labour market being work under job-creation and retraining schemes).[21] The proportion of women among the gainfully employed had dropped from 49 per cent at the end of 1989 to 43 per cent at the end of 1992.[22] 'Of the men gainfully employed in November 1990 every tenth and of the women every fifth was no longer employed a year later, and instead either unemployed, in retraining or in early retirement.'[23] This trend continued in 1993. The officially quoted unemployment rate of 21 per cent among women in East Germany was nearly double that of men (11 per cent). The actual unemployment rate among women, comprising not only those registered as unemployed but also women without regular work, e.g. in further training or retraining, in work under job-creation schemes, or in early retirement, stood at 35 per cent. Thus the official figure of 810,000 women registered unemployed in February 1994 understated the true figure by two-thirds. It can therefore be said that women made up nearly two-thirds of all unemployed persons in East Germany.[24]

This situation was likely to deteriorate further unless vigorously combated by introducing shorter working hours and other steps towards a more effective employment policy.

Women were in any case worse off in the labour market than men: firstly, because they still or again carried the chief burden of family care; secondly, because typical women's jobs in the textile and clothing, leather and shoe-making industries had been lost to a very considerable degree; thirdly, because former domains of women, e.g. banks, the postal service, insurance, were being more and more taken over (again) by men. Thus women were left with only the less attractive segments of the labour market, e.g. the welfare services and cleaning.

Moreover, the dismantling of the GDR social infrastructure, above all inexpensive child-care, had negative effects. For nearly a third of all women the lack of affordable child-care facilities became a problem. The children of East German women not gainfully employed were less likely to be sent to kindergarten than in West Germany.[25]

The status of women with the same qualification level as men in GDR times became more differentiated and underwent a degree of polarisation. For women of 55 years and older, this was an especially painful experience. Their age was emphasised while their qualifications and professional experience were played down. Almost an entire generation was forced to take some form of early retirement. The proportion of gainfully employed women of the 55+ age bracket dropped to 5 per cent by the end of 1992, whereas in 1989 it had still been 13 per cent. Among unemployed women, a disproportionately high 8 per cent were in this age bracket. Many of these women live on the brink of poverty or will do so in old age. This applied particularly to those who had been ousted from gainful employment as early as in 1990. For them, the early retirement pension or unemployment benefits were still based on the lower GDR incomes. Salaries, e.g. for office staff, were at that time less than half the present earnings. In the GDR these low rates were supplemented by a kind of 'second pay packet' composed of subsidised prices for basic commodities, rents and fares. This disappeared.

Women suffered, also, from the experience of not being needed any more, from the abrupt termination of decades of communicative relations, loss in status and social as well as material insecurity.[26] This was complemented by their material situation. Already the incomes of the 50- to 60-year-olds had fallen below that of pensioners and were much lower than the earnings of the under 50s.[27] But this group of women also suffered additional forms of discrimination. The new pension law stipulated that claimants were not granted recognition for periods spent bringing up children if, as was usual in the GDR, they were fully employed at that time.[28] In the GDR, women were granted an additional bonus of five years towards their pension and could retire at the age of 60 (men at 65). This was in recognition of their work in the family as an addition to being in gainful employment.

Five years after unification, East German pensions stood at 70 per cent of the West German level. In addition, pensions of people considered 'close to the GDR state', i.e. those who worked in the civil service, in local government, at universities and colleges, in health or school education, as lawyers, in the army or the police, were further reduced.

Furthermore, a growing gap has opened up between men's and women's pensions. At the end of 1989, women's pensions averaged 108 Marks less than men's; six months later, after monetary union, the difference was DM161.[29] This gap widened, as men's wages differed more from women's than ever before. In January 1992, the difference in gross monthly income in industry of men compared with women was DM298. By October 1992, it was DM481. In trade, banking and insurance the difference was even greater. In January 1992, men employed in this sector earned on average DM322 more than women; ten months later the difference was DM511.[30]

Women of 45 and even of 40 were already at a disadvantage in the labour market. Many had already taken jobs below their qualification levels; they were more ready than younger women, as the situation worsened, to put up with unfavourable working conditions (pay below the rate, part-time work, unprotected employment). In fact, at 45 many women were threatened with long-term unemployment. Single women in particular were potential candidates for poverty in old age.

Even East German girls and young women were more discriminated against than women of their age group in West Germany. Young women could choose freely from a great variety of training courses, but they profited less from these opportunities than young men. Theoretically they had access to a wider range of employment than before. However, in far more jobs than ever men were preferred in united Germany. In some 40 per cent of the training facilities in East Germany only male applicants were taken whereas in West Germany the figure was 25 per cent. Only 30 per cent of the training facilities in the East compared with 63 per cent in the West accepted applicants of either sex.[31] More often than men, women were reduced to undergoing training at institutions unconnected with workplaces, which, in consequence, do not guarantee employment afterwards. Even though 47 per cent of the women took part in training courses, they made up more than 50 per cent of those who failed to get placed afterwards and were left unemployed. This trend increased.[32] Only 18 per cent of the girls compared with 31 per cent of the boys undergoing training at East German firms expected to find employment with their company after completion of training.[33] The training dilemma thus threatened to become a gender dilemma.

The various polarisation trends described exemplify the setbacks which East German women experienced. Their lot looked like matching that of the socially marginalised women in the 'ghettos' of North American cities such as Chicago, Los Angeles or Detroit.

The Mood of Unemployed Women

Unemployed women were affected by a variety of conflicts with which they were unable to cope. Surveys[34] and counselling of those affected showed that the majority of unemployed women were emotionally upset, especially women over 45, the long-term unemployed and single parents. They lost self-confidence, felt marginalised, suffered from hitherto unfamiliar depressions and were afraid of the future.

Yet, women's responses cannot be reduced to passive endurance and resignation. The bulk of East German women rejected their marginalisation in the labour market and the role of housewife. Various surveys showed that only between 1 and 4 per cent of East German women wanted the life of a housewife. And there was not only mute resistance; East German women also developed activities which allowed them to lead full lives.

A considerable minority of the women were actively involved in women's and unemployed pressure groups, in counselling women, or initiating women's or other projects.

In fact, after the *Wende*, East German women developed a higher degree of commitment to education than men. Perhaps they wanted in this way to compensate, at least to some extent, for their disadvantages in the labour market by obtaining additional qualifications. Some 40 per cent of the women interviewed in a survey of East German unemployed had taken part in either further training or retraining courses (as against 30 per cent of the men).[35]

One-third of the new firms in East Germany after 1990 were estab-lished by women. Though in one way remarkable, this also revealed the difficulties experienced by women who lacked financial means and bank securities, factors which exposed them to discrimination by the banks in respect of the loans needed to establish themselves in business. On the other hand, funds for the founders of enterprises were rarely made conditional on their employing and promoting women.

As a rule women opted for individual solutions and tried to 'make the best' of a given situation. One exception, illustrating a collective opposition, was the women's strike on 8 March 1994.[36]

It should be noted that the roots of the muted resistance of East German women are also to be found in behavioural patterns going back to GDR days. As women's inequality was not a topic of public debate even then, women tended to cope with 'their problems' individually, often seeking the fault in themselves.

The fierce competition on the labour market after unification forced women to make greater concessions than men to keep their jobs or to get new ones. Nearly three-quarters of all women (74 per cent) were prepared to accept work of an entirely different type to what they were trained for or employed in as compared to 66 per cent of the men. Nearly 70 per cent were ready to accept a change in the work they were doing as against only 57 per cent of men. And 67 per cent of women were prepared to undergo training to equip themselves for an entirely new type of work as compared with only 20 per cent of men.[37]

More than 60 per cent of the women interviewed, mostly unemployed women with children and academics, said they would accept financial cutbacks. More than half would take up further training or retraining below their level of qualification. The longer they had been unemployed, the greater their financial difficulties, the more readily would they accept a loss in qualified status of this kind.

Similarly they would accept unprotected employment (e.g. jobs where the employer could not pay his share in health and pensions insurance, or paid below the minimum rate for the job). About half of the women interviewed would even accept part-time employment at less than 10 to 15 hours a week.[38]

In many cases women considered such unprotected employment to be their only chance of re-entering the labour market at all. This approach, in turn, jeopardised 'normal employment', so that the women who were still gainfully employed found their own working conditions deteriorating.

Future Prospects for East German Women

The IAB Institute (Institute for Job Market and Vocational Research of the Federal Employment Agency) at Nuremberg predicted that for the 6.8 million prospective jobs in East Germany in the year 2000 there would be 4 million eligible women applicants. Given an employment rate of 43 per cent of women that would mean more than 1.1 million East German women would fail to find gainful employment.[39]

Given a situation in which even a normal (male) gainful employment was becoming more and more of a privilege, with a process of polarisation going on between the highly qualified élite and the less qualified workers, marginalisation and poorly paid work were the unfavourable prospects which large numbers of women were therefore likely to face.

The Gender Segmentation of the Labour Market

In the early GDR, in the late 1940s and early 1950s, the main pillars of a gender-related division of labour seemed under serious attack. At the beginning equal opportunities for both sexes were promoted by means of family, labour and social legislation. However, these steps achieved merely formal equality and eventually ended in stagnation. All the same, women were able to enter traditional men's domains more than before. Some two-thirds of the women interviewed in East Germany after the *Wende* believed that women were entitled to take up traditional men's jobs.[40] And yet, in 1992, only 5 per cent of gainfully employed women were actually still working in technical jobs in East Germany and 2 per cent in the West.[41]

That is to say, women were being forced into ever smaller and inferior parts of the labour market. They were viewed increasingly as just supplementary earners, to be offered the less attractive jobs. The structural disadvantages suffered by women increasingly intensified the gender segmentation of the labour market in East Germany, even more than in the West:

• East German women were worst hit by the cutback in jobs. They were the last to be re-employed.

The share of women among the gainfully employed in industry sank from 41 per cent to less than 20 per cent, in the retail trade from some 72 per cent to less than 50 per cent.[42]

The proportion of women employed was especially low in the expanding branches of the economy such as the building industry and other crafts. Job prospects were poor in the leather and shoe industries, textile and clothing industries, trade, agriculture and forestry, which had traditionally employed many women.

- Women were more or less completely ousted from the male-dominated branches expected to expand. Craftswomen, technicians, mechanics and crane operators retrained for administrative and social services, regardless of the fact that there was practically no demand in this area.
- In the services, traditionally a women's domain, managements favoured an increase of male employees. More women than men lost well-qualified office jobs, especially at the executive and managerial level. There are hardly any women left in such positions.[43]
- East German women earned considerably less than men. In October 1992, women's monthly wages in industry and trade, banking and insurance amounted to an average 83 per cent of that of their male colleagues. A particular problem was that, in West Germany, gender-geared wage differences exceeded those in the East, with women in industry earning 73 per cent and in the services sector 71 per cent of men's wages. As these differences could be expected to affect pay levels in the East, where income levels were anyway lower,[44] women there were at an additional disadvantage.[45]

In West Germany, more jobs for women (many of them part-time) were created, as the services sector and medium-sized businesses expanded. But because of the de-industrialisation of entire regions in East Germany, there was no basis for such a development there. In contrast to trends in West Germany, the number of employees in the services sector in East Germany also dropped, despite a considerable shortage of services there. According to some forecasts, primary services such as retail trade, simple office work and personal services would be expected to grow more slowly than secondary services, e.g. research, organisation, management, counselling, teaching. But the primary services were the traditional areas of women's employment. With the expansion of 'high-quality' services, the simple jobs, mostly done by women, would undergo rationalisation and disappear, e.g. in retail trade, the postal services and banking. No one knew when and what type of services would experience a lasting upsurge in East Germany and whether these services would provide women with jobs. In the short term, this was unlikely, as primarily service jobs like cleaning and many of the postal services had been axed.

Even in the servicing sector in East Germany, women were often refused qualified positions. Shopping chains, for instance, often employed women only as unskilled and poorly paid workers. Women with business qualifications (business colleges/university) were employed below their qualification level.

Further Training Versus 'Dequalification'

A mass devaluation of their qualifications was typical of the situation among East German (and Eastern European) women. Unless a policy to combat it was set in motion, this dequalification could be expected to achieve unique historical dimensions.

GDR women had actually been better represented at the higher qualification levels than in West Germany. In 1989/90, some 40 per cent of the gainfully employed East German women had graduated from college or university as compared with 13 per cent of West Germans.[46] Compared with the percentage of unskilled or semi-skilled women employed in West Germany, namely 27 per cent, the relevant GDR figure was just under 9 per cent. Indeed, East German women had low qualifications more rarely than even West German men.

Contributory factors bringing about women's dequalification in the East after unification were as follows:

* Their qualifications were no longer in demand due to structural changes after the *Wende*. Of the women interviewed, 50 per cent gave this reason.[47]
* Their jobs became obsolete after unification. This happened to more than 30 per cent of the women interviewed. In addition there was a de facto (though not legal) *'Berufsverbot'* (i.e. a politically motivated restriction on appointments) for scholars in certain fields and for a number of teachers.
* Their GDR qualifications and degrees were sometimes not recognised in united Germany because of the difference in job and training specifications. Women were represented more than men in jobs in socio-cultural, educational and economic fields, for which qualifications were either not recognised at all or not treated as being equal to the West German qualifications. Some 35 per cent of the women academics interviewed stated that their degrees were not being

recognised by the Federal German authorities.[48] In this way, academic women were displaced by less-qualified men and obliged to take up retraining courses below their level of qualification. Others felt compelled to accept jobs requiring lower qualifications and accordingly less well paid.

• Further training or retraining courses had little effect and in most cases did not lead to new jobs. Nearly all women needed an additional qualification in order to meet the new requirements. More than men, they attended courses financed by the labour exchanges. In 1993, 57 per cent women took up such courses,[49] which, however, was less than the percentage of women registered as unemployed. Yet this readiness of East German women to undergo training did not always pay off in the labour market. Despite further training and retraining, only 40 per cent found new jobs.[50] More women than men remained unemployed over long periods of time. In the early 1990s, nearly 70 per cent of the long-term unemployed were women. State-funded job policy measures to reduce unemployment (job-creation schemes, financing part of the wages of long-term unemployed etc.) were not adequate to tide women over periods of redundancy.

The Failure of Job Policies, Especially for Women

The Federal German legislation on job promotion, dating back to the 1960s, did not even achieve the target set of achieving full employment in the West, never mind the East.

Certainly, the massive extension of labour market programmes, involving considerable funding, temporarily relieved the labour market. To a certain extent, it mitigated social hardship for many unemployed people. But these programmes were not complemented by structural policy measures; on the contrary, funds were rigorously axed. Instruments of an active job market policy like support for professional training, new jobs and job-creation schemes were curtailed in 1993 and this hit East German women especially hard. Even before the severe cuts in job-creation measures, women were disadvantaged, as they were given only 40 per cent of the jobs financed by the Federal Labour Agency, notwithstanding their disproportionately high rate of unemployment. This unfair treatment of women under job-creation schemes resulted mainly from the fact that most of them were geared to building up the infrastructure to serve industry and commerce, to the improve-

ment of the environment, the dismantling of production plant or reconstruction work. Being physically demanding work in most cases, they
were often reserved for men.

It was clear that these trends would have serious consequences. On
the one hand, they would produce a hierarchy of privileged, less
privileged and underprivileged strata of employed and unemployed. On
the other, this would increase pressure on the employed, reducing
solidarity among workers. It goes without saying that these prospects
would increase the marginalisation of women, who make up the bulk
of the underprivileged groups.

As a trade union report noted:

> The labour market policy for East Germany reveals that, under the
> conditions of the East German transformation, as it became an acute
> regional crisis, the temporarily improved but then curtailed instru-
> ments of an active labour market policy could not take the place of
> an active economic and structural policy.[51]

An effective and integrated labour policy always calls for economic
development and targeted regional structural policies.

Unprotected Jobs for Women Are No Solution

Fear for their jobs forced more and more people still in work to accept
shorter hours without compensation for losses in pay. A growing
number of firms 'discovered' part-time work as an instrument for
putting pressure on staff in times of recession. They introduced 'flexible
working hours' at the expense of their staff. The Institute for Job
Market and Vocational Research found that firms could double the
number of part-time jobs by filling the part-time vacancies with the
unemployed, and then inviting their (still) full-time employed to work
part-time.[52] By the end of 1992, the part-time rate in the West (i.e.
percentage of part-timers of the total number of gainfully employed)
was an overall 16.8 per cent, the rate for women being 36.4 per cent.
In East Germany the overall figures were 9.7 per cent and 16.4 per cent.[53]

Preventing the expansion of so-called 'precarious jobs', especially
among women, would require a determined policy to provide adequately
paid and socially protected part-time jobs, possibly subsidised. Such
subsidies would put women who were working part-time because they

had to take care of young children or relatives on an equal footing with the full-time employed in respect of social insurance and pension claims.

How Do East German Women React to This Totally New Situation?

Are East German women putting up with their new and in many aspects old role? Are they really the 'losers of unification', as critics so often claim? Opinion polls by the Institute for the Analysis of Social Data (*Institut für Sozialdatenanalyse e.V. Berlin*; ISDA) have provided answers to this question. The data indicate that value orientations were changing in a very varied manner. The hopes and fears of East German women differed widely, the 'loser thesis' being just as incorrect as its categorical negation.

Apart from interviews with a selection of women, the ISDA conducted four standardised investigations (representative for the former GDR) to check hypotheses regarding the changes in East German social strata and in the structure of moral values and everyday culture. The first of these series of opinion polls was undertaken in May 1990, i.e. during the last months of the GDR (1,623 interviewees), the following in October 1990 (990 interviewees), another in October 1991 (1,008 interviewees) and the final one in May 1993 (1,953 interviewees). The proportion of women was always about 52 per cent.

According to these empirical findings, women have always regarded social developments in Germany with more scepticism, with greater reservation and also with more resignation than men. According to the ISDA data, the proportion of men who felt they were involved actively in the social process as against those who felt excluded from decision-taking remained more or less stable from 1991 to 1993. The responses of the women, however, changed. Thirteen per cent of the men interviewed felt they had no part in decision-taking in 1991 (as against 14 per cent in 1993), whilst 33 per cent were convinced in 1991 that they were participating in the shaping of society and had a say in important matters (as against 36 per cent in 1993). In 1991 33 per cent of all women interviewed felt excluded from decision-taking. Two years later this figure had risen to 48 per cent. In 1991 only 10 per cent and in 1993 only 7 per cent of women interviewed thought that they had some control over important issues and could influence them. Based on each interview series, the ISDA listed people's main concerns. Nearly 40 per cent of the women interviewed in May 1993 said that for a variety of reasons they were leading more withdrawn lives than before.

There are always marked differences between women and men in respect of employment. The career, the safe job, the personal income, are subjects which women tend to be less optimistic about than men. Here it is worth noting the potential for advance which was achieved in the GDR compared with the state of affairs after the *Wende!*

Whereas in the interview series conducted during the final GDR period, to have a job was considered a matter of course by women, in fact professional success had a low priority, four years after the end of the GDR even having a job at all was tantamount to 'success at work'. This was true especially for the younger but also disproportionately often for unemployed women. In 1993, 44 per cent of all interviewed women and 53 per cent of the unemployed women gave success at work an extremely high priority. This showed that women had become aware of their 'new' position in German society and were calling into question in a radical way the combination of having a job and having a family, which had been a matter of course in the GDR. The higher ranking of success at work in the present value system (as compared to 1989) showed East German women's wish to go out to work had remained as strong as it ever was or had even increased.

East German women, similarly to those in West Germany, were increasingly faced with the alternative of having a job or having children, a situation unknown in the GDR.

After 1990, the birth rate dropped rapidly in the East to a third of the 1989 figure. This was due neither to a 'shock effect' arising from the change of the social system, nor to the migration of younger women to the West. It was rather the beginning of a process of adjustment and re-orientation in which job and family were much more difficult to harmonise than in the past. Such a process of adjustment cannot be reduced to just a change in values. Surveys show that harmonious family relations, children, reliable friends, etc., were still among the most important value orientations of women.

The value placed on 'political freedom' (freedom of expression) underwent a dramatic development in the period after the *Wende*. Not only had the hopes of both sexes in this respect dropped, but the divergence in opinions on this point between the two sexes actually increased considerably. To be politically free, able to speak one's own mind, to have the right to vote freely, to travel anywhere – those were wishes and hopes which had a considerable influence on people in the final days of the GDR. Four years after the autumn events of 1989, political freedom was evaluated solely according to first-hand experience. The following was stated in an interview recorded in spring 1993:

> In the past, I was able to argue with my head of department day in day out without any detrimental effects. Only Honecker was taboo. Today I can attack Kohl day and night, and nobody takes any notice, but I daren't say anything against my employer – I have to keep my criticism to myself. This weighs heavily on my mind.[54]

Political freedom as a source of strength was assessed more critically by women than by men. In May 1990, nearly 50 per cent of the women interviewed put their hopes in what political freedom would allow them to do; in October 1991 this figure was down to 33 per cent and in May 1993 only 18 per cent of the women involved in the survey continued to entertain such hopes.

Apart from the hopes and worries in respect of certain aspects of women's lives, another indicator reveals the change in mood of the East German population and the growing differences in opinion between the sexes. During each of the interview series, the ISDA asked whether the political changes in Germany were approved of or not. In May 1990, some 78 per cent of the women and 81 per cent of the men were in favour of the social transformation; in October 1990 the figures were 73 per cent of the women and 79 per cent of the men; in October 1991 they stood at 64 per cent of the women and 71 per cent of the men; and in May 1993 only 39 per cent of the women and 51 per cent of the men fully supported unification.

Unemployment and fear of poverty had become to an ever-greater extent female and younger[55] was the verdict of the first all-German poverty report. This was the main reason why East German women's approval of the social changes dropped from four-fifths in 1990 to just under two-fifths in 1993.

There are, of course, good reasons why two-fifths of the women nevertheless approved of the social development in general. Women, too, enjoyed a higher average net income (in comparison with the past, not with men). They welcomed the much greater variety of commodities and services, the unfamiliar freedom to travel, the new leisure-time activities, when they have the time or money to make use of them, and the greater opportunities in general.

A sociological study[56] conducted by the East Berlin Academy of Social Sciences of the GDR in January 1989 (before the *Wende*) had looked into comparable issues. The survey related to scales of values in 19 areas of everyday life. Approval of the supply of commodities at that time ranked 19th and thus took last place. Equality of sexes was rated second on the scale of satisfactory aspects. That is, the precise planning by those 'up above' of every aspect of people's lives, secure prospects for the future, but also the lack of spontaneity in the GDR, weighed down young people and obstructed bold or unusual life-plans. 'Why is peace so boring?' asked a young woman in one of Renate Ullrich's[57] interviews, expressing feelings experienced by many young people at that time.

So East German women had an ambivalent approach to their new situation, viewing it in terms of an 'inner conflict'. While critically assessing both past and current official policies on women, they did not give way to an unproductive GDR nostalgia.

An exact analysis of the ISDA data, especially of a 'catalogue of present-day worries' and of comparable empirical findings, leads to the conclusion that, apart from the 'inner conflict' which affects every woman anyway to a greater or lesser degree, there were also other conflicts which divided the East German women into two distinct sections. Special analytical methods reveal that in the period following unification in every interview sequence there was one group of women, a third of all interviewed, who were more worried about their current situation and had less hope for the future. This pessimistic approach covered all aspects of their lives: employment, housing, family, politics. It showed that certain groups of women (and men) felt totally isolated and left out of all economic and social progress, a result which was not surprising to West German social researchers who had worked in this field for many years. 'The exclusion of large sections of the population (i.e. the socially disadvantaged groups) had become lasting,'[58] the report concluded. If by 'losers' one understands those who had definitely given up, then there was definitely a 'loser group'. In May 1993 it was made up mostly of people either already unemployed or on the brink of unemployment. Most of the 'losers' were women industrial and agricultural workers with a relatively low level of education. Woman academics were not affected above average, differing from the relevant findings in 1990 and 1991. In the 40–45 age group, the so-called young elderly,[59] there was a disproportionate number of 'losers'.[60] 'Losers' were poorer than others. The critical figure for the individual average monthly income in 1993 was DM1,500. In the income groups below DM1,500 there were disproportionately large numbers of women, and in those above the proportion of women was unjustifiably low.

Of course, the term 'loser' should be applied discriminately as it relates to a very heterogeneous group of people. From a psycho-sociological point of view, however, it was evident that the 'losers' were neither able nor willing to translate their precarious situation into activity, strength, into fighting back. They withdrew from public life more and more and concentrated on household chores, gardening and taking care of their children or grandchildren. Many of them had given up and lost confidence in themselves. They resigned themselves to being a 'housewife'.

It has, by the way, been established that women who resign themselves to being only a 'housewife' 'incur a higher risk of becoming mentally ill, of their ability to cope with problematical life situations declining. There are no other areas in which they can prove themselves.'[61]

And yet there still remains the second group, the second of the two distinct sections which the reports show have emerged in the period since 1989. These are the women who have shown themselves determined not to give way to pessimism, however daunting the problems might be, who have resolved to stand up for themselves and their rights. The real question lies in establishing what objective chance their optimism has in view of the scale of the predicament which has swept over them since unification. It must be admitted the statistics do not give grounds for positive conclusions.

Notes

1. In addition, many women continued to work after the pension age of 60, either to increase their pensions or just because they enjoyed their work and wanted to maintain the social contacts which were important to them.
2. See Christina Klenner, 'Doppelt belastet oder einfach ausgebeutet?' [Double strain or simply exploited?], *Das Argument. Zeitschrift für Philosophie und Sozialwissenschaften,* No. 6, November/December 1990, pp. 865–74.
3. See Rainer Geißler, 'Die ostdeutsche Sozialstruktur unter Modernisierungsdruck' [The East German social structure under pressure to modernise], *Aus Politik und Zeitgeschichte* supplement of *Das Parlament,* B29–30, 1992, pp.15ff.
4. See Lisa Böckmann-Schewe, Christine Kulke and Anne Röhrig, 'Wandel und Brüche in Lebensentwürfen von Frauen in den neuen Bundesländern' [Changes and breaks in life concepts of women in East Germany], *Aus Politik und Zeitgeschichte,* B 6, 1993, p. 34.

5. See ibid., p.34.

6. For academics, especially scientists and researchers, it was often very difficult to combine this very demanding work with bringing up children. They were not very helpful to a career.

7. Hildegard Maria Nickel, 'Geschlechtertrennung durch Arbeitsteilung' [Separating the sexes through division of labour], *Feministische Studien*, 8, No. 1, 1990, p. 12.

8. Gunnar Winkler (ed.), *Frauenreport '90* [Women's report '90] (1990: Die Wirtschaft, Berlin), p. 68.

9. In the GDR 38 per cent of all people working in agriculture and forestry were women (source: see note 10).

10. *IAB Kurzbericht* (28 May 1991, Berlin) *Frauenbeschäftigung in der ehemaligen DDR in regionaler und wirtschaftlicher Gliederung. Ergebnisse aus der Beschäftigungserhebung 1989*, [Employment of women in the former GDR, according to regional and economic structures], Table 1.

11. Bundesminister für Bildung und Wissenschaft (ed.), 'Berufliche Weiterbildung für Frauen in den neuen Bundesländern' [Further training for women in East Germany], *Bildung-Wissenschaft-Aktuell*, No. 11, 1990, p. 20.

12. Winkler (ed.), *Frauenreport '90*, p. 44.

13. Ibid., pp. 46ff.

14. Deutsches Institut für Wirtschaftsforschung (DIW) *Erwerbsbeteiligung und Einkommen der Frauen in der DDR* [Proportion of women in gainful employment and incomes in the GDR], *DIW-Wochenbericht* No. 19, 1990 (1990: DIW, Berlin), pp. 263ff.

15. DIW-Diskussionspapiere No 7: *Kindererziehung und Erwerbsarbeit – Marktwirtschaftliche Möglichkeiten einer erziehungsfreundlichen Erwerbsarbeit in Deutschland* [Child-care and gainful employment – ways of harmonising child-care and gainful emplyoment in the market economy of Germany] (1990: DIW, Berlin), p. 5.

16. Rainer Geißler, 'Soziale Ungerechtigkeit zwischen Männern und Frauen im geteilten Deutschland' [Social inequality between men and women in divided Germany], *Aus Politik und Zeitgeschichte*, B14–15, 1991, p. 17.

17. Winkler (ed.), *Frauenreport '90*, p. 38.

18. Gensior et al., 'Berufliche Weiterbildung', p. 20.

19. Johannes Steffen, 'Familien auf dem Abstellgleis' [Families pushed aside], *Sozialismus*, No. 5, 1991, p. 41.

20. Ibid.

21. Gerhard Engelbrech, 'Beschäftigungssituation und Arbeitsmark-tschancen von Frauen in Ostdeutschland und Möglichkeiten der Bekämpfung von Arbeitslosigkeit' [Employment situation and job opportunities for women in East Germany and the possibilities of fighting unemployment], *Informationen für die Beratungs- und Vermittlungsdienste der Bundesanstalt für Arbeit ibv*, (No. 26, 1993: Bundesanstalt für Arbeit, Nuremberg), p. 1995.
22. See Engelbrech, 'Beschäftigungssituation'.
23. See ibid., p. 1995.
24. All data in this paragraph were taken from the current statistics of the Federal Employment Agency in Nuremberg or were calculated on that basis.
25. See Gerhard Engelbrech, 'Zwischen Wunsch und Wirklichkeit' [Between wishes and reality], *IAB Werkstattbericht* (No. 8, 11 June 1993, Nuremberg), p. 10.
26. Gunnar Winkler, 'Die künftigen Alten' [The future elderly], *Sozialreport*, III, 1993: *Neue Bundesländer* (1993: Sozialwissenschaftliches Forschungszentrum and Hans-Böckler-Stiftung, Berlin), p. 26.
27. See Engelbrech, 'Zwischen Wunsch', p. 27.
28. Time spent for rearing children was only recognised as such for the pension if East German women could prove that they gave up work for that time.
29. Giesela Helwig and Hildegard Maria Nickel (eds), *Frauen in Deutschland 1945–1992* [Women in Germany 1945–1992] (1993: Akademie Verlag, Berlin), p. 107.
30. Gunnar Winkler, 'Erwerbseinkommen' [Income from gainful employment], *Sozialreport*, III, 1993: *Neue Bundesländer*, p. 26.
31. See Barbara Bertram in ibid., p. 195.
32. In 1992 there were 53 per cent and in 1993 already 56 per cent of women among unemployed school-leavers or graduates. Figures based on Karen Schober, 'Duales System: Nur durch Arbeit trägt Ausbildung Früchte' [Dual system. Work makes training useful], *IAB Kurzbericht* (No 5, 9 March 1994, Nuremberg).
33. See 'Frauen: Ausbildung–Beschäftigung–Weiterbildung' [Women: Training–employment–further training], *Information der Bundesanstalt für Arbeit* (No. 50 1993, Bundesanstalt für Arbeit, Nuremberg), p. 3218.
34. See Anneliese Braun and Michaela Richter, *Befindlichkeiten, Meinungen und Konflikte erwerbsloser und von Erwerbslosigkeit bedrohter Frauen* [Personal situations, opinions and conflicts of unemployed women and those threatened by unemployment] (1992: Arbeits-

losenverband Deutschland e.V., Arbeitsgruppe Frauenerwerbs-
losigkeit, Berlin).

35. *INFO Arbeitslosen-Report Ost – Abschlußbericht* [INFO unemployed report on East Germany] (1993: INFO GmbH, Berlin).

36. On International Women's Day 1994, the East German Independent Women's Association (UVF) and a number of West German women's organisations joined forces and declared a one-day strike. They organised a great many activities, including blocking road crossings, inviting women to rallies, refusing to do their 'women's chores' of child-minding, cooking, etc.

37. See *Sozialreport 1992* [Social report 1992] (1993: Morgenbuch Verlag, Berlin), p. 97.

38. Braun and Richter, *Befindlichkeiten*.

39. Engelbrech, 'Beschäftigungssituation', p. 1995.

40. Ipos report, *Gleichberechtigung von Frauen und Männern: Ergebnisse einer repräsentativen Bevölkerungsumfrage* [Equality of women and men: Results of a representative opinion poll] (November 1991), p. 71.

41. See 'Frauen: Ausbildung–Beschäftigung–Weiterbildung', p. 3218.

42. Based on Winkler (ed.), *Frauenreport '90*, p. 66; and Christian Brinckmann, *Materialien zur Langzeitarbeitslosigkeit in Ostdeutschland und ihrer Bekämpfung* [Materials on long-term unemployment in East Germany and measures to overcome it] (1990: IAB, Nuremberg), VII/10, Table 3.

43. *DIW-Wochenreport*, No. 18/92 of 30 April 1992.

44. The average monthly income of an East German is about 60 per cent of that in West Germany.

45. Based on *Sozialreport*, No. III, 1993, p. 23.

46. See 'Frauen: Ausbildung–Beschäftigung–Weiterbildung', p. 2001.

47. Braun and Richter, *Befindlichkeiten*.

48. Ibid.

49. There was a qualification offensive in East Germany after 1991. Thus, getting qualified was not only a component but a decisive determinant of the transformation process. Following 1989, there were 900,000 participants in further training and retraining courses financed by the labour exchange in addition to training provided by individual companies.

50. According to the statistics of the Federal Employment Agency, Nuremberg.

51. Arbeitskreis AFG-Reform Memorandum, IG Metall, *Für ein neues Arbeitsförderungsgesetz – Eckpunkte* [Advocating new labour promotion legislation] (n.d.: IG Metall, Frankfurt/M), p. 5.

52. Eugen Spitznagel, 'Beschäftigungsförderung durch Veränderung der Arbeitszeitstruktur – eine wenig beachtete Option' [Promoting jobs by changing the structure of working hours – A little considered option], *IAB Werkstattbericht*, No. 11, 25 June 1993.

53. In addition one has to remember that East German women were used to a continuous career and full-time employment. Only 27 per cent of them worked part-time in GDR days. In comparison, in West Germany, many women opted for part-time after the age of 30 or quit working altogether. Compare Institut für Demoskopie Allenbach (ed.), *Frauen in Deutschland: Die Schering-Frauenstudie '93* [Women in Germany: The Schering Study 1993 on women] (1993: Bund Verlag, Cologne), p. 28.

54. Ursula Schröter, unpublished preliminary study within the framework of a project called *Ostdeutsche Frauen zwischen Verlieren und Gewinnen* [East German women between loss and gain] (1993: Berlin), p. 26.

55. Walter Hanesch et al. *Armut in Deutschland* [Poverty in Germany] (1994: Rowohlt Verlag, Hamburg).

56. Akademie der Gesellschaftswissenschaften Berlin, 'Befragung der berufstätigen Bevölkerung in ausgewählten Betrieben und Einrichtungen' [Opinion poll of those employed in selected firms and institutions] – 1,376 interviewees; the data were administered by the ISDA administration, which also carried out the evaluation. However, the survey was not representative of the entire GDR.

57. Renate Ullrich, *Mein Kapital bin ich selber: Gespräche mit Theaterfrauen in Berlin-Ost 1990/91* [I'm my own capital: Talks with theatre women in East Berlin 1990/91], (1991: Zentrum für Theaterdokumentation und -information, Berlin).

58. Helmut Altena, 'Armut: Ursachen, Definition und Lösungsansatz' [Poverty: Causes, definition and solutions], *Rundbrief 1/93*' (1993: Verband für sozialkulturelle Arbeit e.V, Hamburg), p. 41.

59. Rainer Ferchland and Renate Ullrich, *Expertise zur Situation der 'Jungen Alten' in den neuen Bundesländern* [Study on the situation of the 'young elderly' in the new Federal States] (1992: Kommission zur Erforschung des sozialen und politischen Wandels in den neuen Bundesländern, Berlin).

60. However, a more detailed age analysis showed that women around 65–70 and older represented an average proportion of the 'losers',

as the old age pensions had been raised and quite a number of women were eligible for additional pensions which were non-existent in the GDR.

61. 'Frauen im mittleren Alter' [Middle-aged women], *Schriftenreihe des Bundesministeriums für Frauen und Jugend* (1993: Bundesministerium für Frauen und Jugend, Cologne), Vol. 13, p. 26.

6   The End of a European Tradition in Scholarship and Culture?

Horst van der Meer

The fields of GDR scholarship and culture were to experience the same fate as did the economy and social policy. Here, too, there were methods of 'colonisation' and strategies of destruction designed to wipe out the achievements of a 41-year history of one third of the German people within a separate state.

The examples referred to here typify what was a complex process of forced integration of the eastern territories of Germany into the Federal Republic. In the old Federal Republic this in turn led to an all too rosy view of the actual state of affairs there in research, teaching, health and culture and stifled any initiative on necessary reforms. Consequently dubious structures and norms, which had actually long been open to question, were simply thrust upon the eastern Federal States.

Nevertheless, quite a number of scholars and politicians from the West are concerned that opportunities for development are inevitably going to waste. These losses cannot be calculated in monetary terms, but will clearly be detrimental to the German people and European development. These misgivings overlap with the analysis of many East German intellectuals.

During the 40 years of Socialist Unity Party (SED) rule, that party and its satellites usurped all the leading positions, including those in the spheres of scholarship and culture. Thus they were able to manipulate and restrict developments in these areas. These constraints were directly related to the ideological narrow-mindedness of the leading functionaries and the limited economic potential of the GDR. The latter was further exacerbated by the Western embargo, prohibiting the sale of advanced technology to COMECON countries.

For many East German scholars, artists and others working in the area of culture, the transition years after 1989 were difficult. Large numbers of them experienced the collapse of their careers, the end of a secure existence and a total upheaval in their social environment. Nevertheless, they had no desire to turn the clock back. Instead, they wanted to play a role in building a new future.

The following, based on specific facts, figures and analysis, explores some of the most significant developments in the fields of scholarship, art and culture. These changes will be examined not only in the context of the collapse of former GDR structures and the destruction of internationally recognised bodies, but also in the light of intensive efforts towards constructive alternatives.

The Evaluation and Winding Up of the Academies

The political transformation in Europe and Germany created a paradoxical situation in the Federal Republic. On the one hand, the removal of the East–West confrontation opened up the cul-de-sac which existed in German and world politics. On the other hand, the 'colonialist' manner in which German unification took place produced new paralyses and the future consequences remain unpredictable. The opportunities for structural reforms involving and integrating those affected were completely wasted both in East and West. The Western model imposed upon the East itself also urgently required evaluation and renewal.

The new deficits were not even considered in relation to the Western European Union, new developments in Central and Eastern Europe or the global changes taking place in economic and political power. New challenges arising needed to be met, not least by the research and higher education sectors.

The Unification Treaty of 31 August 1990[1] and the CDU Government in Bonn laid down the general terms and conditions for the destruction of East Germany's research in Article 38, entitled 'Scholarship and Research'. They duly proceeded to enforce them following unification, unrestrained by any GDR government as it no longer existed.

Thus the institutes and staff of the Academy of Sciences, the Building Academy and the Academy for Agricultural Sciences had their existence guaranteed only until 31 December 1991. On that day all the remaining institutes of these academies were dissolved, following in the footsteps of the GDR Academy of Educational Sciences and other research institutions, which had already been wound up after the *Wende*.

At the end of 1991 the Council of Sciences of the Federal Republic of Germany, made up of scholars and staff from relevant ministries and directly answerable to the German President, completed a 5,000-page study of the higher education sector and research institutions of the former

GDR.[2] The document's recommendations complied with the instructions set out in the Unification Treaty. Structural reform was not foreseen, only the 'integration of scholarship and research ... into the common research structure of the Federal Republic of Germany'.[3]

Quantified, the following picture emerges: the Council of Sciences proposed 11,000 posts for research establishments, excluding universities,[4] and recommended the creation of 2,000 new positions at the universities for scholars coming from the various academies. There were approximately 30,000 people working in these GDR institutes, so that the proposed appointments would only take care of 35 per cent of them.[5]

To gain a fuller picture, the following should be borne in mind:

• The Council of Sciences assessed the institutes and research teams, not the personnel. Their recommendations, therefore, did not concern the continued employment of research and technical staff or their transfer to other institutions.

• The quota of 35 to 40 per cent of previous posts was determined without reference to either the actual number of staff or their suitability. Hence, many scholars viewed their dismissal as incomprehensible and quite arbitrary.

• The slow progress of the evaluation process and the constant threat of closure of all GDR research institutions outside the university sector led in 1990–91 to an exodus of approximately 20 per cent of research specialists and 30 per cent of technical personnel. It was the older, more experienced academics and the young dynamic members of staff who left in search of better prospects either in West German academic institutions or in local private companies. But many simply resigned and retired from working life altogether.

• The departure of those of managerial rank, the uncertainties inherent in the evaluation process and the filling of senior positions with people from West Germany all combined to weaken the former cohesion and efficiency of once successful research teams. This may be expected to have a long-term negative impact on the capacity and efficiency of research in eastern Germany.

• The Scholars' Integration Programme providing for 2,000 posts to be established under the Higher Education Renewal Programme[6] could well depend to a large extent on the ability of the new Federal States to fund it. These have tried to balance the books by putting through waves of redundancies amongst university staff, thus curtailing the vacancies for scholars created as part of the Scholars' Integration Programme.

• Finally the Council of Sciences effectively ignored Research and Development (R&D) units in industry or attached to special ministerial departments. As a result, there was practically no quantitative or qualitative evaluation of this research sector of the former GDR. The collapse of its industry and the disbanding of the government apparatus therefore meant the irretrievable loss of 80 to 90 per cent of an estimated 86,000 jobs.[7] It is doubtful whether this has been compensated in any way by the setting up of new, private research and development companies.[8]

The Aims of the Evaluation of the Academy of Sciences

Recommendations by leading academics to make use of the high-powered departments of the Academy of Sciences to create a fourth research body alongside the Max Planck Society, the Fraunhofer Society and the Association of National Research Centres was rejected out of hand for political reasons. This foiled the opportunity of utilising the Academy's specific research organisation as a link between higher education and industrial research. The institution's contacts, personal or otherwise, with Eastern Europe, which would have enhanced the road to European integration, were allowed to wither away.

Even when the Unification Treaty was agreed, it was apparent that a reform of scholarship and research in a unified Germany was not intended. The political decision had been taken to change nothing in the old Federal States and everything in the newly emerging ones. The research base developed over 40 years was to be destroyed, the vast majority of institutions dissolved; and what was allowed to remain would be incorporated into West German research institutions. On 3 October 1990 the Academy's previous governing body had to give way to a new board and membership; it was turned into a scholarly society segregated from its research institutes and other academic establishments.

Chairman of the Council of Sciences Professor Dieter Simon admitted his failure to realise his vision of a rational reform of scholarship and research within a united Germany. In an article for the *Frankfurter Allgemeine* he referred to the constructive intentions which had initially predominated in the Federal Republic:

The key point was that the old academic establishments in the GDR and the FRG had become obsolete. It was a matter of abandoning them and building a new structure from joint resources – modern and comfortable – without either addition or assimilation. This unique, historic opportunity would be fully exploited.[9]

Gradually, however, the much criticised Western system began to be advanced as one of the best in the world. From this exalted position it was deemed appropriate to proceed vigorously against the humanities and sciences in the East. And precisely this approach became the guideline for the evaluation commissions of the Council of Sciences. Added to this, many of the very modest proposals of the Council of Sciences were brought to nothing by the machinations of bureaucracy:

> The executive ... consists of civil servants ... When the great concept has duly been ground to a pulp it has become a caricature of itself ... A research group will then be politely directed to a non-existing market. An edition *cannot* be continued in this format, a particular organisational plan does *not quite* meet the requirements. Other institutions are the more appropriate authority and other means more suitable. The measure of the civil servant's table becomes the measure of all things.[10]

The toing and froing over the future of a third of Germany's research potential and over the fate of tens of thousands of highly qualified people went on for months and even years.

The dismemberment process did not of course originate within the bureaucratic administration. It began quite definitely in the action taken by the evaluation teams. The criteria stemmed specifically from the conditions and the experience of the academic bodies in the old Federal Republic. The real issues, however, derived from political considerations as well as from concern over adverse competition. Anything that conflicted with the status quo was wound up irrespective of scientific ability, originality or individual suitability. Nowhere was the slightest effort made to gauge the requirements or indeed the social consequences.

Power struggles, market interests and competition over the ever-diminishing research budgets, combined with arrogance towards and ignorance of the specific research conditions in the GDR, created an unholy alliance. The liberal weekly *Die Zeit* described the situation in the following terms:

Since the end of September these evaluating teams, consisting of scholars and bureaucrats from the Bonn Ministry for Education and Science, have been at large in the institutes of the Academy. In many of the places they go they leave a trail of terror as the officers of the Holy Inquisition once did during their witch hunts.

For many of the Academy's staff this meant 'the dissolution of their institutes, the loss of their posts and the irrevocable end of their careers'.[11]

The quality of the assessments was clearly exposed in the procedure. Prior to the evaluation, each institute had to answer 23 questions relating to duties, activities, equipment, financing, national and international cooperation as well as future objectives.

Due to lack of time the majority of the 20 to 30 commission members, among whom there were rarely more than a few experts, had not familiarised themselves with the documents. As a rule, they only met when the evaluation actually took place. The commission members were not known to the Academy's staff, nor were they introduced to them at the time of the hearing.

The format of the evaluation interviews was practically identical everywhere: consultation with the management bodies; then with staff in the absence of management; followed by a walk-about around the institute; finally an internal discussion among the members of the commission. In a private meeting, the commission's head informed the director of the institute of their preliminary conclusions. The selection procedure remained secret.

The hurried pace with which the talks and inspections took place, the lack of expertise, the lack of in-depth examinations and the commission's incomprehensible recommendations plunged many institute staff into a state of helplessness, disappointment and despair.

Many had hoped that an assessment to determine the staff's prospects would be based on their own level of expertise, the value of their research and the efficiency of their research teams. In fact the opposite was the case. The evaluation became a factor in devaluing their academic qualifications and their life's work.

A Case in Point

In terms of approach there was no fundamental difference between evaluating institutions relating to the humanities or to the natural sciences.

To illustrate an evaluation, the example is taken of a science institute which was among the first to be assessed.

During a visit of only two days' duration, 24 and 25 September 1990, the Central Institute of Electron Physics (ZIE) was assessed by an evaluation commission. At that time the institute had 650 staff working in eight research and three sectional departments.

In preparation for the evaluation the institute had produced a 200-page report. Staff adopted a positive attitude to the assessment and expected the commission to examine the content of their physics research and to decide about the integration of key sectors into overall research in West Germany. However, there were no competent scientists capable of appraising about 60 per cent of the work of the sections and departments. In addition the yardstick employed was inadequate because the institute was being compared to West German university research, when in fact it was comparable to an independent national research centre. All in all it was soon evident that the institute was to become an example of the ruthless elimination of the well-developed East Berlin research scene.

Irrespective of professional competence the leading personnel were removed at every level. In the spring of 1990, Professor Rudi Gündel, a scientist who had always been openly critical of political decisions which hampered research and who had unreservedly promoted the greatest possible independence in research, was elected Director of the ZIE in a secret ballot with 80 per cent of the votes. As a direct result of the intense political discrimination exercised by the commission, he resigned.

In a special publication of the Association of Democratic Scientists entitled *Evaluating the Evaluation*, Peter Carl, former member of staff at the ZIE, wrote: 'From the start the atmosphere at the meetings was hostile, the prejudice of the commission was unmistakable.'[12]

A right-wing conservative member of the commission that assessed the institute, Professor Harald Fritsch from Munich, described their intentions thus:

All professors will be dismissed on a set date, equally all heads of departments in the Academy and the Academy professors. They will not be made redundant immediately but rather demoted to the posts of senior lecturers or assistants on a temporary contract. As I said, I consider the removal of all professors a matter of urgency.[13]

What Remained of GDR Research

The Academy's research team, dissolved at the end of 1991, had consisted of six sections: mathematics and computer science; physics; chemistry; biosciences and medicine; geo- and cosmic sciences; social sciences and humanities. A total of 55 research institutes (including 14 from the social sciences and humanities) belonged to these sections as well as 23 further establishments affiliated to the research sections.

Approximately half of the research potential was in Berlin. Of 23,675 researchers employed (average figure for 1989), 11,942 were working in Berlin. A total of 15,096 were involved in research and development (R&D): 8,079 in research, 7,017 in a scientific-technical capacity. The achievements of that year include nearly 7,000 scientific publications, 1,130 patents registered in the GDR and the holding of 800 conferences and similar events.[14]

It has been established that by 1992 R&D capacity in the former GDR had fallen by 70 per cent. Following this rigorous dismantling of East Germany's research capacity, considerable resources were, however, invested recently in reconstruction on a diminished scale. The Ministry for Research and Technology alone authorised the spending of DM1.6 billion in 1992 and DM1.75 billion in 1993. These funds went to set up three new national research centres and eight branches of existing West German establishments, employing a total staff of 1,700.

Financed by the national and Federal State exchequers, a further 28 research establishments created employment for 3,300 people. On top of this, institutes of the Fraunhofer Society and the Max Planck Society created 1,000 and 900 jobs respectively. Another 1,900 posts for individual scientists were temporarily financed by the Ministry for R&D within the Scholars' Integration Programme.[15] From the former Academy 2,125 academicians were put on temporary low-paid job-creation schemes (max. two years) financed by the Federal Labour Office. By the end of 1993, a total of 10,925 people (46 per cent of the former full-time staff) were in gainful employment of some sort.[16] Naturally, great efforts were made by those affected to keep research teams and therefore jobs going, to find interim solutions, or to create new structures.

The Research and Technology Park Berlin-Adlershof (FTA), situated on the grounds of the former Academy, is one such venture.[17] Of the approximately 15,000 people employed by the Academy in Berlin, in particular in the suburbs of Adlershof and Buch, 11,000 were still working in December 1990. One year later only 8,000 had a contract, and by the end of 1991, only 3,500 staff remained of the 5,500 originally working at the Berlin-Adlershof branch of the Academy. Although the Council of Sciences positively evaluated a number of scientific working groups at that branch employing a total of 1,300 personnel, it slashed at least 2,200 other posts there.

The Research and Technology Park was established in Berlin-Adlershof, authorised by a Berlin Senate decision taken on 15 September 1992.[18] Since 1993, 18 scientific establishments, with a combined staff of 1,448, have operated within this complex, supported by a number of sponsors. There is also a wide-ranging, technologically advanced industrial sector with 132 enterprises having a total workforce of 2,422.[19] By the year 2000 it should employ 10,000 people.

However, at the end of 1993 a third of the employees at the Research and Technology Park were only on temporary and therefore insecure jobs under the job-creation scheme in the field of science and technology. In addition, only 24 people were directly involved in the academic sphere whilst a further 202 researchers were still looking for university posts under the Scholars' Integration Programme.

The main employer of those in employment under job-creation schemes was the 280 member-strong Adlershof Society for Science and Technology, a self-help organisation for scientists.[20] In the existing adverse conditions, this society strove to preserve Berlin's innovative potential, which had given the city an advantage over other locations, until such time as the demand for competent personnel in the economic and research sectors increased again. The Society also provided at least temporary protection against unemployment. The job-creation schemes involved in R&D were likely to remain crucial in providing 'shelter' for highly qualified people who would otherwise be lost to research as a result of redundancies.

The Berlin Senate also set up a whole series of projects including a national research institute for chemistry, BESSY II (High Intensity Synchrotron Radiation Generator), as well as a campus for the natural sciences at Humboldt University.

All in all, however, the collapse of industrial research in East Germany meant a loss of innovative power, a conclusion confirmed by the Ministry for Research and Technology, the German Chamber of Industry and Commerce and the Federation of German Industry. The truth is that out of an original workforce of 85,000 industrial researchers, there 'hardly remained anything worth mentioning'.[21]

Self-Renewal of East German Universities Halted

The transformation of higher education in East Germany after the end of the nazi dictatorship was propelled by a predominantly antifascist pioneering spirit. But this spirit was soon stifled. All autonomy in research and education was withdrawn and constant political interference by the leadership of the state became the order of the day. The SED party hierarchy seized control in particular of all personnel matters. They decided who was to be employed, promoted, and who was not; who could publish what, who gained permission to hold guest lectures or could study abroad.

In practice, however, especially in the 1980s, the party leadership became very careful about upsetting non-party political professors. This was accompanied by increasing liberalisation in research and lecture content. Unfortunately, students did not benefit significantly. Pedantic course planning stunted initiative and independent thought. This, combined with the predominant notion that inside four or five years academic staff had to achieve set targets and produce a graduate out of every enrolled student, had the effect of regimenting university life. Students wasted a lot of time in pointless political activities and work brigades. The student branch of the state youth organisation, the Free German Youth (FDJ), which in the early post-war years had played a role in the democratic reform of higher education, had long since become more or less fossilised. It was an instrument of the party apparatus that simply patronised a reluctant membership. Quite a significant section of the non-professorial teaching staff underwent this regimentation by the party. Some sought refuge in developing reform projects or protected students from reprisals.

The turn towards democratic reform was made possible by the implosion within the GDR in 1989. It was welcomed and enthusiastically supported by the majority of university staff and students.

With one or two exceptions, the long-established and internationally recognised universities and colleges remained. However, academic staff suffered by and large the same fate as that of the GDR Academy of Sciences and other non-university academic institutions. Through direct political intervention, many departments were closed, others were eroded by changes in personnel and by additional devices that appeared politically motivated.

The entire academic staff had to go through a reappointment process under which the applicant was politically vetted by a personnel commission. The outcome was that over 50 per cent of those employed in higher education in 1989 were ousted from their posts.[22]

This made it possible, within a short period of time, to replace at least the core but generally the majority of professors with candidates from the western part of Germany. What unfolded was an unrestrained race from the West to fill these positions, much to the detriment of the East.

It must be of concern that, under various pretexts, recognised academics and specialists, who had for years been pressing for reforms, were excluded and generally eliminated from academic life. In particular this affected those who had been among the opposition forces during GDR times and who, under the new conditions, had set in motion a self-renewal programme at academic institutions.

It was evidently regarded as dangerous that a more autonomous democratic authority, with greater participation by non-professorial academic staff and students, might develop in the East such as might be more radical than in the West. There were examples at almost every university, especially in Berlin. In an effort to avert this development, the new short-lived autonomy was dismantled and replaced with a disguised command structure. The task was shared and carried out by the national and later local ministries (key posts being staffed with 'Western imports'), by West German professors at all decision-making levels as well as by opportunists among the East German academic staff, including a number who had generally been inconspicuous conformists in GDR times.

As a result, everything that was imposed on the universities from outside seemed aimed almost exclusively at changing the institutional aspects, the composition of personnel and the general legal conditions of employment. Consequently, a critical analysis never took place as regards content within the GDR's academic system. The development of 41 years was simply brushed aside. Its experiences went unheeded. Attempts at self-assertion or a constructive critical search for a new, independent direction were all thwarted by threats of redundancy, defamation and dismissals.

Such a blanket condemnation of higher education in the former GDR had not actually been the primary aim of the Council of Sciences of the Federal Republic of Germany, even if there were numerous examples of inquisitorial procedures by commissions and by the temporarily appointed deans from the West. The reason the Council did not achieve meaningful renewal within the East German university system was because it lacked the broad-minded approach that would have generated a constructive and open debate. This would have provided

opportunities for a much needed reform of the *entire* academic scene
in a united Germany. This deficiency was identified by Professor Jürgen
Kocka,[23] one of the principal evaluators in the area of humanities. He
initiated and supervised the establishment of a research centre on contemporary studies at the new regional university of Potsdam. Its purpose
was the reassessment of the development of GDR historical studies independently of political constraints and without avoiding difficult questions.
The dialogue within this research project was marked by openness and
by an interdisciplinary approach as well as a multiplicity of academic
and political standpoints including that of the East German specialists.
Professor Kocka achieved a productive and constructive mix of people
from both within Germany, East and West, and from abroad. And it
is precisely this that has caused overt and covert attacks on this successful
project.[24]

Democratisation Foiled

Unfortunately such positive examples are the exception. A whole maze
of West German legislation, by and large steeped in conservative values
and behavioural patterns, was imposed upon the East German higher
education sector.

This turned the process of unification into a one-way affair, where
there was no exchange of views and experiences on an equal basis among
academics. While East German guest lecturers were few and far between
in the West, frequently second- and third-rate West German professors
have taken over the running of the universities in the East.

In contrast, as early as the autumn of 1989, students, academics and
technical university staff in the East had begun a democratic self-renewal
process which comprised three elements:

- Renewal in terms of personnel and subject matter, creating democratically elected boards of management and carrying out a critical
  reappraisal of the distortions since 1945.
- The utilisation of diverse political, academic, financial and organisational assistance from the West.
- The development of new concepts for teaching and research in
  order to identify a place in the total German academic scene,
  combined with a critical utilisation of the experience of West German
  universities.

The Unification Treaty severely curtailed these endeavours. Based on its provisions, it became perfectly legal to wind up higher education establishments, departments and institutes. This seriously damaged the self-confidence of the movement for renewal and often brought it to an untimely end. Simultaneously it led to the wholesale defamation of academic staff. In December 1990, the regional governments and the Berlin Senate[25] decided to dissolve a whole range of academic establishments, and dismiss staff on a large scale.

Although differences existed there seemed to be essentially three goals:

- To prevent any independent role being played by the East German universities within the German Association of Higher Education. Such a development could have arisen as a result of the renewal process taking place.
- To frustrate the regeneration of socially critical left-wing and Marxist positions.
- To deprive this part of Germany of the human resources and the structures necessary for an honest and critical appraisal of GDR history.

This is how a West German sociologist and academic at Oldenburg's Carl von Ossietzky University summarised his criticism:

The concept underlying the higher education reform in the former GDR is clear: change the legislation, change the institutions, change the staff and then everything will fall into (West German) place. Some things remain: all those institutions which are older than the GDR; those staff who were persecuted or discriminated against; also many of those who were allowed to cultivate international contacts during GDR times;[26] depending on the budget, this included quite a few who were not conspicuous in the GDR and who fit in equally well with the new conditions. The huge number that remain are written off, wound up, forced into early retirement, dismissed, pushed out and sometimes graciously kept on temporary part-time contracts.[27]

These remarks could also be applied to the post-*Wende* developments in primary and secondary education, which many teachers had sought to reform after October 1989. The end of the 'leading role of the party' created the opportunity to develop the inherent potential of the comprehensive schools. This system ensured that all children received a common academic, cultural and physical education and also allowed for early contact with the world of work and industry. It was essential to inject pluralist vitality into a stagnant system which in theory was based on the principles of student self-determination and the co-determination of students and parents in the schools. In the aftermath of unification it was all abolished. Instead, the East got the West German three-tier school system which, as was widely recognised by educationalists and parents alike, was itself crying out for reform. This system allowed for larger class sizes in the primary schools as well as in the non-grammar secondary school sector than was ever the case in the GDR. The grammar schools, deemed the schools for the élite, received more funding and were better equipped. Tens of thousands of teachers were dismissed and joined the ranks of their equally redundant colleagues from the severely curtailed pre-school and after-school care centres.

Surveys conducted in 1993 by the Institute for School Development Research[28] show that, in the meantime, every fifth respondent wanted the GDR school system back. That was four times as many as in 1991. The majority still 'opposed party political educational content' in the curriculum but nevertheless favoured the GDR's school structure and its centralised vocational training. The respondents, usually parents of at least one child of school age, consider only the grammar schools equal to the GDR's secondary schools where students studied to *Abitur* level (equivalent to English A-level). They also demanded that there should be more involvement of parents and students in the schools.[29]

Losses in Academic Potential

All university departments of Marxism–Leninism in Berlin and the new Federal States were closed, even though they had shifted to a pluralist approach to philosophy after the *Wende*. Also wound up were the majority of departments of economics and law as well as a number of faculties attached to the humanities. Some of these were later re-established with a largely West German academic staff. But there was no replacement for the Berlin College of Economics, the College of Law and Administration in Potsdam-Babelsberg, the College of Physical Culture in Leipzig and the College of Agriculture in Meissen.

Also eliminated was the Naval College of Engineering in Warnemünde-Wustrow from which had graduated captains and helmsmen for nearly 200 years. Between 1846 and 1945 some 2,688 students trained as helmsmen and another 1,806 studied to become captains. However, the college underwent its most significant development between 1949 and 1989 when the training and research programme was extended and diplomas were awarded for navigation, marine engineering and marine radio engineering. The college also offered postgraduate research. Four times in its history it was able to avert closure – in 1896/97, 1918/19, 1925 and 1946/47. But in 1989 the opposition from Hamburg and Bremen had a more powerful lobby in Bonn than the East Germans from Wustrow, Warnemünde or Rostock. The abolition of this establishment was one of the saddest events in German maritime history.[30]

Between 1989 and 1993 there was a cut of over 50 per cent of the staff in higher education – 58 per cent of non-professorial academic staff, 51 per cent in the non-academic area. The number of professorships did not change significantly but they were mostly filled by West German personnel, which meant that 60 to 70 per cent of their former East German holders lost their jobs.

Expressed in actual figures, 34,600 posts were cut by the autumn of 1993 from an original number of 66,200 posts in 1989.[31] But this was not the last of the cutbacks. Dismissals continued after that, including those of holders of the large number of temporary contracts as they expired. Of the remaining 10,100 employed in the non-professorial sector, only 20 to 25 per cent were still in permanent full-time posts, all the rest having been given temporary in place of their formerly permanent contracts. The latter group would have to leave the higher education sector within three to five years. This was clearly discriminatory compared to West Germany where the average ratio between permanent and temporary staff was 50:50. In Bremen and Hamburg as many as 90 per cent of the non-professorial academic staff had permanent posts.[32] The alignment of educational standards to Western levels brought to East Germany overcrowded tutorials and the danger that the duration of courses would be exceeded. And on top of that there was the whole issue of graduate unemployment.[33]

The Wrangle over Humboldt University and the Charité University Hospital

On the basis of the Amendment to the Higher Education Act, the Berlin senator for the sciences, Professor Manfred Erhardt (CDU), was able to interfere in a drastic way in East Berlin's higher education sector. He only confirmed the professorships of those he had appointed himself or who were newly appointed under Federal legislation for higher

education. He issued a directive to close Humboldt University's departments of history, education, economics, law and philosophy and to dismiss
all their staff. This put an end to the process of self-renewal and reform
in departments which had initially resisted centralist intervention. On
18 January 1991 Professor Heinrich Fink, the first democratically elected
vice-chancellor, presented a document entitled 'Principles, Aims,
Procedures and Measures to Renew Humboldt University', which had
been fully endorsed by the University's board. In it he stated:

> In particular in the arts and social sciences departments as well as in
> the law faculty, new course and examination regulations will be
> drawn up in conjunction with the Senate committee for sciences and
> research, the Free University Berlin (West) and the judiciary.[34]

Prior to the senator's interference in the University's autonomy, 144
guest lecturers from the old Federal States were teaching at Humboldt
University. Despite this, measures to wind up the existing structures
were passed by the Berlin Senate, measures which directly affected 1,500
employees, 6,500 full-time students and 3,800 extramural students. In
its resolution for renewal, the University board of management had
planned for changes in personnel associated with the new course
contents and on account of the legal and moral misconduct by some
staff in the past. However, it also carried a warning:

> But the intellectual renewal of Humboldt University must not be
> understood to mean the filling of the university's physical and organ-
> isational shell with new people who did not participate in the
> experiences which shaped this university over the past 40 years.[35]

Senator Erhardt was not content merely to dissolve specific departments. He went on to organise a systematic campaign of defamation
against the vice-chancellor, and did not rest until Professor Fink had
been dismissed without notice for allegedly having cooperated with the
Stasi.[36] The senator and his political friends were suspicious of Professor
Fink and other reform-minded people from the former GDR who did
not change into conformists but wanted unification to take place as
between equals. The Sunday newspaper *Das Deutsche Allgemeine Sonntagsblatt* had said in an article about Heinrich Fink's election as
vice-chancellor:

This was a good choice, no doubt. Fink represents the opposition movement in the former GDR. In the autumn he was physically attacked by the *Stasi* outside East Berlin's Gethsemane Church. The 55-year-old is too deeply rooted in the history of this land and people to promote a head-over-heels sell-out.[37]

The attacks on Humboldt University continued. Besides intolerable cuts in the areas of finance and posts, the jewel in the University's crown, the Charité university hospital, was made the object of open and underhand attacks. The hospital, which was founded in 1710, comprised all the clinics associated with the School of Medicine. Efforts went largely into undermining the institution by closing important clinics, cancelling research projects or sacking doctors.

For example among the 152 new appointments, only a third had held the posts previously. Internationally recognised professors such as the surgeon Professor Helmut Wolff, urologist and nephrologist Professor Peter Althaus or immunologist and AIDS researcher Professor Thomas Porstmann were defamed and pressurised out of their posts.[38]

Under the guise of ever-decreasing budgets for Berlin, attempts continued to be made from different quarters to take crucial areas of responsibility away from the Charité, supposedly to fuse them with the West Berlin Steglitz Clinic and the Rudolf Virchow Clinic. This would affect, for example, forensic medicine, paediatric surgery, radio therapy and heart, kidneys and liver transplant surgery. These moves brought the staff of the Charité, the dean of the School of Medicine, Professor Harald Mau[39] and the University's chancellor Marlis Dürkop into the arena. It became an ongoing conflict. Even the enormously improved situation in technical equipment after 1989 and the more modern and open-minded approach in some fields hardly compensated for the loss of specialists.[40]

Destroying the Health System

In the final years of the GDR, it became increasingly apparent that the material resources of East Germany's health system were out of date. The GDR produced high-quality medical equipment but almost all of it was exported. Only a handful of prestige hospitals and research establishments received imported or top-quality home-produced equipment. By the mid-1980s it was an open secret that almost all hospitals were in need of a total overhaul and re-equipment which would, even by conservative estimates, have cost the GDR between 60 and 80 billion Marks.[41] Those in power were not prepared to fund this. There was in the GDR a deep gulf between workable concepts and insurmountable obstacles, caused by the country's economic weakness, an over-emphasis on ideology, and the party leadership's arrogance and anti-intellectualism.

The political *Wende* in 1989 brought with it a rapid improvement in medical technology, which was soon translated into better patient care. All the same, the GDR had excellently trained medical staff and a high per capita ratio of doctors. In this respect there was little difference compared to the old Federal Republic. In addition, despite all the material shortages, a medical system operated which cared for all, from the very young to the very ill and very old. Improvements in the sphere of medical equipment following the *Wende* coincided with the destruction of the GDR's complex and diverse health system. The patients' interests were not the primary consideration; ignorance and a mania for change caused irreversible damage.

Thus, for example, prophylaxis in childhood and the obligatory immunisation of children were thrown overboard even though they had proved successful in maintaining public health, and had, indeed, been much admired by doctors in the West. The same fate befell research and treatment in specialised areas, as well as in the outpatient health centres, which had found international recognition.

In the health system, too, the rigorous devaluation and elimination of GDR achievements were central features following unification with the West. Immediately after 1989, several issues were addressed as a matter of urgency. Not among these, however, was the state of buildings and equipment, which needed improving. Instead, the social and health insurance system was totally restructured in line with the Western model, and the apparatus itself became bloated, with the number employed increasing fivefold from 6,000 in the GDR system to 30,000. Many doctors and physiotherapists had become self-employed, and owed large sums to the banks. Most health care establishments at the workplace, and outpatient health and social care centres, were dissolved. Older doctors, who were reluctant to take out huge bank loans for equipment and who used to work in health centres, were by and large forced into early retirement, unless they were lucky enough to be able to go into partnership in one of the few joint or group practices. The social care and health care system experienced a range of entirely new requirements resulting from mass unemployment, early retirement and homelessness, but also from formerly marginal problems such as drug abuse and AIDS.

Just as was the case in the research and higher education sectors, so too the West German norm was imposed in the sphere of health insurance and medical care. It very soon became abundantly clear that the system itself required fundamental reform. People arrived at this conclusion on account of higher insurance contributions and increased charges for prescriptions and prophylactic cures. Despite the poor standard of equipment and financial provisions in the GDR health system, most people had trusted the system as it was free and accessible to all. It had guaranteed a complete network of care and preventive medicine, thanks especially to the efficient, highly qualified personnel.

The West German health system proved to be increasingly expensive. With the profits for the pharmaceutical industry and more and more commercialised private practices, costs escalated. Many East Germans questioned the decision to destroy the GDR health system and abandon its structures and cohesion, which had proved to be more effective and more economical than those of the West.[42]

The General Medical Council for Berlin and its president, Dr Ellis E. Huber, did everything in their power to save the GDR health centres, but they failed because of the political narrow-mindedness of the establishment.[43] The Medical Council had sought to use the GDR health experience to create a socially oriented, cost-efficient and integrated outpatient health care system within a united Germany. But that was not to be.

Getting Back to Private Practice

Administrative interference in medical research and teaching was accompanied by the closure of important non-university establishments. This first happened to the Sports Medical Service, employing 1,500, and to the Academy for Further Medical Qualification. The latter had played a role in collating international research and making it available to doctors, in order to keep them up to date with the latest developments in medicine.

Under the conditions of the German market economy, the state steadily downgraded its responsibility and obligations towards its citizens. This tendency made itself felt especially in the health system in the area of the former GDR. It was apparent to the general population that health care for children was suffering particularly, as was the integrated system of preventive medicine, outpatient and inpatient treatment and after-care. This system was totally destroyed regardless of the consequences to patients:

• In 1988, 84 per cent of children under the age of 2 were being looked after, medically as well, in crèches in the GDR. From the age of 2 until they reached school age, 94 per cent attended kindergartens and, during the primary school stage, 83 per cent went to after-school child-care centres. From a medical viewpoint, this guaranteed continuous medical care including obligatory immunisation. These services were greatly reduced. Parents were no longer invited at regular intervals to present their children for immunisation. They were responsible for having the children inoculated at the overcrowded GP's practices.

• In 1989 the GDR had 622 health centres (of which 151 were at workplaces). These were quite considerable establishments, employing on average 21 doctors. In addition there were 1,023 outpatient departments (of which 364 were at workplaces). A half-hearted clause contained in the Unification Treaty guaranteed the continuation of these health centres for three to five years, but that did not prevent most of them closing. Workplace health centres went along with the collapse of industry, and so too did those based in the residential areas, because local authorities were unable to support them financially. Massive pressure from the national organisation for GPs, backed by certain political and judicial tricks, sounded the death-knell for a medical tradition going back to the period of the Weimar Republic. The first health centres were set up immediately after the First World War in Berlin, for example at the *Haus der Gesundheit* (House of Health) at Alexanderplatz. They were supported by the national health system in an attempt to protect poorer patients from profiteering private physicians. In the GDR these health centres became standard for public health care and private doctors were the exception.

• Of 100 former health centres and outpatient departments in East Berlin in 1989, only twelve remained, the only ones the Berlin Senate was prepared to finance. Approximately 1,000 doctors were either made redundant or forced at short notice into self-employment. This effectively meant the winding up of a cost-effective alternative to the Western system of private practices. It has also adversely affected the integrated medical approach, which had combined prophylaxis, therapy, dispensary and socio-psychological treatment.

• Other centres which were also decimated were those for ante-natal and post-natal care, child and youth health care, health care for diabetics or rheumatics, for the mentally or the chronically ill, the handicapped, and treatment centres for patients with tumours and lung diseases.

Doctors in the East now had to gear their work to the principle of profit. Competition replaced cooperation. Keen to follow the trend of using as much high-tech equipment as was the custom in the West, they found themselves under constant pressure to offer patients super-fluous services. Most of them lacked the special know-how required and moreover had less time compared to before,[44] which led to an increased number of inaccurate diagnoses. In this respect the improved standard in technical equipment proved a mixed blessing, despite the undeniable improvement this equipment brought to patients, after years of shortages.

A medical association, Medicine and Society, was established in October 1991, mainly by East German and East Berlin doctors, to cope with some of these predicaments. The association set out to dissemi-nate information to physicians and the general population, and to encourage doctors and other medical personnel to undergo further training. The association played an important role in identifying defi-ciencies and developing alternatives. Publications, lectures and conferences were organised in which the GDR health system was critically appraised with a view to drawing attention to its positive features as an option for united Germany.

GDR Cultural Heritage

Culture and the arts were always an integral part of GDR society. It would be wrong to conclude, however, that they were merely the handmaids of the system.

GDR culture and arts were accessible to and enjoyed by broad sections of the population – literature was read and discussed widely; everybody knew the Dresden Art Gallery; subsidised tickets ensured that theatres and concerts were open to all. Writers' workshops for non-professionals and countless other cultural activities were promoted, from stamp-collecting to local dancing and fine arts groups.

Part of this broadly based concept of culture was the principle of sports for all – the very foundation of competitive sports. It also included children's summer camps organised by the trade union movement, free library facilities in the workplace and in hospitals, extra-curricular clubs and societies at school run by parents. On the one hand, the aim was to promote pleasure in the arts and to enhance people's creativity; but it also generated a sense of community for all irrespective of social background, sex and age.

But of course the SED leadership insisted on determining the type of culture to be promoted. Restrictions which seemed acceptable immediately after 1945 as a safeguard against disseminating nazi literature and art deformed into control and censorship by the party apparatus over the entire output of artists and all those working in the area of culture. Inevitably this filtered down in a patronising fashion to the recipients of culture, the population at large. More often than not, it meant the suppression of initiative and self-reliance, where artistic and cultural activities impinged on the public domain. Right up to the 1960s, the SED art gurus tolerated only works of art which they deemed socialist and realist. The German, European and world cultural heritage was indeed acknowledged and made accessible; but because the SED officers' criteria for evaluating works of art and their creators were frequently philistine, they often banned literature, music, plays or films which happened to conflict with the received norms, and did not allow the general public unrestricted access to these works. This happened to Franz Kafka's novels, kept under lock and key for many years.

The attitude eventually changed. In the 1970s and 1980s, artistic quality came to be almost exclusively determined by the degree of recognition obtained in West Germany. Artists were guaranteed a number of privileges such as freedom of travel and a good income at home, but only if they were politically well behaved, desisting from public criticism of society, and generally conformed to the norms expected of them. There was less direct censorship, although on occasion novels, paintings, films and television programmes would be withdrawn. The ban placed on some *perestroika* films at the end of the 1980s gave rise to considerable protest by large numbers of people who wrote to the papers and the SED leaders censuring this decision.

Through its dogmatic approach, the establishment not only created conformity steeped in hypocrisy, but also came up against an increasingly effective, diverse and to some extent successful resistance. There is ample evidence of this in the way GDR novels were received by the general public in the 1970s and 1980s, and in a growing number of independent groups with agendas that diverged to a greater or lesser degree from the official party line – for example, gay and lesbian groups, feminists, environmentalists, artists', writers' and music workshops.

Thus, large sections of the cultural intelligentsia grew increasingly disillusioned, particularly during the last 20 years of GDR existence, although many, especially the older generation, continued to believe that the system could be reformed and never gave up their hopes for democratic openness and economic prosperity. After the war they had committed themselves to building a socially caring alternative to the system of profit-making and it was naturally difficult for them to face up to the fact that their convictions and aspirations might have been in vain. Others, in particular the younger generation of artists, became increasingly vocal in their criticism of political conditions, and openly demanded reform. This gave rise to a new affinity between artists and their public. And it was in this spirit that artists organised the biggest free mass rally experienced in the GDR on 4 November 1989 in East Berlin's central square, Alexanderplatz. Their hopes were high and so possibly were their illusions. They were determined to transform the GDR into a better country with a democratic and pluralist culture, a land nobody would feel compelled to leave.

In the aftermath of the fall of the Wall on 9 November 1989, anyone interested in politics soon realised that it was the beginning of the end for the GDR. From then on, East Germans lived within an all-German political framework. And from the outset, it was the old Federal Republic which took the initiative.

If the post-*Wende* political leadership in Germany had had its way, four decades of development would be ignored or denigrated and GDR history banned from living memory. The cultural identity of eastern Germany, the product of 40 years of common historical development within the GDR, was, after all, shared by the five new Federal States – Mecklenburg-West Pomerania, Brandenburg, Saxony-Anhalt, Saxony and Thuringia – despite their regional differences.

Theatres and libraries were initially to be preserved but lack of public funds increasingly put them at risk. Other former state establishments such as youth clubs, where they still existed, struggled for survival. GDR publishing houses, record companies and concert promoters were taken over by Western companies or put out of business through competition. They were wound up or went bankrupt because their former sponsors, the industries in the East with their cultural funds, disappeared. West German agencies, film-makers and television companies only rarely employed East German actors and actresses. West German publishers only took on board the most prominent of GDR authors.

Many composers, sculptors, singers, dancers and others in the entertainment industry faced great financial difficulties.

The experience of life in the GDR over 40 years, with all its contradictions, hopes and disappointments, had provided potent creative impulses which GDR art, literature and the stage reflected. It constituted a potential for the constructive assessment of the *Wende* and the new challenges arising from it.

A central motive of many cultural activities and debates in the wake of the *Wende* was to prevent East German culture from being discarded, to approach it in the spirit of critical and constructive appraisal, and to protect all the grassroot activities.[45] It was hoped that the East Germans would be allowed to contribute to a critical and constructive cultural perspective for unified Germany.

Such a development depended of course on whether united Germany would find the strength to critically reassess the cultural deficiencies that had developed in both states over 40 years. Indeed, in this way Germany might have made an important contribution to European unity. After unification, however, the cultural scene in East Germany underwent profound upheavals, and money rather than ideas tended to dominate the debates in the fields of culture.

To maintain and reform theatres, museums and libraries required not only financial resources but also political vision. The sudden loss of even the viable sections of industry, the de facto removal of many well-known artists and entertainers from public life and the exodus of young and dynamic talent to the West[46] all contributed significantly to people losing their self-confidence. Initially, the euphoria in the East led to an uncritical acceptance of Western norms, causing people to disregard their own history. Subsequently, however, this gave way to a more discriminating view, not only of everyday life[47] in general but also of the cultural tradition.[48]

A new approach gradually made itself felt in the East but also, to some extent, in the West, counteracting the trend to erase all facets of GDR history or present a biased picture of them. It involved all areas of culture ranging from creative art and criticism to the preservation of historic monuments.

Contradictory Features of the New Cultural Life

This cultural revival could have availed itself of certain material facilities which had been established during and even prior to the *Wende*. But the German Government and the established political parties, including the SPD, decided, after some hesitation, to wind up the GDR politically and economically. They gave neither the Modrow interim government nor the first and last democratically elected de Maizière GDR government any breathing space. Pressure was increased by the demand for monetary union on the part of about 40 per cent of the electorate. In the cultural field the mad rush towards unification pursued in other areas was, thankfully, avoided. The policy adopted by Herbert Schirmer,[49] last GDR Minister of Culture, was to 'buy time for culture'. This proved most advantageous and did in fact save a certain fraction of the GDR cultural heritage.

The biannual cultural agreements between the GDR and the FRG with monthly meetings to ensure their smooth running, a practice in operation since 1986, contributed to this. On 19 December 1989, three months before the last parliamentary elections, another two-year agreement was signed in Dresden by GDR Prime Minister Dr Hans Modrow and Chancellor Dr Helmut Kohl. It was scheduled to expire on 31 December 1991, and its aim was to guarantee a broad range of cultural activities. An all-German cultural commission was established comprising representatives of the Federal Government, the local governments, the GDR Government and four groups of experts. The commission met three times and on 29 September 1990, at its last meeting, a resolution was passed to preserve the cultural achievements of the former GDR and continue to contribute to its cultural funds out of the fund for 'German unity'.

Financial means could, therefore, be made available to a number of needy GDR artists. Cultural assets of European standing were safeguarded and the cultural infra-structure preserved. A number of areas were identified for special attention: acting; fine arts; music; literature; film and media; libraries; museums; archives and collections; the preservation of historical monuments; youth and adult education; social culture; the upkeep of local traditions; folk-art and the study of local history. Article 35 of the Unification Treaty acknowledged the importance of culture in the unification process and laid down that 'the cultural fund will be continued transitionally until 31 December 1994 to promote culture, the arts and artists'.[50]

Although it was those in power who decided which cultural assets were worth preserving, the financial aid made available in this sector was, on the whole, significant. Thus the Ministry of the Interior allocated a total of DM3.3 billion in its budgets for 1991, 1992 and 1993 for the areas mentioned above and for important individual cultural institutions in the new Federal States. However, when the Federal Government decided to transfer responsibility for cultural funding to the Federal States and local authorities by the end of 1994,[51] it was clear that this would lead to cutbacks in the cultural area.

Whether culture and the arts would thrive would depend largely on the personal commitment of those in charge of the administration and of the politicians, on whether there remained a sound cultural infrastructure and sufficient funds were available. Although the state withdrew increasingly from its cultural sponsorship, there were men and women who proved that individual commitment can achieve things.

The Berlin Senate decided to erect a memorial, both as a reminder and as a warning, to the burning of the books by the nazis on 10 May 1933 on Bebelplatz.[52] On that site, an empty library was to be visible through a window in the ground. While this would recall the GDR's rather formal treatment of the nazi past on the one hand, it would also remind people of the more recent past when, after the *Wende*, the East Berlin and East German libraries had undergone a rigorous 'cleansing' of GDR books and East German publishing houses had wheeled out new books, fresh from the printers, among them prestigious reference books and licensed editions by internationally recognised authors,[53] to dump them on the rubbish tips.

In Beeskow, a small town in Brandenburg, a cultural and educational centre was established. The thirteenth-century Wasserburg, a fortress built on the lake, was reconstructed at the expense of the Federal, State and local governments. Altogether DM4 million was invested in this project and in the setting up of two museums and a number of studios there. A series of events took place to recapture aspects of East German intellectual life.

A collection of GDR 'Commissioned Art' was likewise exhibited there. The initiator and director of the institution was Herbert Schirmer, last GDR Minister for Culture. He had collected 300 paintings and 2,000 drawings from GDR days, hoping their exhibition would stimulate an unbiased assessment of GDR art.[54]

In Mecklenburg-West Pomerania, too, much was done at Federal State and regional levels to promote culture. Art and artists' societies were set up, national parks created, theatres reformed and, among other things, a cultural map published.[55]

Notwithstanding such isolated positive developments, however, the overriding impression was of a dearth of general creative concepts and little chance for art to flourish. The disastrous financial situation of the regional and local authorities seriously impeded all plans to promote the arts. In the old Federal Republic a whole network of structures had emerged which kept the cultural infrastructure independent of the market. Such structures were non-existent in the new Federal States. Long-term state subsidies were therefore indispensable if profit was not to be the only criterion by which to decide what should survive.

In Berlin there was no plan on how to combine the two separate cultural entities of East and West Berlin, with their often twin structures. Decisions were generally based on budgetary considerations only, without any consideration for cultural or historical parameters. This is not, of course, to underestimate the gigantic undertaking involved in assessing and reorganising the different cultural activities in the two parts of Berlin, bearing in mind their duplication,[56] traditions and new requirements.

However, there were those who with great commitment made every effort to reform the cultural and educational scene. They encouraged people to critically analyse the past, and develop visions of the future.

Thanks to the tireless efforts of voluntary or poorly paid enthusiasts on job-creation schemes, some of the GDR's cultural heritage was preserved. The Unification Treaty gave culture and the arts a slightly better deal than agriculture, industry and scholarship. Nevertheless, on the whole, capital is certainly not the champion of art for the people.

Notes

1. *Vertrag zwischen der Bundesrepublik Deutschland und der Deutschen Demokratischen Republik über die Herstellung der Einheit Deutschlands* [Unification Treaty between the Federal Republic of Germany and the German Democratic Republic] (6 September1990: Presse- und Informationsamt der Bundesregierung, No. 104, Bonn), p. 887.
2. Hans-Jürgen Block, 'Die Empfehlungen des Wissenschaftsrates für die Forschungslandschaft in den neuen Bundesländern' [Recommendations of the Council of Sciences for research in the new Federal States], in Hilde Schramm (ed.), *Hochschule im Umbruch: Zwischenbilanz Ost* [Academic training transformed: Interim report on the East] (1993: BasisDruck Verlag, Berlin), pp. 347–8. This work was commissioned by the teachers' trade union.
3. *Einigungsvertrag*, p. 887.
4. In terms of posts: 1,600 in national research centres; 850 in Max Planck institutes; 4,300 in *Bunte Liste* (miscellaneous) institutes; 950 in Frauenhofer institutes; 1,200 in Federal research centres; 2,100

in regional research centres – so far not sanctioned. These figures are taken from Block, 'Empfehlungen', pp. 347–8.

5. Figures provided by the Council of Sciences: 18,500 in the institutes of the Academy of Sciences; 10,000 in the institutes of the Academy of Agricultural Sciences; 1,100 in the institutes of the Building Academy; 500 in the institutes of the Metereological Service and the Department of Health: Block, 'Empfehlungen'. There are also other data available which do not represent any significant difference. Quoted in the same publication on p. 350 are the following figures: Academy of Sciences – employees in 1989: 23,665, of which 18,285 in R&D (excluding humanities and social sciences).

6. The figures for agreed posts in the regional research centres (2,100) and the Scholars' Integration Programme (2,000) were merely designed to set the trend and did not commit the authorities to abide by their pledges. No data were ever officially released to show whether or to what extent they had been implemented.

7. During the parliamentary debate of 13 January 1994 the situation in industrial research was presented in detail and there was agreement that of the 86,000 to 87,000 persons once employed in that area, there would be 13,000 left. *Das Parlament* (1994: No. 3, Bonn), p. 11.

8. More detailed data in Charles Melis,'Was ist von dem DDR– Forschungspotential übriggeblieben?' [What remained of the GDR research potential?], in Schramm (ed.), *Umbruch*, pp. 350–1.

9. *Frankfurter Allgemeine*, 19 March 1991.

10. Ibid.

11. *Die Zeit*, 14 December 1990.

12. 'Evaluation der Evaluation', special edition of *Forum Wissenschaft* (1990: No. 4, Marburg).

13. *Süddeutsche Zeitung*, 6 December 1990.

14. *AdW-Informationen*, published by the Public Relations Office at the Academy of Sciences, Berlin, 17 May 1990.

15. Block, 'Empfehlungen', p. 357.

16. *DGKK-Mitteilungsblatt der Deutschen Gesellschaft für Kristallwachstum und Kristallzüchtung* e.V., No. 58, Berlin, November 1993.

17. *Wirtschaft und Wissenschaftspark Berlin Adlershof/Johannisthal* [Research and Technology Park of Berlin-Adlershof/Johannisthal], Vol. 4 (1993: Schriftenreihe des Wissenschaftssoziologie und -statistik e.V. Berlin).

18. Resolution No. 2264/92.

19. Dr Eberhard Brink, address on behalf of the sector for economic innovations at the Research and Technology Park Adlershof (FTA) to the Senate of Berlin, 23 November 1993.
20. Peter Knieß, 'Durch ABM-Förderung zum Technologie- und Wissenschaftsstandort Adlershof' [Establishing a technological and scientific centre at Adlershof by means of job-creation schemes], in *Wirtschaft und Wissenschaftspark*, pp. 36–7.
21. *Berliner Zeitung*, 10 January 1994.
22. Estimated figures: job cuts between 1989 and 1993: higher education from 14,000 to 7,000; non-university research from 32,000 to 10,000; R&D in the economy from 86,000 to 20,000-25,000; humanities and social sciences from 8,000 to 2,000; in Melis, 'DDR-Forschungspotential', p. 357. (See n.6 – no data were officially released.)
23. Professor Jürgen Kocka, historian, served on the evaluation commission of the Council of Sciences for humanities and social sciences, professor at the Free University Berlin and at the Regional University Potsdam.
24. An American guest professor attending the research project in contemporary studies at Potsdam Regional University wrote a very positive letter about it to the *Frankfurter Allgemeine*, 4 November 1993.
25. During GDR days the old Federal States were dissolved and transformed into districts. In 1990 the old structure was re-established.
26. This observation only applies in certain exceptional cases. As can be seen in the case of Klinkmann, even international recognition will not protect a person who is unwilling to renounce his or her reformist views. Horst Klinkmann was Director of a Clinic for Internal Medicine at University Hospital Rostock and an internationally recognised nephrologist. He played a significant role in the establishment of a dialysis centre and was the last freely elected president of the GDR Academy of Sciences. 'Der Riß im Leben des Horst Klinkmann',[The rift in the life of Horst Klinkmann], *Die Zeit*, 2 April 1993.
27. Hansjürgen Otto, 'Öffnung statt Austausch der Köpfe' [Opening up rather than changing the staff], in Schramm (ed.), *Hochschule im Umbruch*, p. 23.
28. *Neues Deutschland*, 7 February 1994.
29. On education cf. Chapter 7, p. 201.
30. Trauriges Ende einer Kapitänsschule' [Sad decline of a school for captains], *Das Parlament*, No. 52, 24/31 December 1993.

196   Horst van der Meer

31. Ulrich Jahnke and Hansjürgen Otto, 'Stellen- und Personalabbau an den Hochschulen 1989 bis 1993: Zwischenbilanz 1992' [Staff cuts at universities and colleges], in Schramm (ed.), *Hochschule im Umbruch*, pp. 414–5.
32. Karla Schmidt und Ursula Werner, '(K)eine Chance für den Mittelbau' [(No) chance for the middle strata], in Schramm (ed.), *Hochschule im Umbruch*, p. 418.
33. Horst van der Meer, 'Abwicklung der Universitäten' [Dismissals at the universities], in *Ex-DDR vom Industriestaat zum Entwicklungsland?* [Ex-GDR from industrial state to development country?] (1991: Dieter Jöster Vertriebsgemeinschaft GmbH, Frankfurt/M), p. 157.
34. Ibid.
35. Ibid.
36. See Chapter 1, p. 21 above.
37. *Deutsches Allgemeines Sonntagsblatt*, 8 June 1990.
38. See, for example, Knut Holm, *Das Charité-Komplott* [The Charité conspiracy] (1992: SPOTLESS-Verlag, Berlin).
39. He had previously tolerated and supported Senator Ehrhardt's policy.
40. *Bleibt von der Charité bald nur noch der Name?* [Will there soon be only the name of Charité left?], *Frankfurter Allgemeine*, 21 February 1994.
41. This figure was cited by Professor Seidel, then deputy head of department at the Central Committee of the Socialist Unity Party, in a lecture delivered in autumn 1988 at the GDR Institute of International Politics and Economics, Berlin.
42. Regine Hildebrandt (Minister for Social Affairs in Brandenburg), 'Die Einrichtungen des Gesundheits- und Sozialwesens in der DDR und in den neuen Bundesländern' [The health and social institutions in the GDR and in the new Federal States], *Aus Politik und Zeitgeschichte* supplement of *Das Parlament*, B3/94, 21 January 1994.
43. Dr Heinrich Niemann, 'Polikliniken – ein rotes Tuch für die Profitmedizin' [The polyclinics – a red rag to the profit-oriented health service], *Neues Deutschland*, 20 December 1991.
44. Doctors need either a receptionist or else plenty of time to do their accounts, a job which used to be dealt with centrally.
45. Manfred Ackermann, *Der kulturelle Einigungsprozeß Schwerpunkt: Substanzerhaltung* [The process of cultural unification: Focus on preservation of the substance] (1991: Friedrich-Ebert-Stiftung,

Forum Deutsche Einheit, Perspektiven und Argumente, Bonn–Bad-Godesberg), No. 7, pp. 14–15.

46. Different estimates exist of the number of those who migrated to the West after the fall of the Wall, there being no reliable statistics. Between 1989 and the end of 1993 4,847 people left Weimar for the West. Of these 1,204 were aged between 16 and 30. That left a population of 58,565 (*Neues Deutschland*, 10 January 1994). In 1990 there was a population of 2 million living in Mecklenburg-West Pomerania. By June 1993 150,000 had migrated to the West.

47. Rainer Gries on the revival of East German products, 'Aus dem Osten: Daher gut!' [From the East: Therefore first-rate!], *Das Parlament*, No. 4–5, 28 January/4 February 1994.

48. GDR films were shown regularly and successfully on various television channels; popular GDR bands had made a come-back and their records sold very well. GDR actors and actresses became very popular again.

49. Herbert Schirmer, art expert, journalist, active member of the opposition movement *Neues Forum* in the Frankfurt/Oder district in GDR days, was, for six months, Minister of Culture in de Maizière's government.

50. *Einigungsvertrag*, p. 886.

51. 'Debatte des Deutschen Bundestages am 10. Dezember 1993 über die Lage der Kultur in den neuen Bundesländern' [Parliamentary debate of 10 December 1993 on the situation of the cultural institutions in the new Federal States], *Das Parlament*, No. 52, 24/31 December 1993.

52. Early in January 1994 the Berlin Senate decided to erect this memorial based on blueprints by the Israeli artist Micha Ullmann. It symbolises the library that was robbed of its approximately 20,000 books which were burnt.

53. Klaus Dieter Stefan, 'Bücher auf der Kippe' [Books on the refuse dumps], *Freitag*, 14 January 1994. Fr. Martin Weskott from Katlenburg near Göttingen undertook the commendable task of gathering tens of thousands of such books and looked after them for future use.

54. Dirk Schümer, 'Kombinat mit Kassenbrille: Ex-DDR-Kultur-minister Schirmer sammelt Propagandakunst' [National trust looked at through national health service spectacles: Ex-GDR Minister of Culture Schirmer collecting propagandist art], *Frankfurter Allgemeine*, 15 January 1994.

55. *Kunstlandkarte 1993 Mecklenburg-Vorpommern*, [1993 map of art works in Mecklenburg-West Pomerania], published by the Federal State Department for Culture and Industry (1993: Verwaltungs-Verlag, Munich); *Mecklenburg-Vorpommern Kultur* [Culture in Mecklenburg-West Pomerania], published by the Tourist Office and the Federal State Department of Trade and Industry (1992: Konrad Reich Verlag, Rostock).
56. Article by two former museum directors in Berlin on the dispute over Berlin's Island of Museums in *Frankfurter Allgemeine*, 13 January 1994.

7 Right-wing Extremism in East Germany Before and After the '*Anschluß*' to the Federal Republic

Manfred Behrend

In February 1994 a dispute arose between leading public figures in the two parts of Germany which is characteristic of East–West relations within the reunited country. Kay Nehm, Chief Federal Prosecutor, who is from the West, held foreigners to be responsible for the rise in xenophobia and extremism. At the same time he claimed that right-wing radicalism had spilled over from the East into the West. This latter thesis incurred the wrath of former GDR citizens. It led Regine Hildebrandt (SPD), social welfare minister in Brandenburg, to accuse the country's top prosecutor of being 'deplorably uninformed'. She declared that '[right-wing] radical organisations and strategy have clearly spilled over from the West'.[1]

Both sides here were using vocabulary which stemmed originally from the offices of the Socialist Unity Party (SED). In the late 1980s, when neofascist activities within the GDR could no longer be disclaimed, these same offices coined the official phrase to the effect that right-wing extremism had 'spilled over from the West'.[2] In Frau Hildebrandt's case she – probably unconsciously – took over the usage, while Herr Nehm, who also pressed it into service, turned it around. He argued further that self-confident East German right-wing radicals had encouraged their West German cronies to greater activity.[3]

The fact is that both versions of the 'spill-over' theory are one-sided and thus wrong. There is surely no serious movement anywhere which arises solely from being imported or exported, just as there is none which is not subject to influences from outside. We shall attempt below to summarise the development of East German right-wing extremism. The following nine theses have been elaborated on the basis of relevant studies made both before and after the *Wende*.[4]

Reasons for Right-wing Extremism in the Lifetime of the GDR

1. In the years following 1945 a process of transformation took place in the Soviet occupation zone, later to become the German Democratic Republic, which had no equivalent in Western Germany. At the outset this transformation was largely in keeping with the agreements reached by the Allies at Yalta and Potsdam. The expropriation of the *Junkers* and the big companies responsible for war crimes meant that the socio-economic roots of fascism and militarism were eradicated in the East. The combing out of nazis from the organs of state and the judiciary, the hunting down of nazi criminals, and thoroughgoing reforms at all levels of education, etc., created the basis for radical democratic development. However, the green shoots of further progress and advance towards socialist democracy were largely thwarted by the rapid imposition of Stalinist methods of administration, the creation and consolidation of a party and state bureaucracy, and the effects thereof. What was ostensibly the property of the people became mere state property, managed and misused by apparatchiks who were responsible to no one beyond the top bureaucracy. The result was that in the end nobody respected this property, which is why it was possible to reprivatise it after 1990 without any real resistance on the part of those who worked there. The GDR political top brass of all shades developed into a new ruling caste enjoying unwarranted privileges. The bloc parties, led by the Socialist Unity Party, plus the various organisations of the broad masses (particularly the trade unions) saw themselves degraded into mere rubber stamp bodies. The institutions of popular representation and the media were brought into line. The Ministry of State Security (*Stasi*) inflated itself out of all proportion, especially under Erich Mielke. In the end it employed hundreds of thousands of professionals and part-timers and amassed mountains of dossiers on millions of citizens. It was, however, poorly equipped to deal with real enemies of the state and tended, on the whole, to be rather ineffective. Openings for a measure of resistance to the high-handedness of bureaucrats existed. But the lack of democracy hindered progressive forces in their development and favoured careerists. And this ultimately also weakened the state's ability to defend itself against right-wing extremists.

2. Fascist and racist attitudes survived in the GDR under a polished veneer of thoroughgoing antifascism. They were transmitted to younger generations by older people who had experienced Hitler's Germany, the Second World War and the defeat of 1945, with its dire consequences

for so many Germans. This transmission was mainly from grandfather to grandson. The increasingly authoritarian and undemocratic character of the GDR regime and its leading party, the SED, served both as a model for individual attitudes and behaviour patterns and as a trigger which set off sharp anticommunist responses to it. Like all reactionary trends, this one also equated Stalinist 'actually existing socialism' with communism and socialism as such.

3. State policy and education in the GDR took on formal and hier-archical features, particularly after Erich Honecker became General Secretary of the SED Central Committee and his wife Margot Minister of Education. The chance to encourage the development of human beings able to think critically and act independently was missed and a renewed spirit of knuckling under fostered. The history presented in history classes and books ran to seed in bloodless clichés.[5] Significant complex processes, particularly in the recent and immediate past, were omitted or smoothed over. What had been a combative antifascist culture in the immediate post-war years degenerated into mere ritual. There was no longer any attempt to get to grips with nazism, its activists and fellow-travellers, its day-to-day history and the attractiveness of certain aspects of it. Instead of facing up to tasks like these, the people in power in the GDR – and this included old resistance fighters and victims of the nazi regime – proclaimed themselves and the people lock, stock and barrel to be the 'victors of history' – a group of people who no longer had any need to grapple with the nazi legacy. Ranging from the regimentation of voluntary work to the pretentious but vacuous parades and what amounted to a new *Führer* cult, there was a copying of both Stalinist and reactionary models from Germany's own past. The result was a widespread lack of knowledge of and insight into fascism and political reaction. There was little ability to judge and act when confronted with that prettified image of German national socialism conveyed by the West German media and neonazis as well as by some older people. Revanchism, xenophobia and racism encountered low levels of political and ideo-logical resistance and immunity within broad sections of the population.

4. Internationalism in the GDR suffered a fate parallel to democracy, antifascism and socialism, frequently degenerating into mere ritual. Sig-nificant parts of the world remained unknown to most GDR citizens, particularly the young. Within the country the Stalinist form of 'vigilance' based on mistrust of one's own comrades also ensured isolation from the Soviet army units who made up the largest contingent of foreigners in the GDR. The same was true of embassy and consular staff and of foreign citizens working or training in the country. At times the party

and state bureaucracy itself practised xenophobia, particularly against Poles. This was inter alia used to divert popular anger over shortages on to shoppers from outside.[6] Gorbachev's initial attempt to transform the USSR into a modern socialist country was perceived by the GDR bureaucracy as an onslaught on power structures identical to their own. Their answer was a ban on films and periodicals plus an undercurrent of anti-Soviet propaganda. In the 1970s and 1980s, with the exception of costly prestige projects such as microelectronics, the GDR leadership blocked the thrust of modernisation in the economic-technological as well as the political fields. In their propaganda they disputed the continuing existence of the German nation and sought to generate an indigenous GDR nationalism under the slogan 'socialism in GDR colours'. They failed in this, and in the second half of the 1980s they increasingly aligned themselves with West German political interests, particularly after the first billion Marks loan arranged by Franz Josef Strauß, Bavarian Prime Minister and leader of the CSU. This also found expression in the way the GDR authorities, following requests by the CDU/CSU and the SPD, deported Tamil refugees after having stopped them from travelling from the East Berlin airport at Schönefeld to West Berlin. Even research studies into political developments in the Federal Republic would sometimes be suppressed, for tactical reasons. The GDR leadership, in distancing themselves sharply from the USSR, were in fact encouraging those who saw the Federal Republic as the better Germany. So already under Honecker, the ground was being prepared for the obsequiousness of GDR citizens towards their later West German masters.

5. Extreme right-wing elements in the country also benefited from the GDR leadership's moralising appeals to the nation to raise work morale and improve performance in the interests of the common good. These elements, too, demanded 'German workmanship', cleanliness, a sense of duty and 'soldierly virtues'. Some who grew up at that time in the GDR established themselves as good workers and reliable members of the armed forces and police, winning the goodwill of their superiors and the trust of their peers. Simultaneously the frequent discrepancy between word and deed on the part of the party and state leadership gave rise to dissatisfaction, as did the hypocrisy of official propaganda, sloppy workmanship condoned 'from above', failure to meet plan targets, economic disorganisation and the frequent supply bottlenecks. The extreme right were able to exploit this dissatisfaction for their own ends. Objective criticism almost always met with an authoritarian

response 'at the top'. Hence certain sections of predominantly young people began to gravitate towards new ultra right-wing 'authorities'.

6. Under the conditions sketched above a whole gamut of significant right-wing extremist tendencies developed within the GDR.[7] From the 1960s on, revanchist groups known as *Landsmannschaften* (associations of Germans from territories outside the Federal Republic, generally in Eastern or Southeastern Europe) met secretly, first in Potsdam and later near the Polish western frontier as well. Neonazi cadres were active at times among the riot police stationed at Basdorf near Berlin and within the National People's Army in the Leipzig military district. Secret trials arising from fascist activities took place in the GDR on several occasions. Some activitists fled to the Federal Republic, where they later joined the militaristic 'sports club' known as *Wehrsportgruppe Hoffmann* (the paramilitary group organised by Karl-Heinz Hoffmann). The Federal Republic bought others out of captivity – for instance Arnulf-Winfried Priem, the present director of *Hauptschulamt Wotans Volk* the neo-pagan Odin's People's Chief Education Office, a crypto-fascist group. In 1986 in the town of Schmiedeberg near Dresden, the first meeting took place of members of right-wing student fraternities at 15 universities and colleges in the GDR, although this type of reactionary association was prohibited. Groups of so-called 'nazi punks' established themselves, especially among young workers, apprentices and school students, including the sons of party and state officials. This was in the first half of the 1980s. The second half of that decade saw the rise of groups of skinheads and *Faschos*. The latter included the '30 January group'[8] in East Berlin, the forerunner of the National Alternative (*Nationale Alternative*). Some of the amalgamations fell apart again, and none achieved the degree of organisation and cohesion characteristic of the groupings in the 'old' Federal Republic. However, given the existing social basis, they undoubtedly had the potential for development.

7. The relationship between the extreme right, on the one hand, and the state, on the other, was fraught with contradictions. Officially the GDR was looked upon both at home and abroad as the antifascist German state per se. But the extreme right was already active well before the 1980s, which was the time generally held to be the moment when ultra-reactionary forces first emerged in an organised way. With their image in mind, the GDR powers of that period took pains to ensure that nothing concerning this development leaked out. For years they succeeded in so doing, thus preventing the much-needed public confrontation with the problem. This helped the right-wing extremists to expand in both illegal and semi-legal forms. In the second half of the 1980s, however,

the neonazis became active to a degree which it was no longer possible to hush up, although attempts were again made to do so. Particularly alarming was the attack by right-wing skinheads on a punk concert in East Berlin's Church of Zion on 17 October 1987. The state at once played down the incident, calling the rampaging neonazis 'hooligans', i.e. non-political bully-boys. However, under pressure from antifascists both inside and outside the SED, the judiciary saw itself obliged to pass harder sentences than had been planned and to open legal proceedings against neonazis in around 50 trials at various venues in the GDR. For a time the far right skinhead scene was subjected to heightened surveillance. Nevertheless the responsible security organs and the upper echelons of the party were loth to acknowledge neonazis as a serious threat. Frequently all skinheads had to do in order to carry on undisturbed under the vigilant eye of the Ministry of State Security was to let their hair grow, transform themselves into 'respectably' turned out *Faschos* and hold back for a while from all too blatant actions. The SED and the authorities went on ignoring warnings which the Lutheran Church had been issuing since as far back as the late 1970s concerning neofascist and xenophobic tendencies. Research studies on the skinhead scene undertaken by the police and (commissioned by the Ministry of State Security) at Humboldt University in Berlin were looked upon with suspicion and soon discontinued.

8. The right-wing extremists became de facto allies of the bureaucracy when the SED Politburo finally declared the advocates of democratic and socialist reforms and of truthful reporting in the GDR media to be the main enemies of socialism within the country. It was these extremists, after all, who, like the People's Police and State Security, fell upon civil rights campaigners and other 'trouble-makers'. During the clashes on and around 7 October 1989 (the fortieth anniversary of the founding of the GDR) provocateurs in the black costumes of the neonazis went into action alongside uniformed security forces. As and when required these men in black were able to produce legitimation showing them to be employees of the State Security Service. In detention centres in Bautzen and Berlin and in various police stations fascist-minded members of the police and its riot units harassed the arrested, who included mere passers-by as well as demonstrators. Where responsibility for this lay was never established. The Federal Republic of Germany was as little interested in doing so as was the GDR in its days. GDR State Security connections to West German neonazis remained equally obscure. They were very likely pretty close at certain points. The Ministry of State Security had, after all, lent massive support on occasion to right-wing terrorists and aided the escape of persons under

threat of prosecution in the Federal Republic.[9] Throughout the GDR's existence the Ministry of State Security's extensive arsenal of files on nazis and neonazis was closed to all outsiders, and neither researchers nor journalists, neither the Central Office for the Investigation of Nazi Crimes at Ludwigsburg, nor even the Federal Office for the Defence of the Constitution, had right of access to these files. In this connection, the Rev. Joachim Gauck – the Federal Officer responsible for documents of the State Security Services of the former GDR – and the Gauck administration named after him declared the records compiled by the Ministry of State Security on extreme rightists and their activities to be victim-dossiers and entitled to particular protection by law.[10]

9. At the same time as the bloc parties, mass organisations such as the Free German Youth (FDJ), and the GDR organs of state were frequently guilty of seriously neglecting the struggle against neonazis, this was taken up by what were known as 'Autonomous Antifascists', a movement which arose in the second half of the 1980s. Acting at times as part of the 'grassroots Church', they were involved in investigating and documenting neofascist activities and activists and in taking counter-measures. In addition they provided help and support to foreigners living in hostels and took part in protests against the election rigging of 7 May 1989 in the GDR. They were such a source of annoyance to the Berlin area head office of the SED and its leader Günter Schabowski, an SED Politburo member, that, at the end of September 1989, the latter were moved to send out a circular denouncing the Autonomous Antifascists as a neofascist group under the aegis of the Church.[11] Their pretext was the sew-on badge with the slogan 'Against Nazism', depicting a shattered swastika. In this the SED's Berlin office followed the example of the other German state's courts and police, who had frequently justified their persecution of antifascists on the basis of their allegedly pro-nazi insignia, despite it being clearly recognizable as antifascist. On 7 and 8 October 1989 members of the Autonomous Antifascists along with civil rights groups were subjected to assaults by the security forces. After the *Wende* they cooperated in establishing 'safety partnerships' with the police and organised actions against neonazis.[12]

Right-wing Extremism and Neofascism after the Autumn of 1989

The fall of the GDR in 1989 was part of more comprehensive developments in all European COMECON countries, as well as in Yugoslavia.

The system of 'actually existing socialism' disintegrated because it had become inwardly eroded and brittle as a result of a lack of broad participation in decision-making. An ever-increasing number of GDR citizens, particularly young people, were leaving the country for economic and in part political reasons. After 7 October 1989 civil rights campaigners backed by popular support achieved a certain easing of the dictatorship. One month later the opposition within the SED itself forced through the resignation of the Politburo and the Central Committee and the convening of an extraordinary party congress to transform the SED into a non-Stalinist party.

For a short time a chance existed for the GDR to take an independent democratic and socialist course. At the same time this offered an opportunity to curb the ultra-right forces in the country. The most significant obstacle on this road was the sudden opening of the GDR's western border on the orders of the SED Central Committee under Egon Krenz on 9 November 1989. This immediately brought the obvious predominance of the Federal Republic and its economic attractiveness fully to bear on millions of GDR citizens, and gave an enormous impetus to nationalism. The East German left which could have countered this was seriously weakened. Those on the left were put at a severe disadvantage by disclosures concerning the crimes of Stalinism in general and the crimes, hypocrisy and corruption of the top men in the Honecker and Krenz regimes in particular. There were about 2,000 political activists and 15,000 sympathisers in and around the extreme right in the GDR at that time.[13] Up to the opening of the Wall, for all their orientation towards Western models and their sporadic contacts with Federal German neonazis, they were their own people. When the border was opened, right-wing extremists from the West entered the GDR on a recruitment drive. Some were from West Germany, some from West Berlin, others were ex-GDR people who had fled into the 'old' Federal Republic or had been brought out of captivity by the latter. By and large, West German structures which had proved their viability over decades were the ones which established themselves in the East, although some independent formations came into being too.

The West German Component

The West German component in German right-wing extremism was stronger and more experienced than its East German equivalent. On the one hand, the extant economic basis and the old civil service and judiciary were kept in existence on the territory of West Germany after 1945. On the other hand, organised fascism continued to exist almost without interruption after the demise of Hitler's nazi party, the National Socialist German Worker's Pary (*Nationalsozialistische Deutsche Arbeiterpartei*; NSDAP).[14] First to become active were undercover channels such as the secret association of former SS members (ODESSA). Working with certain Catholic Church dignitaries they helped nazi war criminals evade the Allied military tribunals by providing escape routes to South America. After the establishment of the Federal Republic of Germany in 1949 (and even in some cases before that) a multiplicity of extreme right-wing groupings came into being in West Germany. Among them were associations of Germans who had been expelled from the former 'eastern territories' (*Vertriebenenverbände*), war veterans' associations including those of the former *Waffen-SS*, civilian organisations and institutions of a right-wing conservative and nazi complexion, and various newspaper and book publishers. In the early 1950s one-time nazi officers grouped around Werner Naumann, who had been permanent secretary to nazi Minister of Propaganda Josef Goebbels, made an attempt to infiltrate the Free Democratic Party (FDP). The British military authorities blocked this, however. Of the new groupings it was Otto Ernst Remer's Socialist Reich Party (*Sozialistische Reichspartei*; SRP) which initially came through most strongly, but this party went so far in its declaration of loyalty to Hitler fascism in all its 'purity' that it became an embarrassment to official political circles in Bonn. The SRP was banned by the Federal Constitutional Court in 1952 at the request of the Government. The other neonazi groups including newly formed onces went on unhindered for the most part. In periods of economic and political crisis some of them even did well at elections. In this way the National Democratic Party of Germany (*Nationaldemokratische Partei Deutschlands*; NPD), an amalgamation of various other groups, won seats at local government and Federal State level in 1964. They came to grief, however, at the general election of 1969, after which their electoral basis shrank to a fraction of what it had been previously, and membership gradually dropped from 23,000 to 5,000 in 1992.

The new *Ostpolitik* policy towards the East pursued by the Brandt/Scheel Government led to a caesura in the history of the Federal Republic. In the struggle against this policy a proto-form of terrorist neonazism came into being for a short time in the guise of Operation Resistance (*Aktion Widerstand*), a kind of rallying point for the extreme right. Building on this, certain groups and parties emerged in the 1970s whose aim was to rebuild the nazi party, NSDAP, and the 'Greater German Reich', aims and actions which were in flagrant breach of the Constitution. Their most important leader was, up until his death from AIDS in 1991, the ex-*Bundeswehr* lieutenant Michael Kühnen. He was instrumental in setting up a fascist network comprising variously named groupings – for instance German Alternative (*Deutsche Alternative*; DA); founded in Bremen in 1989 – and extending over Germany, Austria and the Netherlands. The umbrella organisation for this network was the Community of Adherents of the New Front (*Gesinnungsgemeinschaft der Neuen Front*; GdNF). At the same time it functioned as the legal arm of a new and illegal NSDAP and called itself, in true nazi style, 'the movement' (*die Bewegung*). The NSDAP's Organisation for Expansion Abroad (*Auslands- und Aufbau-Organisation*; NSDAP-AO) in the US gave support and instruction to German, Austrian and Dutch neonazis.

Also in opposition to the new *Ostpolitik,* Gerhard Frey founded the German People's Union (*Deutsche Volksunion*; DVU) in 1971. (Frey is the publisher of the pro-nazi weeklies in the Federal Republic with the highest circulation figures.) This organisation – since become a party – cultivates fascist traditions, whitewashing Hitlerism, whose crimes it denies or plays down. On of the leading speakers at DVU meetings was, alongside Frey, the British neonazi historian David Irving. At elections the DVU often made common cause with the NDP, in contrast to the roughly 1,000-strong combined membership of the GdNF, the like-minded Nationalist Front (*Nationalistische Front*; NF – since banned) and the Freedom-loving German Workers Party (*Freiheitliche Deutsche Arbeiterpartei*; FAP). The DVU, with, according to its own figures, 26,000 members, is the largest ultra-right organisation in the Federal Republic.

Changes in the *Ostpolitik* also led, among other things, to the formation of the party known as the Republicans (*Die Republikaner*; REP) in 1983. In this case, the catalyst was the change of course towards the GDR on the part of Bavaria's Prime Minister Strauß, in particular the loan he negotiated. At first it was in essence a splinter group of the CSU. Later, however, the REP developed into an independent party of the extreme right, under the leadership of Franz Schönhuber, journalist and one-time SS man. In 1992 membership numbered nearly 25,000. Its policies were on the whole right-wing conservative with certain pro-nazi features. The world view of its leaders was that of the so-called 'New Right' rather than of the traditional right wing. Following the example of the French *Nouvelle Droite*, it subscribed to a seemingly modern, seemingly scientifically based nationalism and to a racism cosmetically retouched as 'ethnopluralism'. It saw its historical models not so much in Hitler as in the activitists of the 'Conservative Revolution' who worked against the Weimar Republic and finally helped heave Hitler into the saddle. It also found further models in the Strasser brothers and the 'left' inside the Nazi Party – forces which lost the power struggle within that party.

The main tendencies within West German right-wing extremism differed from one another in their attitude to the Constitution of the Federal Republic. Whereas the Republicans, and to a lesser degree the NPD and DVU, accepted the Constitution as a basis for their activities, openly fascist groups like those of the GdNF were fiecely hostile to the parliamentary system and the Constitution.

The Eastward March of Right-wing Organisations

As already mentioned, after 9 November 1989 right-wing extremists of every shade entered the GDR from West Germany and West Berlin. They distributed their literature, canvassed for members and stayed put. Practically the only action taken by the GDR parliament and executive against the onslaught was a *Volkshammer* ban on all political activity by the Republicans and having Schönhuber warned off at the Potsdamer Platz border crossing point in Berlin. The Presidium of the *Volkshammer* unhesitatingly granted legal status to all groups who handed in statutes and a declaration of programmatic intent, regardless of their nature. Antifascist constitutional principles and corresponding laws were no longer applied. Provocative acts such as the hunting down by nationalists of citizens loyal to the Constitution, the ripping up and burning of the national flag or putting up a swastika in the middle of Marx-Engels Forum in Berlin remained unanswered for. If on occasion the police had no alternative but to intervene, the right-wing inciters were let off lightly. A case in point was the march by a thousand neonazis, skinheads and hooligans, celebrating Hitler's birthday on 20 April 1990, and the rampage which followed it. The National Alternative, for a time the Berlin subsidiary of the neonazi German Alternative, were given permission by the Housing Office to move into 122 Weitling Straße in the borough of Lichtenberg. It was only after a house search revealed, besides fascist cult objects, a list of the names of 'left-wing enemies' and evidence of attacks having been launched from there, that the authorities banned the organisation from participation in East Berlin's regional elections. On 23 June 1990 the Autonomous Antifascists demonstrated in Weitling Straße against the neonazis. There they ran into squads of police, brought in, seemingly, to defend the neonazis, and clashed with them. Some of the media displayed great indignation, not on account of the neonazis and police but against the Autonomous Antifascists. The East at that time was looked upon as a kind of eldorado by far-right extremists. All the groups involved developed regional subsidiaries in the GDR on the basis of an already existing potential. Initially the West German NPD had made an effort to persuade its East German namesake (NDPD)[15] to merge with it. It failed in this bid despite the interest shown by certain officials of that bloc party. After this the NPD temporarily set itself up in the East as the Central German National Democrats (*Mitteldeutsche Nationaldemokraten*; MND – which title implies the party's revisionist plans towards the former eastern German territories). It was not long, however, before it took on the name National Democratic Party of Germany in the GDR too.

Membership gains within the GDR failed to stem that party's overall contraction. The German People's Union and the Republicans, on the other hand, succeeded until 1994 in largely compensating for losses incurred in the 'old' Federal Republic through gains made in the East. The Republicans then also expanded their leadership pool, for instance through the acquisition of a former colonel in the GDR National People's Army, a professor of Marxism-Leninism, several local and municipal councillors who deserted from the SPD and CDU and *Bundestag* member Rudolf Krause from Bonese, also formerly CDU.

From the very beginning, the parties on the extreme right were unable to harvest the fruits of unification in the form of votes. Rather it was the Chancellor's party, the CDU, which cashed in on the windfall. In 1990, at the elections to the Federal State and national legislatures respectively, the Republicans, NPD, and far-right splinter groups together received 0.89 and 1.8 per cent of the vote in the East, i.e. a mere fraction. This remained so in all subsequent elections including the 1994 general elections. Only at Berlin's district council elections in 1990 did the Republicans manage to win 9.9 per cent of the vote in the West and 5.4 per cent in the East.

Of the openly fascist groups, it was in the main the German Alternative who established a basis in the East, while the Nationalist Front, the Freedom-loving German Workers' Party and the Viking Youth (*Wiking Jugend*), founded in West Germany as far back as 1950, also gained a foothold. The DA was formally established for 'Central Germany' on 7 July 1990 at Kiekebusch near Cottbus. Present at this event were Michael Kühnen and Gottfried Küssel, head of the Austrian People's Loyal Extra-parliamentary Opposition (*Volkstreue Außerparlamentarische*

Opposition). In October 1991, East Germans in the persons of Frank Hübner from Cottbus and several of his supporters took over the leadership of the DA as a whole.

A special phenomenon in the right-wing spectrum was the German National Party (*Deutsch-Nationale Partei*; DNP). It was set up by neonazis from the ex-GDR at Wechselburg in Saxony on Hitler's birthday in 1992. Its chairman, Thomas Dienel, had a career behind him which had led him from a course of studies at the SED District Party School at Erfurt, to the full-time job as an officer of the state youth organisation, thence to a secretaryship of the Sex League in Thuringia, and after that to chairmanship of the DNP there.

The Rise of Extreme Violence

On 3 October 1990 German unity became a fact. The date itself brought no basic change, since destinies in the East had already lain in Western hands for some time previous to this. It did mean, however, that opportunities for extreme right-wing elements, and for openly fascist groups in particular, now became even greater than in the ex-GDR. Neonazis made their presence felt in the form of spectacular parades in Halbe and Halle, Dresden, Arnstadt and Rudolstadt. They committed countless acts of terror. They desecrated Jewish cemeteries, Russian military cemeteries and German antifascist memorials. They attacked anarchist squats and left-wing youth clubs, and assaulted handicapped and homosexual Germans, Russian soldiers and Jewish immigrants from Russia. Their brutality against asylum seekers and foreigners on contract work became more and more vicious. Among the first to be murdered by German neonazis following the '*Anschluß*' were the Angolan Amadeu Antonio in Eberswalde and the Mozambican Jorge Gomondai in Dresden.

The forces of law and order, the established parties, and the neonazis did some ball-passing on the question of unwelcome guests from foreign parts. In a circular of 12 September 1991, Volker Rühe, then General Secretary of the CDU, called upon full-time officers and elected representatives of the party to initiate a campaign to limit the fundamental right to political asylum. Shortly afterwards the neonazis and skinheads made their own contribution to this. Beginning on 18 September 1991 and without interference from the police they staged the biggest reign of terror to date against asylum seekers – a whole week of pogroms at Hoyerswerda in Saxony. A section of the townspeople applauded. The powers that be gave in to the fascists and had all foreigners removed to other places.

Both the CDU and the CSU in the meantime stepped up the pressure towards modification of the right to asylum. On 5 June 1992 they got the FDP and SPD to join them in a vote to speed up asylum application proceedings. The law in question provided for summary proceedings, internment camps and deportation of rejected asylum applicants within six weeks. This did not satisfy most conservatives, however. What they demanded was the alteration of Article 16 of the Constitution through supplementary provisions. This aim was to abolish de facto the constitutional principle that 'politically persecuted persons enjoy right to asylum'. At that time the FDP and SPD opposed this move. At their previous party congress the Social Democrats had taken a decision in favour of strict adherence to the principle of the right to political asylum.

On 22 August 1992, hundreds of skinheads and hooligans under the command of mainly West German neonazi leaders and armed with stones, fireworks and molotov cocktails launched an attack on the Central Reception Point for Asylum Applicants (ZAST) for the catchment area of Mecklenburg-West Pomerania in Rostock-Lichtenhagen.[16] This major neofascist operation against the right to asylum had been openly and repeatedly announced in advance. Authorities in Rostock and the provincial capital Schwerin in effect lent support to their preparations by concentrating more and more asylum applicants in and around the ZAST. This led to an unacceptable breakdown of hygiene and set the local inhabitants against the immigrants. At that point began, on 22 August, a battle lasting several days, in which senior police officers at first callously exposed their unsuitably equipped constables to the stones and Molotov cocktails of the neonazis. When the battle was at its fiercest the police units which had been sent in to protect the ZAST were suddenly withdrawn, so that the neofascists were able to set fire to the building. More than a hundred Vietnamese and their families living in the same building, a German television team and the Rostock commissioner for foreign nationals would have perished in the smoke and flames had they not been able to extricate themselves at the last minute by escaping over the roof into another house.

The nights of arson at Rostock-Lichtenhagen were the signal for a series of similar attacks, particularly in the East. In Lichtenhagen – as had been the case in Hoyerswerda – asylum applicants were moved to other locations. The victors were the neofascists. They were given kidglove treatment even in cases of life-threatening assaults on the police.

On the other hand, the forces of law and order launched onslaughts on antifascist counter-demonstrators, among them French Jews, and arrested several of them.

This terror, reminiscent of the Brownshirts, was partly instrumental in bringing the SPD and FDP over to the CDU line in Bonn. At the Petersberg on 22–3 August 1992, senior Social Democratic officials voted to limit the right to asylum. By mid-November an extraordinary party congress of the SPD had approved this decision, so typical of the general rightward slide within the party. In a parallel development, the FDP turned its back on fundamental liberal principles with regard to the rights to asylum. Helmut Kohl, chairman of the CDU and Federal Chancellor, conjured up the danger of a national emergency should a modification of the Constitution fail to be adopted and demanded that in such a case the Government would have to be permitted to apply methods 'which are no longer within the Constitution'.[17] The coalition parties and the SPD voted, in the Federal parliament on 26 May 1993, to severely restrict the right to asylum. The law altering the Constitution came into effect on 1 July 1993. The various opponents of the Constitution, including the neofascists, had forced the acceptance of their position in a series of actions which demonstrated a certain de facto division of labour, even though no actual alliance existed between them. The absolute hard-liners even pressed for the abolition of the individual right to asylum (which continued to exist in a formal sense) and also the relevant examination of a case in a court of law.

Hooligans and trouble-makers from the 'old' Federal Republic were among the main instigators of the battle of Rostock-Lichtenhagen. Regardless of this, West German politicians and media were quick to place blame for the escalating xenophobia solely on the door of the former GDR with its 'dreary pre-fabricated high-rise blocks' and a population who never had an opportunity to get used to outsiders, having themselves been ghettoised for years. A series of outrageous arson attacks in the 'old' Federal States brutally disproved this propagandistic thesis – most infamously in the murder of eight women and young girls at Mölln and Solingen in November 1992 and May 1993. Thus the realm of neofascist terror was among the first to see German unity realised.

Statistics published by the Federal Office for the Defence of the Constitution indicate 270 acts of violence stemming from the extreme right in 1990, 1,483 – five and a half times as many – in 1991, and 2,584 – another 74 per cent rise – in 1992. All the figures applied to Germany as a whole. According to the same source, 90 per cent of these acts were committed against foreigners in 1992, whereby there were 17 fatalities

(3 in 1991).[18] Frightening as these statistics were, the Party of Democratic Socialism/Left-wing List (PDS) submitted to the Federal parliament proof based on press reports that the number of people killed by right-wing extremists was at least ten in 1991 and 30 in 1992.[19]

The Federal Office reported a drop in extreme right-wing acts of violence to a figure of 1,814 in 1993 – still above that of 1991, with the number of killings down to eight.[20] This reduction might be partly accounted for by organised protests against the terrorisation of foreigners – protests like the candle-light chains at the turn of the year 1992/93 which brought together hundreds of thousands of Germans, some from within the CDU camp itself. Fading applause for neonazi offenders also showed how the popularity of acts of violence against foreigners had ebbed.

It appears, however, that the basic motivation for this reduction derives from a shifting of emphasis undertaken by the right-wing extremists themselves. The latter went over more and more to an 'anti-antifa' campaign (i.e. anti-antifascist) stimulated by an offensive against antifascist opinions and the political left launched by establishment politicians and political scientists.[21] The call was published in April 1992 by Christian Worch in his magazine *Index*. Worch is chairman of the Hamburg National List (*Nationale Liste*) and the most important leader of the GdNF. He gave an overview of left-wing groups and properties to be reconnoitred, kept under surveillance and attacked, and expressed the hope that a 'people's front of the right' would emerge as a result of the campaign – a closer amalgamation of openly fascist and other far-right groups. At the end of 1992 this target was further confirmed in a neonazi strategy document. Regional 'anti-antifa' groups came into being, connected with each other by means of telephone information lines and boxes. They spied systematically on 'enemies of the movement', prepared hit lists and committed acts of terror. All this was facilitated by the fact that the growing wave of assaults on antifascists since the turn of the year 1992/93 was largely made light of by the police and for the most part remained unreported beyond the regional level.[22]

In contrast to the scarcity of publicity on anti-antifa activities in general, a sensation was created by the appearance in autumn 1993 of a hit list of antinazis in the pamphlet entitled *Der Einblick: Die nationalistische Widerstandszeitschrift gegen zunehmenden Rotfront- und Anarchoterror* (Insight: The Nationalist Resistance Pamphlet against Increasing Red Front and Anarchist Terror). Hit lists of antinazis which had come to light long before this one had received nothing like as much attention, if any. And all this was despite the fact that the *Einblick*, which was distributed from Denmark, was badly researched and contained large gaps and inaccuracies as a result. The main reason for the proportionately greater stir was that, in this first centrally compiled list, there appeared not only names of left-wing antifascists and of related institutions and organisations, but also those of respectable journalists and judges, business people and mayors. Consequently, even the frequently rather hesitant Federal Prosecutor in Karlsruhe reacted immediately and initiated investigations into the author and the disseminators of the pamphlet in connection with the formation of a criminal association.[23].

Regarding the aims of the project, it says in the introduction to the *Einblick*:

We will make every effort to avoid issuing calls for acts of violence, killings, etc., against our opponents. Each one of us must make his own decision as to how he wants to use the data made available to him here. All we want is that it be used!!![24]

The phrasing is typical of fascists in its call for carnage on the one hand and the attempt to shirk responsibility for it on the other. That the threat of terror was made in earnest was demonstrated by letter-bomb attacks on anti-racists in Austria. These attacks started immediately after the appearance of the *Einblick* and were carried out by people of like mind to those editing the journal. The fact that the terror was also directed against members of the ruling élite was too much for the representatives of government.

The Facilitation of Right-wing Extremism by Establishment Forces

As a result of their having previously operated in two separate states, differences continued to exist between the two sections of German right-wing extremism – for instance in the level of aggressiveness, in matters of strategy and tactics, etc. In the meantime, however, the two sections formed themselves into a combined camp. Their strength and muscle increased. This, on occasion, came to the notice of the representatives of law and order in Germany. In July 1993, for instance, Günther Beckstein (CSU), Minister of the Interior in Bavaria, stated that whereas ultra-left violence had declined in significance, the rule of law was coming under acute threat from an increase in ultra-right violence.[25] Following on this, Federal Minister of the Interior Manfred Kanther (CDU) stated that the Government had grounds for concern regarding ultra-right extremism.[26] Eckart Werthebach, President of the Federal Office for the Defence of the Constitution, finally pulled himself together, and after repeated denials declared that operational alliances existed among neonazis which amounted to the beginnings of a united front.[27]

Partial insights of this kind, however, were, for tactical reasons, frequently modified and relativised. They changed nothing in the Federal German practice of favouring ultra-right extremists and neonazis. Methods remained as described below.

In the case of attacks and murders committed by neofascists, the police frequently came too late, or, if they were present, turned a blind eye or simply stood and watched. The police contingents sent in against these nazi thugs tended to be small and badly equipped – particularly in the East. In the case of left-wing demonstrations, on the other hand, the forces of law and order were usually present in large numbers and excellently equipped. The march held in Fulda on 14 August 1993 in memory of Rudolf Hess was made possible by the fact that the police had been withdrawn to ward off antifascists converging on the town from outside. The officers remaining within the town directed the traffic to facilitate the smooth running of the neonazi march.

Evidence against the men of violence on the extreme right was frequently obscured, in the course of sloppily pursued investigations, rather than uncovered and followed up. As a rule the political background was not taken into account. The same was true of ties to other neofascists at home and abroad and to government institutions and the political establishment in West Germany. The fascist thugs were usually presented as lone wolves. Only in exceptional cases – for instance in the proceedings against the perpetrators of the Mölln arson – were right-wing extremists accused of murder. Usually the worst they had to face was prosecution for manslaughter or grievous bodily harm. On the whole the sentences were extremely lenient and often took the form of suspended sentences. The fact that the continuation or the reconstruction of the NSDAP contravenes the Constitution was, in East Germany too, no longer of any consequence. Displays of nazi symbols such as the swastika and the Hitler salute went for the most part unpunished, particularly if given a slightly distorted appearance. It was only in 1993 that the Kaiser's imperial war flag was banned in some Federal German States. It had been pressed into service for decades by extreme rightists as a legal surrogate for nazi symbols.

Certain representatives at various levels of government also played down or facilitated neofascist activities. Chancellor Kohl declared the Rostock-Lichtenhagen pogrom nights to be the work of men of violence on both the extreme right *and* extreme left.[28] In so doing he largely exonerated the former while slandering the latter, who could be shown to have had no part in the pogrom. Later, backed by Foreign Minister Klaus Kinkel (FDP), he described the Solingen murderers as 'individual offenders on the fringe of society',[29] despite the fact that their ties with organised neofascism were known. In the case of Rostock-Lichtenhagen, representatives of both the State Government and the town senate aided and abetted the arsonist assassins. A Social Democratic critic who pointed this out was immediately suspended. On the other hand it was many months before two of those mainly responsible for not holding the nazis back, Mecklenburg's Minister of the Interior Lothar Kupfer (CDU) and Rostock's mayor Klaus Killmann (SPD), lost their posts in 1992. Meanwhile no penalties were imposed for the fact that, within the competence of Federal Minister Angela Merkel (CDU), neonazi-dominated youth clubs and extreme right-wing social workers were financed out of state funds earmarked for an anti-violence programme.[30]

Compared to this, the action taken by the Federal Minister of the Interior and interior ministers of several German states in banning neofascist groupings as from November 1992 displays a martial determination. In this way the German Alternative and Nationalist Front were made illegal. Proceedings were instituted to also ban the Freedom-loving German Workers' Party: there are, however, serious defects in these bans. They are directed against only a small segment of the ultra-right scene, and have been, as a rule, given effect only after several days' notice. This gave those concerned the opportunity to clear their bank accounts, to spirit away incriminating material and to go over to new organisational forms. Wherever the authorities moved in against successor organisations, the game began all over again. This happened, for instance, in the case of the NF and the Support Scheme Central German Youth (*Förderwerk Mitteldeutsche Jugend*; FMJ). Once again the neonazis emerged unscathed. So the effect of the bans remains slight while at the same time lending the far-right extremists the aura of being persecuted.

From December 1992 onwards the Federal Office for the Defence of the Constitution had the Republicans also under surveillance – something it previously had not done. What lay at the bottom of this change of heart on the part of the CDU and CSU was not a sudden awakening of antifascism within the parties. Rather it was the fact that the Republicans had become a serious competitor for the CDU and CSU as a result of electoral successes in Berlin and in various West German

Federal States. To be under surveillance by the secret service was hardly likely to damage their image. In the meantime they had become the party with the best prospects among those on the extreme right, having tailored themselves to appeal to the mood and social needs of a potential clientele in the East. However, by adopting REP slogans and demands, particularly the call for restricting immigration legislation, and by isolating Herr Schönhuber by means of some of his former camp-followers, the CDU and CSU succeeded in preventing the Republicans from expanding. They managed to relieve the latter of a considerable portion of their voters which reduced the REP vote well below the 5 per cent mark which it needed to get into the *Bundestag* at the 1994 general elections.

Developments beyond their actual sphere of influence as well as the climate of the times as such had been encouraging to the growth of the extreme right. With the collapse of 'actually existing socialism', the forces opposed to right-wing extremism and neofascism were, for a time after unification, seriously weakened as a result of the campaign waged by the West German political establishment assisted by East German aides against socialist and antifascist traditions. This campaign comprised the onslaught on relevant monuments and street names, pension cuts for former GDR state employees, the impounding and/or confiscation of almost the entire funds of the PDS and organisations like the GDR association of the victims of nazi persecution, etc. All this both encouraged and lent credence to the anticommunist and anti-antifascist campaign launched by the extreme right, while both coalition and opposition were feeding neonazi xenophobia through the de facto abolition of the right to asylum.

Although the 1994 general elections did leave right-wing extremism very much in the cold, there is no cause for complacency. It should never be forgotten that ever since the Hitler era these people have been ideally cut out for the job of channelling the helpless rage of the masses into forms of protest advantageous to the powers that be but inflicting terrible harm on the vast majority of the people.

Notes

1. *AP (Associated Press)*, 13 and 14 February 1994.
2. In an editorial of 29/30 April 1989 the widely read *Berliner Zeitung* commented that 'neonazism is impossible in *our* country. Fascism in all its forms is a product of the monopoly capitalist system. We

have torn it up by the roots. If this kind of muck does on occasion spill over the Wall in the form of a handful of skinheads, the socialist state, though a humane one, will strike without mercy.' In an interview with the Warsaw *Polytika* at the beginning of September 1989, head of state and party chief Honecker said: 'Xenophobia, the nationalism of a Greater Germany, neonazism, revanchism and racism find no sustenance in our socialist society, and, in contrast to other countries, can never establish themselves as a political force. Nor can the ideological influence of our enemies, emanating therefrom, change this.' (Quoted from *Neues Deutschland*, 7 September 1989.)

3. *Berliner Zeitung*, Berlin,14 February 1994.
4. The following depiction is based largely on studies by Margitta Fahr, 'Skins – extreme Randgruppe oder soziale Erscheinung mit qualitativ steigender Dimension?' [Skins – extreme fringe group or social phenomenon of increasing importance?], *Antifa-Infoblatt*, 1 July 1989; Norbert Madloch, 'Zur Entwicklung des Rechtsextremismus in der DDR und in Ostdeutschland von den 70er Jahren bis Ende 1990' [The development of right-wing extremism in the GDR and in East Germany from the 1970s to the end of 1990] and 'Rechtsextremismus in der Endphase der DDR und nach der Vereinigung von DDR und Bundesrepublik Deutschland – Chronologie' [Right-wing extremism in the terminal stage of the GDR and after the merger of GDR and Federal Republic], in Robert Harnischmacher (ed.), *Angriff von Rechts: Rechtsextremismus und Neonazismus unter Jugendlichen Ostberlins* [Attack from the right: Right-wing extremism and neonazism among young people in East Berlin], 1993: Hanseatischer Fachverlag für Wirtschaft, Rostock; Loni Niederländer, 'Zu den Ursachen rechtsradikaler Tendenzen in der DDR' [Causes for right-wing radical trends in the GDR], *Neue Justiz*, No.1, 1990; Konrad Weiss, 'Die neue alte Gefahr. Junge Faschisten in der DDR' [The new old menace: Young fascists in the GDR], *Kontext*, Evangelische Bekenntnisgemeinde Berlin–Treptow, 8 March 1989; Manfred Behrend, 'Rechtsextremismus und Neofaschismus in der DDR – eine verharmloste Gefahr' [Right-wing extremism and neofascism in the GDR – a menace played down], *Der antifaschistische Widerstandskämpfer*, No.12, 1989, and 'Rechtsextremismus in der DDR: Anerkannte antifaschistische Traditionen – negative Wirkung stalinscher Strukturen' [Right-wing extremism in the GDR: Acknowledged antifascist traditions – negative effects of Stalinist structures], *Antifa*, No.1,

1990; Bernd Siegler, 'Auferstanden aus Ruinen ... Rechtsextremismus in der DDR' [Arisen from the debris ... Right-wing extremism in the GDR] (1991: Edition Tiamat, Berlin).

5. See Chapter 6, pp. 178–80.

6. Many Poles made shopping trips to the GDR when visas were temporarily abolished in the 1970s.

7. Data used here are mainly taken from Madloch, 'Zur Entwicklung' and 'Rechtsextremismus'.

8. Called after the 30 January 1933, the day the nazis took power in Germany.

9. *Junge Welt*, 12 June 1991, and 23 July 1991.

10. *Junge Welt*, 30 December 1992, 2 January and 3 May 1993.

11. Today Günter Schabowski is one of the West's star witnesses for the 'inevitable and just demise of the GDR'.

12. *die andere*, 3 January 1991.

13. *Berliner Zeitung*, 16 February 1994.

14. This depiction is largely based on studies by Thomas Assheuer and Hans Sarkowicz, *Rechtsradikale in Deutschland: Die alte und die neue Rechte* [Right-wing radicals in Germany: The old and the new right wing] (1990: Verlag C.H. Beck, Munich); Uwe Backes and Patrick Moreau, *Die extreme Rechte in Deutschland: Geschichte – gegenwärtige Gefahren – Ursachen – Gegenmaßnahmen* [The extreme right wing in Germany: History – the present menace – causes – countermeasures] (1993: Akademischer Verlag, Munich); Peter Dudek and Hans-Gerd Jaschke, *Entstehung und Entwicklung des Rechtsextremismus in der Bundesrepublik* [Genesis and development of right-wing extremism in the Federal Republic of Germany], vols 1 and 2 (1984: Westdeutscher Verlag, Opladen); Reinhard Opitz, *Faschismus und Neofaschismus* [Fascism and neofascism] (1984: Verlag Marxistische Blätter, Frankfurt/M).

15. See Chapter 2, p. 48. The East German NDPD membership were mostly small tradespeople and craftspeople. Originally founded to offer a political homestead for the grassroots members of nazi organisations, these had, by 1989, long been replaced by younger people who had never had any nazi leanings and who, therefore, wished to have no truck with the East German nazi organisations. The MND, DVU and Republican Party recruited their members from a cross-section of the GDR population, ex-SED members among them. With the right-wing drive of the CDU/CSU and SPD, the formerly right-wing parties lost followers massively to the established parties.

16. For the following information I am indebted to the work of Hajo Funke, *Brandstifter: Deutschland zwischen Demokratie und völkischem Nationalismus* [Arsonists: Germany between democracy and jingoist nationalism] (1993: Lamuv Verlag, Göttingen),

17. *Der Spiegel*, 2 November 1992.

18. *Verfassungsschutzbericht* [Report by the Office for the Defence of the Constitution] for 1991 (1992: Bonn), p. 76 and for 1992 (1993: Bonn) p. 91.

19. PDS/Linke Liste, material presented at press conference held in Bonn on 1 July 1993: 'Über den schonenden Umgang der Bundesregierung mit dem Rechtsextremismus' [Regarding the Federal Government's leniency towards right-wing extremism], part III, and, 'Morde in Deutschland mit und vor rechtsextremistischem Hintergrund seit der Wiedervereinigung' [Murder in Germany by right-wing extremists and against a right-wing extremist background], p. 1. Arbeitsgruppe zur Bekämpfung rechtsradikal motivierter Kriminalität und Selbstjustiz der Hauptabteilung Kriminalpolizei des Ministerium für Innere Angelegenheiten, 'Neofaschisten und Rechtsradikale − wer sie sind und wie sie auftreten' [Neofascists and right-wing radicals − who they are and how they present themselves], *Neues Deutschland*, 3 January 1990.

20. *AP*, 13 January 1994; Federal Minister of the Interior, *Bedeutung und Funktion des Antifaschismus,* [Significance and function of antifascism] (1990: Bonn).

21. Hans-Helmuth Knütter, 'Antifaschismus und politische Kultur nach der Wiedervereinigung' [Antifascism and political culture after unification], *Aus Politik und Zeitgeschichte* supplement of *Das Parlament*, (22 February 1991, Bonn). Here antifascism is condemned as 'a weapon of the left in their internal and foreign policy', 'Marxist' and hostile to the Federal Republic of Germany.

22. *Berliner Zeitung,* 10 June 1993; *Antifa*, No.1, 1994. In November 1992 the left-wing squatter Silvio Meier was stabbed to death in Berlin by an ultra-rightist. Following upon this there was a rise in murders committed against antifascists and in attacks on left-wing youth centres. Despite massive evidence the criminal investigators refused to recognise a number of these murders for what they were and so they did not appear in the statistics.

23. *AP* and *dpa (Deutsche Presse-Agentur)*, 2 December 1993.

24. *Der Einblick* (n.d., n.p.), p. 4.

25. *Neues Deutschland*, 31 July/1 August 1993.

26. *dpa*, 16 August 1993.

27. *ZDF* [Second German television channel], 29 August 1993.
28. *Bild am Sonntag*, 30 August 1992.
29. *Neues Deutschland* and *Frankfurter Allgemeine*, 3 June 1993; *Berliner Zeitung*, 10 June 1993.
30. 'Panorama', television-documentary on ARD television channel, 9 September 1993; *Junge Welt*, 27 November 1993; *Berliner Zeitung*, 10 December 1993.

Index

Abortion, 65, 142, 146
Academy for Agricultural
  Sciences, 168, 194n
Academy for Further Medical
  Qualification, 185
Academy of Educational
  Sciences, 168
Academy of Sciences, 39, 168,
  170, 172, 173, 174, 176, 194n,
  195n
Academy of Social Sciences,
  159, 165n
Act on the Privatisation and
  Reorganisation of Nationally
  Owned Assets, 93
Agrarian reform fund, 15
Agricultural Adjustment Law,
  126, 130
Agricultural cooperatives (LPG),
  105, 118n, 120, 121, 122, 124,
  126, 128, 129, 130, 131, 135,
  136n, 137,
AIDS, 183, 185, 208
Aktion Widerstand, 207
Albrecht, Ernst, 14
All-German cultural
  commission, 191
Alliance 90, 56, 63, 64, 65, 66
Alliance 90/The Greens, 4, 53,
  56, 64, 66, 71, 72, 73, 77n
Alliance of Free Democrats - the
  Liberals (BFD), 48, 54
Allied Military Tribunals, 207

Alternative Enquiry
  Commission, 23
Althaus, Peter, 183
Amendment to the Higher
  Education Act, 181
Anschluß, 4, 5, 6, 8, 15, 29, 46,
  49, 51, 54, 68, 69, 82, 91, 93,
  111, 112, 119, 120, 125, 199,
  211
Anti-antifa campaign, 214
Antifascism, 176, 200, 201, 205,
  214, 215, 216, 219n, 221n
Antonio, Amadeu, 211
Association of Democratic
  Scientists, 173
Association of Farmers and
  Cooperatives, 120, 125
Association of National Research
  Centres, 170
Asylum, 59, 60, 63, 211, 212,
  213, 218
Austrian Freedom Party, 59
Autonomous antifascists, 205,
  209, 210
Awakening 1989 – New Forum,
  41

Baby year, 142
Bahr, Egon, 49
Bahro, Rudolf, 22
Barbe, Angelika, 42
Bauer, Leo, 22
Beckstein, Günter, 71, 215

Berlin 30 January Group, 203
Berufsverbot, 154
Biedenkopf, Kurt, 58, 72
Biermann, Wolf, 39, 55
Birthler, Marianne, 66
Birthler, Wolfgang, 62
Birthrate, 113
Bischofferode, 9, 24, 61
Bisky, Lothar, 70, 71
Bloc parties, 200, 205
Blum Robert, 74n
Böhlener Plattform, 42
Bohley, Bärbel, 40, 42, 64
Böhme, Ibrahim, 40, 42, 53
Brandt, Willy, 3, 207
Branitzki, Heinz, 101
Breuel, Birgit, 11, 12, 13, 14,
    15, 32n, 33n, 100, 111
Building Academy, 145, 194n
Bundeswehr, 4, 31n, 59, 60, 66,
    208
Burning of the books by the
    Nazis on 10 May 1933, 192

Candle light chains, 214
Carl, Peter, 173
Central Association of the
    German Building Trade, 101
Central German National
    Democrats (MND), 210,
    220n
Central Institute of Electron
    Physics (ZIE), 173
Central Office for the Investiga-
    tion of Nazi Crimes at
    Ludwigsburg, 13, 205
Central Reception Point for
    Asylum Applicants (ZAST),
    212
Central Round Table, 45, 46,
    54, 68, 75n

Christian Democratic Union
    (CDU), 3, 8, 16, 35, 38, 46,
    47, 49, 50, 51, 52, 53, 55, 56,
    57, 58, 59, 61, 62, 65, 70, 72,
    73, 75n, 79n, 120, 125, 130,
    135n, 137n, 181, 202, 210,
    211, 213, 217, 218, 220n
Christian Social Union (CSU),
    8, 46, 51, 53, 54, 55, 56, 58,
    59, 62, 70, 72, 73, 75n, 79n,
    119, 120, 136, 181, 202, 212,
    215, 217, 218, 220n
Church of Zion, 204
Club of Rome, 5
College of Agriculture in
    Meissen, 180
College of Law and Administra-
    tion in Potsdam-Babelsberg,
    180
College of Physical Culture in
    Leipzig, 180
College of Economics in Berlin,
    180
COMECON countries, 1, 2,
    122, 167, 205
Commissioned Art, 192
Communist Party of Germany
    (KPD), 35, 73n, 135n
Communist Party of the Soviet
    Union, 36
Communist Platform of the PDS
    (KPF), 71
Community of the Adherents of
    the New Front (GdNF), 208,
    209, 214
Conservative Alliance, 119
Council of Sciences, 168, 169,
    170, 171, 177, 193n, 194n,
    195n
Credit Transaction Fund, 110
Cultural agreement, 191

Cultural Association
(*Kulturbund*), 38

de Maizière, Lothar, 49, 50, 52,
53, 54, 57, 76n, 77n, 93, 95,
117n, 124, 191, 197n
Delors, Jacques, 6
Democracy Now (DJ), 40, 47,
48, 63, 75n
Democratic Awakening (DA),
42, 119, 136n
Democratic bloc, 38, 44
Democratic Farmers' Party of
Germany (DBD), 36, 74n, 119
Democratic Women's
Federation (DFD), 35
Dienel, Thomas, 211
Dresden Art Gallery, 187
Dresden Bank, 7
Dreßler, Rudolf, 60
Duchac, Josef 57
Dürkop, Marlis, 183

East German Greens Party, 66
Ebeling, Hans-Wilhelm, 76n
Echternach, Jürgen, 16
Eichbauer, Fritz, 101
Election rigging, 205
Embargo politics, 84
Engholm, Björn, 60
Environmental Library, 40
Eppelmann, Rainer, 40, 42, 75n
Equal (gender) opportunities
policy, 139, 140, 141, 142,
160, 164n
Erhardt, Manfred, 181, 182, 195n
European Council, 6
European Community, 104,
105, 125, 130
European parliamentary
elections, 62

European Regional Fund, 112
European Union, 6, 168
Evaluation, 23, 30, 110, 168,
169, 170, 171, 172, 173, 175,
178, 194n, 195n
Extraordinary Party Congress of
the SED, 67, 68, 206
Extraordinary Party Congress of
the SPD, 213

Family farms, 125, 127, 128,
129, 130, 131, 136n
Family policy, 142
Farmers' mutual aid association
(VdgB), 38
Faschos, 203, 204
Fascism, 75n, 176, 188, 192,
200, 201, 203, 204, 205, 207,
210, 214, 215, 216, 218, 219n,
220n
Federal Audit Office, 95
Federal budget, 111
Federal Constitution, 209, 212,
213, 216
Federal Constitutional Court
(*Bundesverfassungsgericht*), 16,
54, 56, 95, 105, 107, 118n,
131, 207
Federal cooperative laws, 126
Federal Council (*Bundesrat*), 17
Federal Employment (Labour)
Agency, 31n, 131, 138n, 147,
155, 163n, 164n
Federal national debt, xi, 7, 13,
56, 108
Federal Office for the Defence of
the Constitution, 31n, 213,
214, 216, 217, 221n
Federal parliament (*Bundestag*),
33n, 72, 75n, 110, 138n, 197n
Federal Prosecutor, 215

Federal State elections, 37, 72
Federation of German Industry
    (BDI), 6
Fink, Heinrich, 21, 182, 210,
Fischbeck, Hans-Jürgen, 41
For Our Country appeal, 45
Fraunhofer Society, 170, 174,
    193n
Free Democratic Party (FDP),
    48, 50, 51, 55, 56, 59, 60, 69,
    70, 72, 207, 211, 213, 217
Free German Trade Union
    Federation (FDGB), 35, 38
Free German Youth (FDJ), 35,
    37, 38, 176, 205
Freedom and Prosperity – Never
    again Socialism, 49
Freedom-loving German
    Workers' Party (FAP), 208,
    210, 217
Frey, Gerhard, 208
Fritsch, Harald, 173
Fulda march, 216

Gauck, Joachim, 20, 21, 205
Gauck-authority, 9, 21, 70, 205
GDR army (NVA), 203, 2210
GDR association of the victims
    of nazi persecution, 218
GDR Constitution, 37, 54
GDR elections of 1990, 119,
    123
GDR Family Code, 141, 152
GDR Government (Provisional),
    92, 124
GDR Government of 1990, 45,
    47, 52, 54, 92, 168, 191
GDR Green Party, 44, 48, 50,
    66
GDR Housing Construction
    Law, 110

GDR Institute of International
    Politics and Economics, 196
GDR Law on the Assets of Local
    Communities, 105, 106, 107
GDR Liabilities Repayment
    Fund, 110
GDR Ministry of State Security
    (Stasi), 20, 21, 22, 39, 40, 41,
    43, 45, 49, 53, 55, 57, 60, 62,
    63, 64, 65, 69, 70, 182, 183
    200, 204, 205
GDR national debt, 108, 110
General elections of 1969, 207
General elections of 1990, 55
General elections of 1994, xii,
    59, 72, 210, 218
General Medical Council for
    Berlin, 185
Gerlach, Manfred, 44, 47
German Alternative (DA), 208,
    209, 210, 211, 217
German Antimonopolisation
    Commission, 9
German Association of Higher
    Education, 179
German Bank (Bundesbank), 7,
    20
German Central Office for the
    Prosecution of Crimes
    Involving the Government,
    12, 13
German Chamber of Industry
    and Commerce, 175
German Confederation, 85
German Economics Institute, 87
German Forum Party (Deutsche
    Forumpartei), 50
German Greens Party (West),
    55, 65, 66
German National Party (DNP),
    208, 209

German People's Union (DVU), 136n, 210, 211, 220n,
German President, 169
German secret service (BND), 71
German Social Union (DSU), 47, 49, 51, 53, 54, 55, 56, 119, 136n
German Trade Unions Federation (*DGB*), 61
Germany Forum, 59
Gethsemane Church, 183
Gies, Gerd, 57
Gläser, Wolfgang, 48
Goebbels, Joseph, 53, 207
Goldhammer, Bruno, 22
Gomolka, Alfred, 58
Gomondai, Jorge, 211
Gorbachev, Mikhail, 3, 46, 47, 67, 202
Government guarantees (*Hermes Bürgschaften*), 14
Government settlement programme, 105
Gramlich, Horst, 62
Grass roots church (*Kirche von unten*), 41, 205
Grass Roots Round Table, 63
Greens, 55
Grenzfall, 40
Grünewald, Joachim, 33n
Gündel, Rudi, 173
Gysi, Gregor, 31n, 33n, 53, 67, 70, 71, 72

Haider, Jörg, 59
Hamm-Brücher, Hildegard, 60
Harich, Wolfgang, 22, 39
Hauptschulamt Wotans Volk, 203
Haus der Gesundheit, 186
Havemann, Prof. Robert, 22, 39, 40, 42

Heitmann, Stefan, 58
Henrich, Rolf, 42, 48
Herrnstadt, Rudolf, 39
Herzog, Roman, 59
Hess, Rudolf, 216
Heym, Stefan, 10, 39, 65, 72
High Intensity Synchrotron Radiation Generator (BESSY II), 175
Higher Education Renewal Programme, 169
Hildebrandt, Regine, 61, 133, 196n, 199
Hilsberg, Stephan, 42
Hintze, Peter, 62
Hitler, Adolf, 15, 64, 75n, 200, 207, 208, 209, 211, 216, 218
Hoffmann, Lutz, 87, 117n
Honecker, Erich, xiii, 19, 30n, 40, 43, 65, 67, 159, 201, 202, 206, 219n
Honecker, Margot, 201
Hoyerswerda, 211, 212
Huber, Ellis E., 185
Hübner, Frank, 211

Imperial war flag, 216
Independent Commission for Vetting the Assets of all GDR Parties and Mass Organisations, 53, 68
Independent Women's Association (UFV), 44, 48, 50, 66, 164n
Initiative for Peace and Human Rights (IFM), 40, 41, 42, 48, 54, 63
Initiative for a Green League and a Green Party, 44
Insight (*Einblick*), 214, 215

Institute for Labour Market and Vocational Research (IAB), 138n, 152, 156, 162n, 163n, 168n
Institute for School Development Research, 180
Institute for the Analysis of Social Data (ISDA), 157
Institute of World Economics, Kiel, 109
International Labour Organisation (ILO), 6
International Monetary Fund, 6
International Women's Day, 138n, 164n
Iron Curtain, 2
Iron Foundry Works East at Eisenhüttenstadt (EKO), 14
Irving, David, 208

Janka, Walter, 22

Kafka, Franz, 188
Kanther, Manfred, 215
Killmann, Klaus, 217
Kinkel, Klaus, 217
Klein, Thomas, 40, 42
Klinkmann, Horst, 195n
Kocka, Jürgen, 178, 195n
Köhler, Otto, 32n
Kohl, Helmut, x, 3, 4, 7, 8, 46, 47, 49, 50, 51, 52, 55, 56, 57, 58, 59, 73, 75n, 76n, 79n, 86, 91, 159, 191, 213, 216
Krause, Günter, 52, 57
Krause, Rudolf, 59, 77n, 210
Krenz, Egon, 41, 43, 44, 67, 206
Kühnen, Michael, 208, 210
Kupfer, Lothar, 217
Küssel, Gottfried, 210
Kutzmutz, Rolf, 62, 71

Lafontaine, Oskar, 61
Lambsdorff, Otto, 50, 59
Land reform 1945-49, 16, 17, 36, 53, 105, 117n, 119, 125, 131, 135n
Landsmannschaften, 203
Langnitschke, Wolfgang, 68
Law on Compensation and Conciliation (EALG), 16
Law on Pensions Adjustment, 146
Law on the Structural Adjustment of Agriculture in the GDR to the Social and Economic Market Economy (LAG), 125
Leutheusser-Schnarrenberger, Sabine, 60
Liberal Democratic Party of Germany (LDPD), 35, 38, 44, 48, 50, 51, 135n
Liebknecht/Luxemburg demo of 1988, 41
Ludendorff, Erich, 75n
Luft, Christa, 10, 32n, 47, 72
Lummer, Heinrich, 59

Medicine and Society, 187
Magdeburg option, 73
Maleuda, Günter, 74n
Management Buy-Out (MBO), 96, 103, 111
Matthäus-Maier, Ingrid, 52, 87, 117n
Mau, Harald, 183
Max Planck Society, 170, 174, 193n
Meckel, Markus, 42
Meier, Silvio, 221
Merkel, Angela, 57, 217, 221n
Merker, Paul, 22

Mielke, Erich, 200
Modrow, Hans, 3, 10, 45, 47, 52, 92, 117n, 191
Mölln outrage, 213, 216
Momper, Walter, 46
Monday demos, 3
Monetary Reform of 1948, 85, 86, 87, 88, 89, 90
Monetary Union of 1990, 3, 19, 52, 80, 85, 86, 88, 90, 91, 93, 95, 108, 110, 116n, 117n, 124, 127, 149, 191
Movement for a Democratic Socialism, 42
Müller, Manfred, 72
Münch, Werner, 57

National Democratic Party of Germany in FRG (NPD), 207, 208, 209, 210
National Democratic Party of Germany in GDR (NDPD), 35, 36, 38, 44, 48, 50, 51, 220n
National Front of the GDR, 37, 38, 74n
National Socialist German Workers' Party (NSDAP), 207, 208, 209, 216
National Socialist German Workers' Party for Expansion Abroad (NSDAP-AO), 208
Nationale Alternative, 203, 209
Nationale Liste, 214
Nationalist Front (NF), 208, 210, 217
NATO, 40, 48, 56, 58, 66
Naumann, Werner, 207
Naval College of Engineering in Warnemünde-Wustrow, 180, 195n
Necker, Tyll, 6

Nehm, Kay, 199
Neofascism/neofascist, 29, 59, 203, 204, 205, 206, 207, 213, 214, 216, 217, 218n, 219n, 220n, 221n
Neoliberalism/neoliberalist, 5, 6, 11
New Economic System of Planning and Management, 37
New Forum, 41, 48, 54, 63, 64, 66
Nickel, Hildegard-Maria, 143, 162n, 163n
Nooke, Günter, 64, 66
Nouvelle Droite, 208
Nuremberg Trial, 64

ODESSA (Assistance Society for former SS officers), 207
Ogger, Günter, 100, 102, 117n
Old liabilities, 103, 105, 107, 108, 109, 110
Opening of the Wall, 206
Ostpolitik, 207, 208

Parker, John, 31n, 32n
Party of Democratic Socialism (PDS), 28, 31n, 48, 49, 50, 53, 55, 56, 61, 62, 64, 65, 66, 67, 68, 69, 70, 71, 72, 73, 78n, 79n, 123, 138, 214, 218, 221n
People's Chamber (*Volkshammer*), 37, 38, 44, 45, 47, 48, 49, 50, 51, 53, 54, 55, 69, 71, 76n, 93, 209
People's Congress Movement for Unity and Just Peace, 37
People's Front of the Right, 214
Permanent tenancy (*Erbbauzins, Erbpacht*), 19

Pohl, Wolfgang, 68
Poppe, Gerd, 40, 65
Poppe, Ulrike, 40, 41
Porstmann, Thomas, 183
Potsdam Agreement of 1945, 18
Priem, Arnulf-Winfried, 203
Principles, aims, procedures and
    measures to renew Humboldt
    University, 182
Privatisation-related bonus
    system, 103, 104
'Prosperity for the East'
    programme, 112, 137n
'Prosperity instead of Socialism',
    120, 124
Provisional government of the
    GDR, 45
Przybilski, Helmut, 62
Punk concert in East Berlin in
    1987, 204

Rau, Johannes, 59
Red Army Fraction (RAF), 11,
    32n
Reich, Jens, 54, 59, 65
Reiche, Steffen, 61, 62
Reichenbach, Klaus, 52
'Rejection of the Practice and
    Principle of Segregation', 40
Remer, Otto Ernst, 207
Reparations Balancing Plan, 109
Republican Party (REP), 51, 55,
    59, 65, 71, 208, 210, 217,
    218, 220n
Research and Development
    (R&D), 170, 174, 175, 194n,
    195n
Restitution before compensation
    provision, 18
Rexrodt, Günter, 9, 30n, 31n,
    59

Richter, Hans, 103
Richter, Edelbert, 42, 47
Rohwedder, Detlev Karsten, 10,
    11, 108
Romberg, Walter, 52
Rostock-Lichtenhagen, 212,
    213, 216, 217
Rühe, Volker, 57, 211

Salzgitter Commission, 14
Saxony elections of 1990, 120
Saxony state elections of 1994,
    60, 62, 71, 72
Saxony-Anhalt state elections of
    1994, 60, 73
Schabowski, Günter, 43, 205,
    220n
Scharping, Rudolf, 60, 61, 62,
    71, 73, 79n
Schäuble, Wolfgang, 52, 58, 73
Scheel, Walter, 207
Schirdewan, Karl, 39
Schirmer, Herbert, 191, 192,
    197n
Schnur, Wolfgang, 42, 47, 49
Schöde, Wolf, 13
Schönhuber, Franz, 208, 218
Scholars' Integration
    Programme, 169, 170, 174,
    175, 194n
Scholz, Rupert, 59
Schorlemmer, Friedrich, 42, 47
Schult, Reinhardt, 64
Schulz, Werner, 65
Schumacher, Kurt, 36, 73
Schwaetzer, Irmgard, 59
Science and Technology Park at
    Berlin-Adlershof (FTA), 174,
    175, 194n, 195n
Science and Technology Society,
    175, 194n, 195n

SED-PDS, 48, 49
Seelig, Marion, 42
Seelig, Roland, 42
Seite, Berndt, 16
Senate of Berlin, 21, 28, 174, 175,
  179, 182, 186, 192, 195n, 197n
Sex League, 211
Skinheads, 203, 204, 211, 209,
  212, 219n
Simon, Dieter, 170
Sinn, Hans Werner, 96, 117n
Social Democratic Parliamentary
  Party, 87
Social Democratic Party of
  Germany (SPD), 3, 4, 8, 9, 10,
  13, 16, 35, 36, 42, 46, 48, 49,
  50, 51, 52, 56, 59, 60, 61, 62,
  63, 64, 69, 70, 72, 73, 75n,
  77n, 123, 135n, 210, 212,
  213, 217, 220n
Social Democratic Party of the
  GDR (SDP), 42, 46, 48, 49,
  50, 51, 53, 55, 56, 75n
Socialism in GDR Colours, 202
Socialist Reich Party (SRP), 207
Socialist Unity Party of Germany
  (SED), 2, 35, 36, 37, 38, 39,
  41, 43, 44, 45, 48, 63, 66, 67,
  74n, 83, 119, 123, 131, 167,
  176, 188, 199, 200, 201, 204,
  205, 206, 211, 220n
Society for the Protection of
  Nature (NABU), 15
Solingen, 213, 217
Stalin/stalinist/stalinisation, 22,
  25, 36, 37, 46, 62, 69, 70,
  200, 201, 206, 219n
Stolpe, Manfred, 17, 22, 40, 62,
  64
Strasser brothers, 209
Strauss, Franz Josef, 51, 202, 208

Süssmuth, Rita, 65
Support Scheme Central
  German Youth (FMJ), 217
Swastica, 216

Templin, Wolfgang, 65
'Ten Point Programme to
  Overcome the Division of
  Germany and Europe', 75n
Thatcher, Margaret, 56
Thierse, Wolfgang, 53, 61, 62
Tiananmen Square massacre, 43
Tränkner, Ludwig, 12, 32n
Treuhand controlling committee,
  94
Treuhand Law, 93, 98, 102, 108
Treuhand managers, 9, 11, 12,
  13, 14, 32n, 93, 97, 99, 101,
  102, 103, 108
Treuhand President, 10, 32n, 108
Treuhand property, 99, 113
Treuhand sales, 99
Treuhand shares, 93, 96
Treuhandanstalt, xi, xivn, 9, 10,
  12, 13, 14, 15, 17, 26, 32n,
  33n, 52, 59, 60, 68, 92, 93,
  94, 95, 96, 97, 98, 99, 100,
  101, 102, 103, 104, 105, 106,
  108, 110, 111, 113, 114, 115,
  116, 117n, 131
Tschiche, Hans-Jochen, 42
Tynek, Karl, 12

Ulbricht, Walter, 37
Ullmann, Micha, 197n
Ullmann, Wolfgang, 41, 53, 54,
  55, 64
Unification Treaty, 3, 15, 18,
  52, 54, 55, 59, 93, 106, 107,
  118n, 126, 131, 168, 169, 170,
  179, 186, 191, 193n, 197

Union of German Forest
   Owners' Associations, 15
United Left (VL), 42, 47
United Left/The Carnations, 50
Unlawful state (*Unrechtstaat*), 22,
   26
Unofficial informant of the Stasi
   (IM), 21

Vaatz, Arnold, 76n
Vertriebenenverbände, 207
Victims of the nazi regime, 201
Viking Youth, 210
Vogel, Bernhard, 58
Volkstreue Außerparlamentarische
   Opposition, 210
Volmer, Ludger, 66
von Weizsäcker, Richard, 58

Waffen-SS, 207
Waigel, Theo, 12, 52
Wall, The 2, 6, 30n, 55, 64, 119,
   189, 197n, 206, 219n
Walther, Joachim, 53
Warsaw Treaty, 48
Wehrsportgruppe Hoffmann, 203

Weimar Letter, 44
Weiske, Christine, 66
Weiß, Konrad, 41, 53, 55, 64,
   65, 66, 219n
Wende, The 3, 17, 19, 26, 66,
   144, 150, 152, 154, 158, 159,
   168, 179, 180, 189, 190, 192,
   199, 205
Werthebach, Eckart, 215
Weskott, Fr. Martin, 197n
Wisser, Claus, 14, 101
Wolf, Christa, 40, 46
Wolff, Prof. Helmut, 183
Wollenberger (Lengsfeld), Vera,
   41, 65
Women's dequalification, 154
Women's Strike of 1994, 151,
   164
Worch, Christian, 214
World Bank, 6
Writers' Workshops, 187

Young Comrades Association, 71
Young Socialists, 63

Zaisser, Wilhelm, 22, 39

Published by Pluto Press

Bonn & the Bomb

German Nuclear Weapons Policy from Adenauer to Brandt

Mathias Küntzel

After the Second World War, Germany was denied access to nuclear technology. Dr Küntzel's study reveals, however, that German politicians of all persuasions have planned to develop nuclear weapons for the last forty years. Although walls of secrecy surround investigations into Germany's nuclear intentions, Dr Küntzel has succeeded in providing, for the first time, an in-depth study of Germany's involvement in the Non-Proliferation Treaty (NPT) and the prospects for a German Bomb. The research is based on interviews with government officials and diplomats and comprises an important study in German–American relations.

'*Bonn & the Bomb* is surely the best book written about this chapter of German history' *Der Spiegel*

'a unique and illuminating study of the postwar policies of the Federal Republic of Germany' Professor Robert Jungk

'An extremely well-researched, in-depth work, easy to read and altogether very interesting' Ben Sanders, Chairman of the Programme for Promoting Nuclear Non-Proliferation

ISBN 0 7453 0910 0 hbk   0 7453 0909 7 pbk

Order from your local bookseller or contact the publisher on
0181 348 2724.

Pluto Press

345 Archway Road, London N6 5AA
140 Commerce Street, East Haven CT 06512, USA

Published by Pluto Press

States of Injustice

A Guide to Human Rights and Civil Liberties

in the European Union

Michael Spencer

There is a broad consensus in most member states of the European Union – with the flagrant exception of the United Kingdom – that the Union is in general a good thing, and that fostering closer economic links between member states through the abolition of internal border controls will be of benefit to all concerned. But will it? States of Injustice focuses on the unintended consequences of abolishing border restrictions: the deeply racist and anti-libertarian agenda of Fortress Europe.

While member states continue to pay lip-service to the international conventions on human rights, they are concurrently encouraging greater intergovernmental cooperation in sensitive areas of policy not subject to democratic scrutiny or control – in particular asylum and immigration policy, policing, employment rights and protections, women's, gay and lesbian and children's rights and data protection. Michael Spencer offers a succinct country-by-country summary of civil rights in representative member states, together with a clear explanation of the complementary roles of Union institutions and the Council of Europe.

ISBN 0 7453 0979 8 hbk   0 7453 0980 1 pbk

Order from your local bookseller or contact the publisher on
0181 348 2724.

Pluto Press

345 Archway Road, London N6 5AA
140 Commerce Street, East Haven CT 06512, USA

Published by Pluto Press

WORLD ORDERS, OLD AND NEW

Noam Chomsky

In this new, ambitious and expansive study of global politics, Noam Chomsky challenges conventional definitions of the 'New World Order', examining the acts of imperialism and economic manipulation which have produced the unbalanced world order of the 1990s. Chomsky begins with a reconsideration of the Cold War, revealing how it became a pretext for the USA to expand politically, economically and militarily under the guise of self-defence.

In the post-Cold War era, he argues, the break-up of the Soviet Union has clouded a convenient distinction between 'good' free market westerners and 'evil' communists. The book also offers a startling new commentary on the Gulf War, and the relationship between America and Britain and the 'enemy' before, during and after hostilities. In a detailed analysis of the strategic manoeuvres between the West and the Third World, Chomsky concludes that George Bush's New World Order has become a domestic and international propaganda tool in the hands of the powerful.

Noam Chomsky is Professor of Linguistics at the Massachusetts Institute of Technology and an internationally acclaimed scholar and political activist.

ISBN hardback: 0 7453 0920 8   softback: 0 7453 0919 4

Order from your local bookseller or contact the publisher on 0181 348 2724.

Pluto Press

345 Archway Road, London N6 5AA

Published by Pluto Press

Pax Americana?

Hegemony or Decline

Jochen Hippler

Is there a new world order? This is the key question that Jochen Hippler addresses in *Pax Americana?* In answering it, Hippler explores the rise of the post-war order, the future of the Third World, the crises in the Gulf and the ideology and power centres of the 'new world order'.

In a powerful summary, Hippler concludes that we are living in a world where the USA, armed to the teeth, remains the only global military power. Yet this occurs at a time when the USA, now a major debtor nation, is internally weak. *Pax Americana?* is a succinct and incisive analysis of global power and an excellent text that aids an understanding of the world as a whole.

ISBN 0 7453 0695 0 hbk   0 7453 0696 9 pbk

Pax Americana? is published in the Transnational Institute series – critical studies of seminal themes in contemporary development, aid and international relations. Details of other titles are available from Pluto Press.

Order from your local bookseller or contact the publisher on
0181 348 2724.

Pluto Press

345 Archway Road, London N6 5AA
140 Commerce Street, East Haven CT 06512, USA